Artistic Ecologies

New Compasses and Tools

Artistic Ecologies: New Compasses and Tools

EDITED BY
Pablo Martínez • Emily Pethick • What, How & for Whom / WHW (Ivet Ćurlin, Ana Dević, Nataša Ilić, Sabina Sabolović)

CONTRIBUTIONS BY
Luna Acosta • CAConrad • DAAR (Sandi Hilal & Alessandro Petti) • Yael Davids • Eva Ďurovec • Marina Garcés • Teuta Gatolin • Yayo Herrero • Max Jorge Hinderer Cruz • Margherita Isola • Jammers • Pablo Martínez • Dan Perjovschi • Emily Pethick • Pirate Care • The Sensing Salon (Valentina Desideri & Denise Ferreira da Silva) • Cecilia Vicuña • WHW (Ivet Ćurlin, Ana Dević, Nataša Ilić, Sabina Sabolović)

MANAGING EDITOR
Milica Vlajković

SPANISH-ENGLISH TRANSLATIONS
Nicholas Callaway • George Hutton

COPYEDITING AND PROOFREADING
Jaclyn Arndt

GRAPHIC DESIGN
Dejan Kršić

PRINTING AND BINDING
Tiskara Zelina d.d, Croatia

PUBLISHED BY
What, How & for Whom / WHW
Bogovićeva 1
10000 Zagreb, Croatia

Sternberg Press
71–75 Shelton Street
London WC2H 9JQ
United Kingdom
www.sternberg-press.com

DISTRIBUTED BY
The MIT Press, Art Data, Les presses du réel, and Idea Books

ISBN 978-3-95679-633-3

The publication *Artistic Ecologies: New Compasses and Tools* is a part of the two-year project *Education from Below*, realized in collaboration with the Rijksakademie van beeldende kunsten, Amsterdam • MACBA – Museu d'Art Contemporani de Barcelona • What, How & for Whom / WHW, as a part of the Creative Europe Programme of the European Union.

Artistic Ecologies: New Compasses and Tools is co-funded by the Creative Europe Programme of the European Union. The European Commission's support for the production of this publication does not constitute an endorsement of the contents, which reflect the views only of the authors, and the Commission cannot be held responsible for any use which may be made of the information contained therein.

Co-funded by the Creative Europe Programme of the European Union

Through project grants to WHW Akademija this publication is supported by FfAI – Foundation for Arts Initiatives; Kontakt Collection, Vienna; and ERSTE Foundation, Vienna.

This publication is also co-funded by City Office for Culture, International Relations and Civil Society, Zagreb, and the Ministry of Culture and Media as well as the Office for Non-Governmental Organizations of the Government of the Republic of Croatia. The views expressed in this publication are the sole responsibility of the editors and authors and do not reflect the position of any of the aforementioned funders.

Artistic Ecologies
New Compasses and Tools

EDITED BY

Pablo Martínez
Emily Pethick
What, How & for Whom / WHW

Sternberg Press

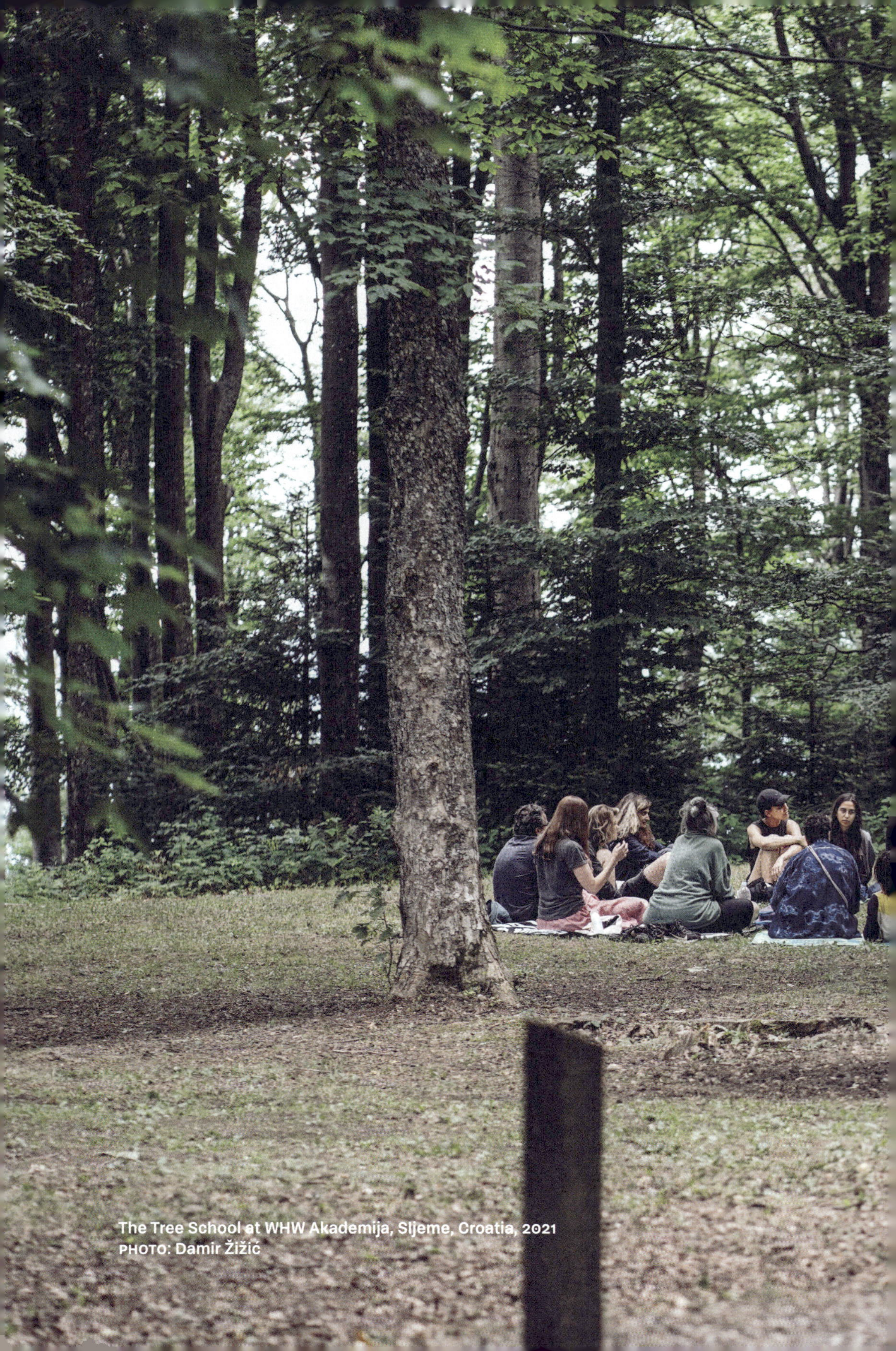

The Tree School at WHW Akademija, Sljeme, Croatia, 2021
PHOTO: Damir Žižić

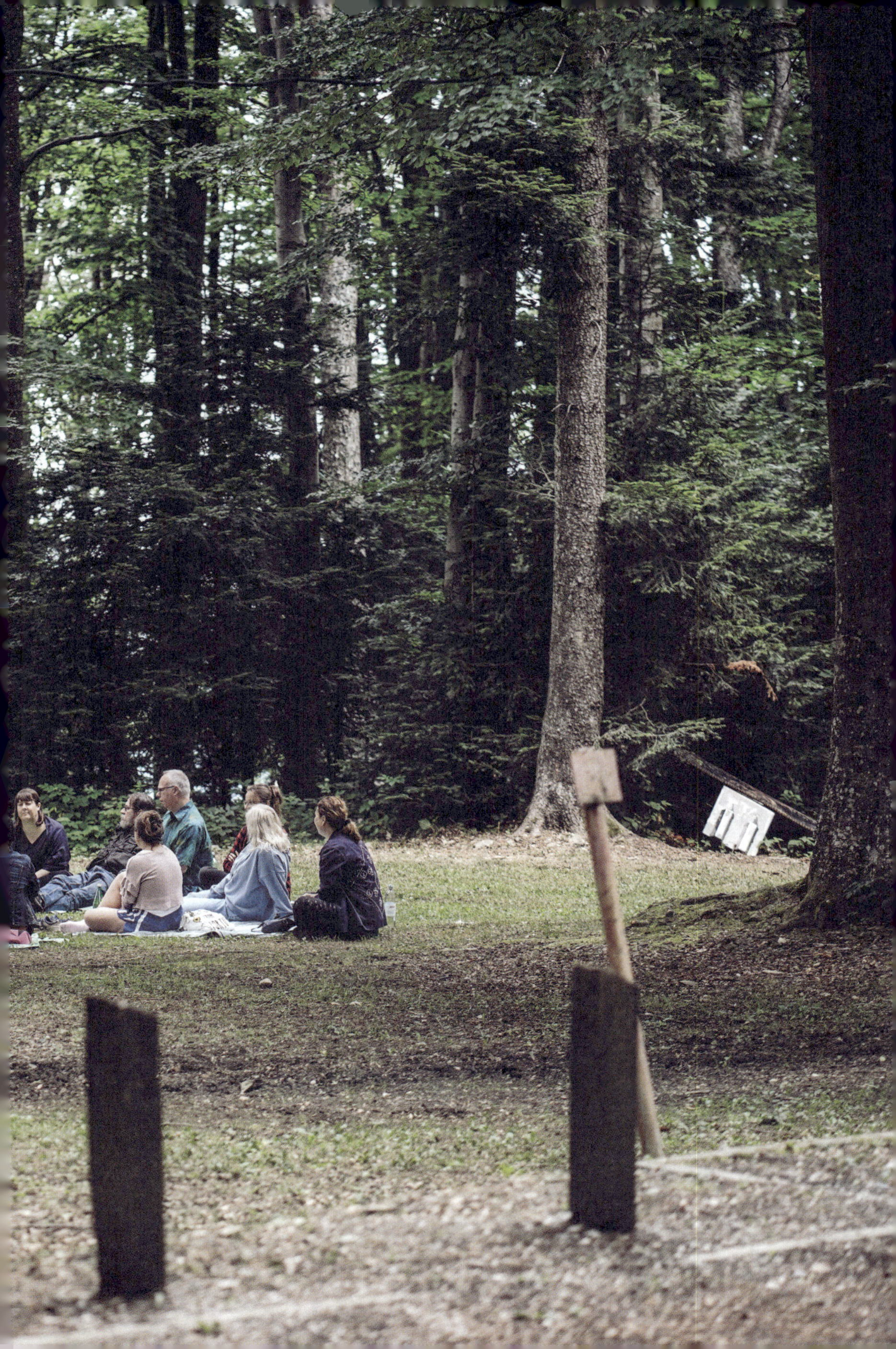

Contents

Cecilia Vicuña

Sabor a Mí (1973)

una celebración de los comandos
comunales, de los cordones indu
striales, de los centros de ref
orma agraria, de los centros de
cultura popular, de las JAP, de
los CUP.

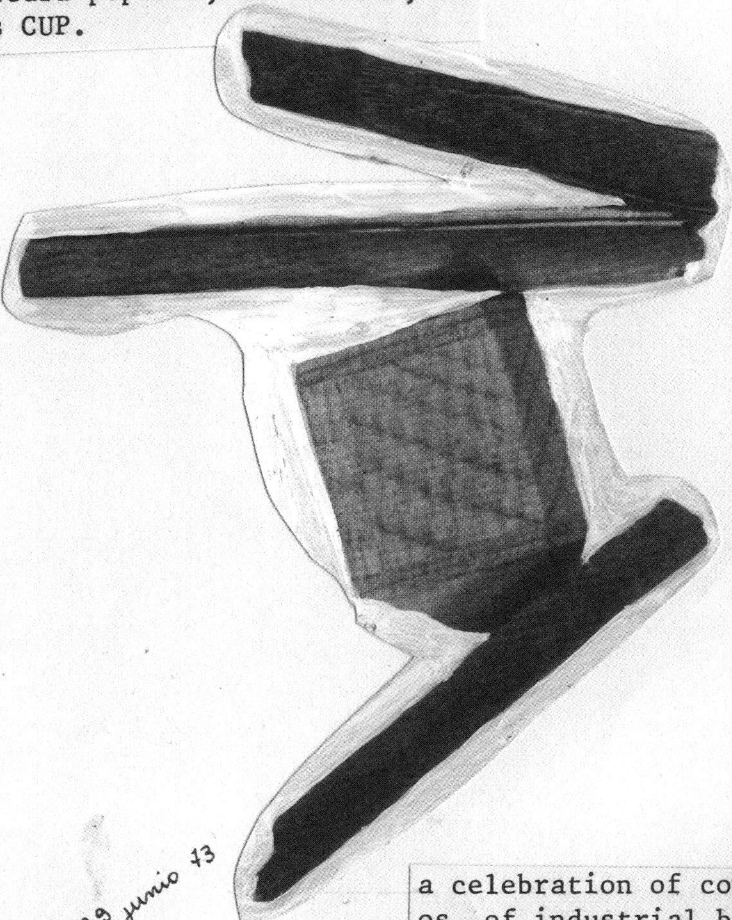

29 junio 73

a celebration of commune comand
os, of industrial belt organiz
ations, of agrarian reform cent
ers, of people's cultural cente
rs.

La lucha hay que darla en el frente cultural; para conso
lidar el proceso revolucionario debemos crear un movimient
o cultural, una nueva visión de la realidad debe reemplaza
r a la antigua. necesitamos muchos activistas culturales.
todos los trabajadores de la cultura deben reunirse en un
largo congreso que dure noche y día para discutir hablar y
pensar hasta venir a un acuerdo y crear un solo bloque; que
todos los diarios, radios, revistas, T.V. cine, teatro,pin
tura mural pongan el dedo en la llaga, actuando como un só
lo animal, un organismo de pensamiento y visión al servici
o de la revolución. una sola organización donde todos está
n inscritos para la coordinación. ¿tú que quieres hacer?
¿donde lo quieres hacer? házlo. ¿cuántos C.C.P. hay? cuánt
os artistas hay? uno para llá otro para acá, que ninguno
quede fuera, y así nada funciona al lote, ni la t.v. ni lo
s diarios ponen lo que se les antoja, todos somos un solo
cuerpo para destrozar el pensamiento reaccionario, la ideo
logía burguesa, el individualismo, la seriedad y la angusti
a, la manera blanca, europea, capitalista de existir.

The struggle must be waged in cultural fronts. To consoli
date the revolution we must create a cultural movement and
change people's realities. We no longer need mere changes
in individual consciousness, but a change in social consci
ousness. A new vision of reality must replace the old one.
All workers of culture must gather in a long congress durin
g days and nights, until aims and agreements are reached,
creating a unified block.All papers, radio, mags,t.v. cine
ma, theatre,mural painting should point out the open sores,
acting like one single creature, like a thought machine in
the service of the revolution. One single organization coor
dinating all; how many commando communes are there? How
many artists are there? Choose where you want to work, cho
ose. invent your task, do it! All together to destroy react
ionary ideas, bourgeoisie ideology, individualism,solemnity,
all white, european, capitalist ways of existence.

As industries are nationalized, I am nationalized.
From individual to communal property.

12 julio 73

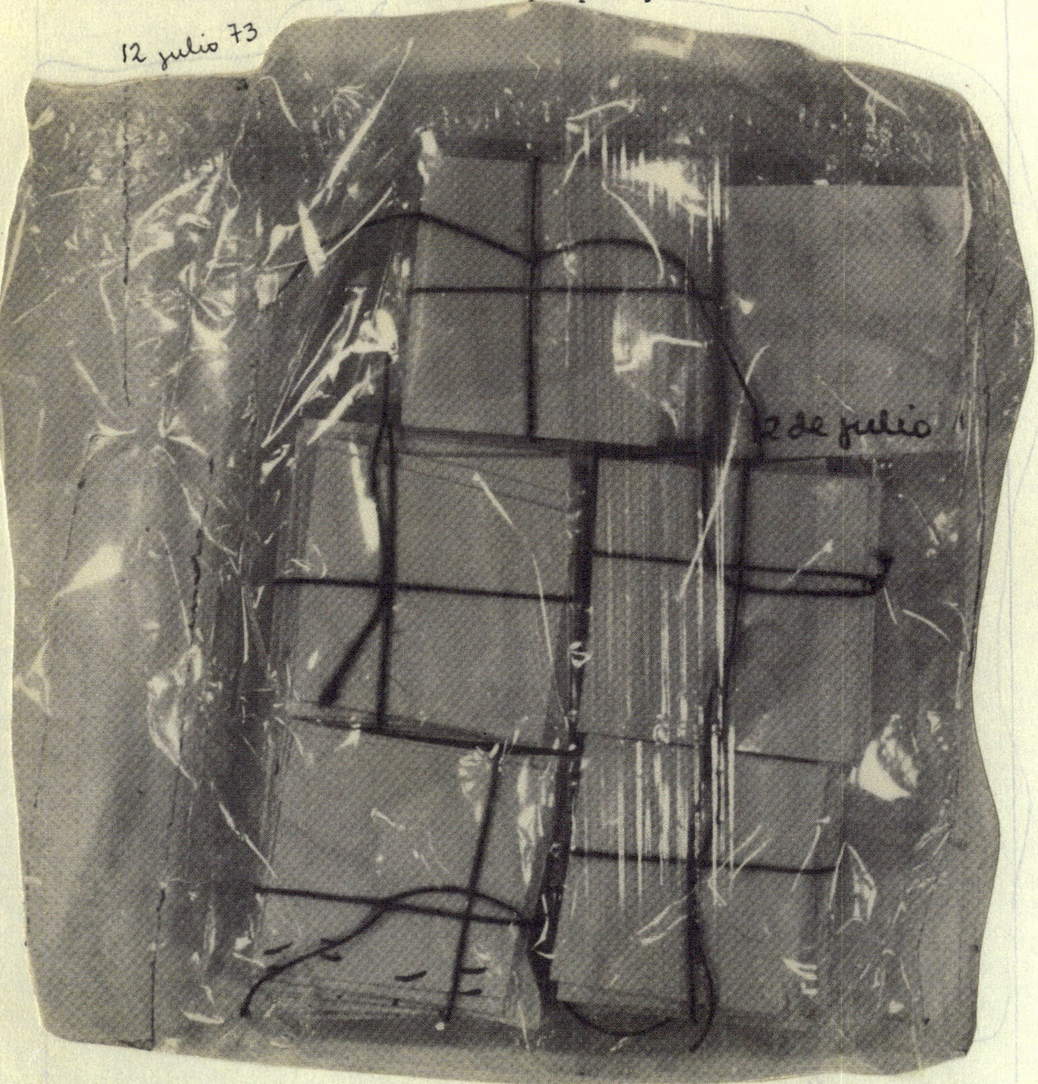

Así como las industrias pasan al área social, yo pasé al área social, de la propiedad individual a la comunal.

Calcomanía
chilena:
el efecto
del femin
ismo revo
lucionari
o será el
nacimient
o de una
relación
distinta
entre ho
mbre y m
ujer;ni
poder
ni

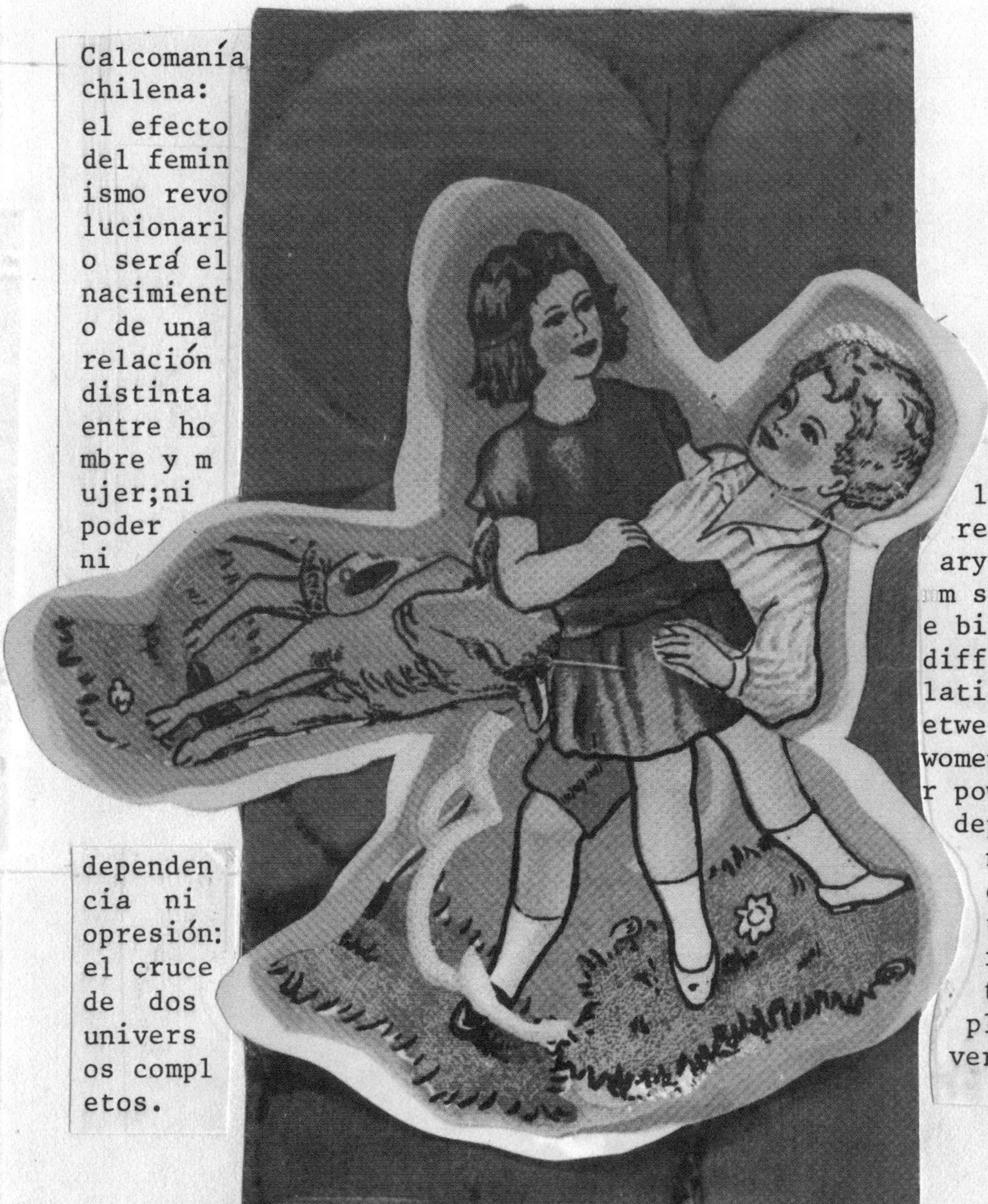

dependen
cia ni
opresión:
el cruce
de dos
univers
os compl
etos.

28 julio 73

A decal
from chi
le:
revolution
ary feminis
m shall giv
e birth to a
different re
lationship b
etween men &
women;neithe
r power nor
dependance
nor oppr
ession;
the meet
ing of
two com
plete uni
verses.

◄
Excerpts from Cecilia Vicuña, *Sabor a Mí*, artist book. Published in 1973, Beau Geste Press. Reissued in 2007, Ediciones Universidad Diego Portales, and 2011, ChainLinks.

Artistic Ecologies: New Compasses and Tools

FOREWORD

The struggle must be waged in cultural fronts. To consolidate the revolution, we must create a cultural movement and change people's realities. We no longer need mere changes in individual consciousness, but a change in social consciousness. A new vision of reality must replace the old one. Choose where you want to work, choose, invent your task, do it!

These words are not ours, nor are they new. They are fragments of a poem by Cecilia Vicuña from the 1970s, which opens this volume. It might seem strange to use old words to introduce a book subtitled *New Compasses and Tools*—however, one of the things this book aims to address is the way in which the new has often operated in the art world, and in society at large, since modernity, to produce an image of change in which many things in fact stay the same. It is evident that we need to rearrange the logic of cultural production and institutions as mere elements of a cultural industry that demands a regular substitution of formats and topics, over and again. As Vicuña does, we believe that "a new vision of reality must replace the old one": it is time to think from and in a different direction, and this vision—it is increasingly clear—must be more respectful of life in all its forms.

This book is part of a project, titled *Education from Below*, through which we came together from three different institutions (in scale, place, mission, and nature): the MACBA - Museu d'Art Contemporani de Barcelona,[1] Rijksakademie van beeldende kunsten (Amsterdam), and WHW Akademija (Zagreb). As practitioners that all work with artists, artistic development, and critical culture, we wished to create a shared space through which we could exchange thoughts, practices, and methodologies and create environments in which artists and thinkers can develop new projects, from the ground up. The project seeks to resignify the notion of "education" by collectively reimagining ways of organizing, creating, and exchanging knowledge, both in artistic as well as institutional practices. What structures of learning do we need in order to build alternative pedagogies? How can these nourish and be nourished by non-extractive art ecologies?

Through the *Education from Below* program, we gathered to share concerns and speculate together about possible alternatives to the current state of art practice and artistic institutions. For that purpose, project partners and participants put their experiences and imaginations to work, collectively, thereby building—not just with ideas but also with affects—a structure of mutual support.

Although we could not foresee the shaking brought to our lives by the ongoing-never-ending waves of the pandemic, some elements from our experiences—even prior to COVID-19—seemed to foreshadow a crisis yet to come: the lack of time to implement changes in the art world, the required ceaseless mobility of people, goods, and labor, the demand on artists, curators, and other cultural agents to be flexible and adaptable in the face of increasingly rigid structures, the bureaucratization of artistic work ... These discomforts led us to think of other ways of working, and to think about "education from below." In the midst of the project, the pandemic got us thinking more strongly about the need for new ways to navigate such a crisis, and to open up the question of what kinds of compasses and tools we need, as artists and cultural workers, to be able to continue working in this new global situation.

Under a condition of ongoing all-encompassing crisis, possibilities for concrete artistic ecologies nurtured through self-organization, reciprocity, adaptability, collectiveness, antifragility, and mutual care became relevant on a larger scale. Although the pandemic period has been challenging, many artistic and educational practices—including some presented in this volume—broadened their capacity to embody agile and responsive modes. Essayist Nassim Nicholas Taleb offers the notion of "antifragility" in differentiation to "resilience": whereas resilience "resists shocks and stays the same," antifragility is a newly acquired, transformative quality that does not exist prior to a crisis.[2] Through systems of support, the artistic ecologies we have tried to co-create through this project are able to hold the capacities for intimacy and resistance beyond mere resilience. Pedagogical contexts have always involved aspects of care, from the basic support of participants, listening, and sharing to mutual respect among all involved. Now more than ever, an awareness and practice of care needs to be incorporated into the structure of situations of cultural production and exchange as a shared responsibility. For education in particular, in essence, is care.

We believe that art can help define new ways of reconfiguring our relations to Earth and its inhabitants. To generate new worlds, it is first necessary to break down the top-down Enlightened notion of the institution as a space for the dissemination of knowledge (the good kind). This is why we looked for strategies to imagine more porous models of artistic and institutional practice through which we can learn from and with others. We knew this challenging process would not simply consist of inverting hierarchies—that would not make any sense. Rather, we set out to investigate modes that could make the artistic institution a more democratic and hospitable place. The guiding question of "What can we learn from others?" was not used as a tool to merely look for other sources from which to acquire and accumulate knowledge. This question is not about "knowing more" but about learning with others what might be useful in collectively freeing ourselves and lowering our ecological impact. As feminist theorist Donna Haraway exposes, the current spiraling planetary devastation requires *sym-poiesis*, which can be translated as "making with," rather than *auto-poiesis*, "self-making."[3]

This publication is a mélange of textual and visual contributions that explore sites where and practices through which new institutionalities can emerge. Commissioned essays (Pirate Care, Marina Garcés) and new translations of two previously published texts (Yayo Herrero, Max Jorge Hinderer Cruz) build the analytical backbone of the book. Conversations with art practitioners (the Sensing Salon, DAAR - Decolonizing Architecture Art Research) and a transcript of a workshop (Yael Davids) portray alternative ways of forming knowledge through artistic practice. Poems and drawings (by CAConrad, Dan Perjovschi, Cecilia Vicuña)—some published before, some commissioned for this book—together with interventions and contributions by residents of the Rijksakademie in Amsterdam and participants of WHW Akademija in Zagreb and the Independent Studies Programme at the MACBA in Barcelona (Luna Acosta, Eva Ďurovec, Margherita Isola, Jammers, Teuta Gatolin) offer different heterodox channels through which education from below can emerge.

These collected essays, conversations, drawings, and poems offer analysis, but also speculation, that fosters imagination and helps in thinking through and creating alternatives—to hierarchized pedagogy, to technocratic institutions, to extractive practices. This book aims to enable us go somewhere else: those of us who have written it, those of you who read it, and all those with whom we discuss it. It is not meant to just affirm what we already know and do. Nor does it aim to represent particular identities or positions. It should instead help us to continue working together and impact our practices. It is a book with its own agency, one that inspires and calls to action. We need to access more transformative and playful energies in order to reconfigure the cultural and educational fields, to transgress boundaries, to cross over into an unknown future. In a time when public institutions are under all kinds of pressure, it is essential to continue being critical of institutions but also to passionately defend their significance and to acknowledge their essential role in the civilizatory change brought about by the material scarcity and global warming of the growth economy. Without a powerful institutional network, we cannot implement the changes required if we want to continue living on this planet as a species. Without radical imagination, dialogue through practice, and the invention of new compasses and tools, we cannot progress and invent the institutions of the future.

—Ivet Ćurlin • Ana Dević • Nataša Ilić • Pablo Martínez • Emily Pethick • Sabina Sabolović

NOTES

1 Shortly before the end of the *Education from Below* project, Pablo Martínez was dismissed from his position as Head of Programming at the MACBA as part of the museum's organizational restructuring. He continued to work on the project and this publication without institutional affiliation with the MACBA.

2 Nassim Nicholas Taleb, *Antifragile: Things That Gain from Disorder* (New York: Random House, 2012), 36.

3 Donna J. Haraway, *Staying with the Trouble: Making Kin in the Chthulucene* (Durham, NC: Duke University Press, 2016).

Dan Perjovschi

virus
EUROPE

Drawings (2020–21)

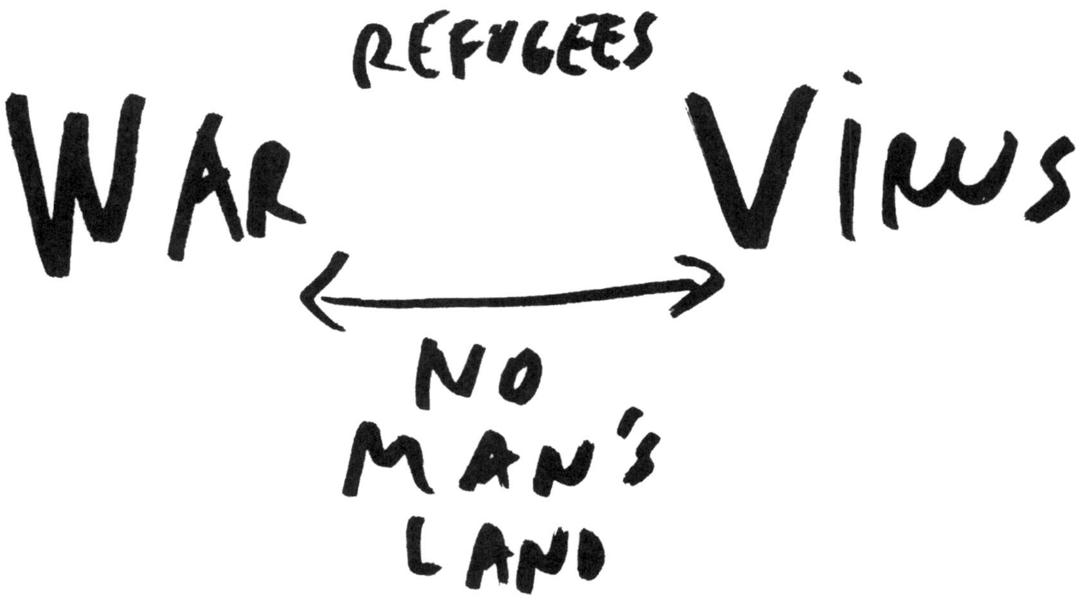
REFUGEES
WAR
VIRUS
NO MAN'S LAND

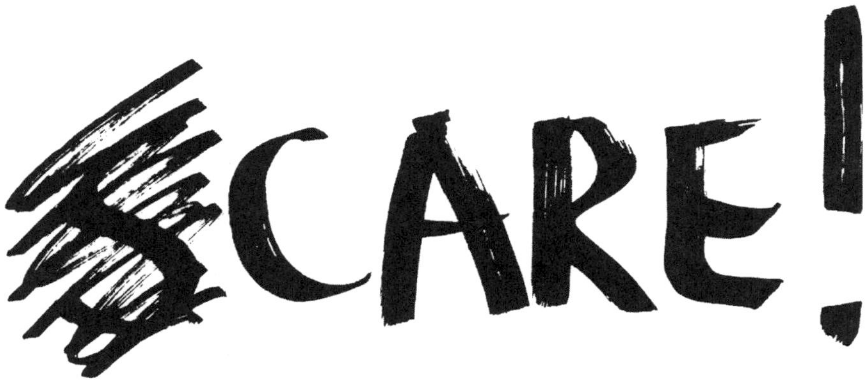
SCARE!

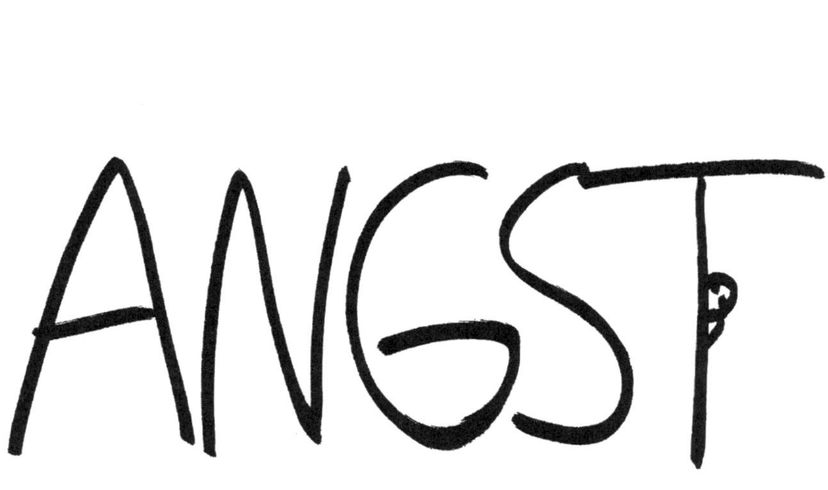
ANGST

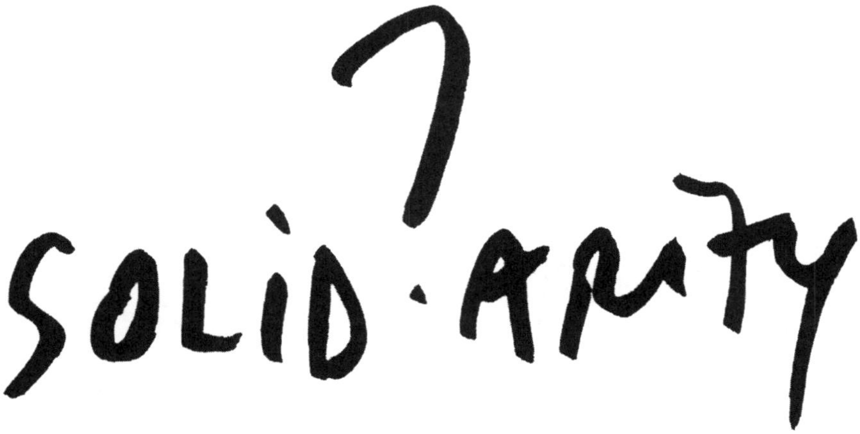
SOLIDARITY

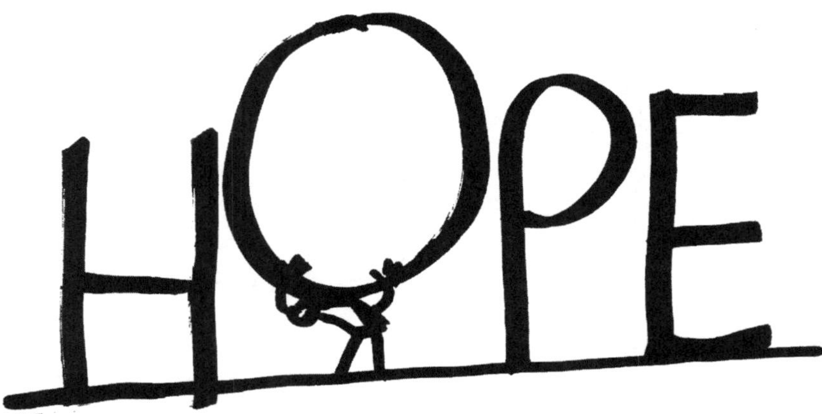
HOPE

Subjects Rooted to the Earth and Bodies:

Toward a Human Culture that Recognizes Limits and Vulnerability

—Yayo Herrero

Our society, entirely enthralled by its own achievements, calls itself the "society of knowledge." Over the last few decades, Earth's biocapacity has been surpassed, biodiversity is vanishing at ever increasing rates, and the biosphere's dynamic processes have been completely disrupted—and yet, this crisis of life itself is going largely ignored, both socially and politically. All our human knowledge, of which we are so proud, cannot save us from ourselves. Those who enjoy great economic and political power, and to a large extent the social majorities who let them have it, do not seem to realize that our species depends on these natural assets. They are evidently unaware that humankind is altering the same specific biogeophysical conditions that are necessary to its survival: we rely on the great thriving branch of biodiversity, and we are hacking away at it with great zeal.

Western culture, historically forced upon the rest of the world by means of trade and war, has a fundamental flaw: that is, the belief that the human species and its cultures are separate from (and more valuable than) the rest of the living world. Unlike Indigenous communities around the planet, we in the West believe that people can live beyond nature's limits, thereby disregarding the inherent weakness of our vulnerable, finite bodies. We feel that we are adjacent to the complex web of life itself.

The fiction that humans can live "emancipated" from nature, from our own bodies, or from other people is a pillar of the Western civilizing project. Ignoring individual immanence and vulnerability, and the existence of physical limits, has been possible for Westerners only because natural resources and cycles, other territories, other species, and women and other subjugated peoples have borne the brunt of the environmental, social, and day-to-day consequences of these lives, which are so falsely detached from ecodependence and interdependence. The architecture of today's neoliberal societies, built upon patriarchal, anthropocentric, and capitalist foundations, endangers the ecological harmony that enables all human life (and that of other species), and it threatens to bring about genuine anthropological collapse.[1]

Humankind finds itself in a tricky situation. The best scientific information available suggests that ecosystems are already languishing and that it is impossible to keep denying the depletion of energy sources and materials. It is no longer credible, furthermore, to claim that environmental deterioration is the inevitable price to pay for living in societies in which most people feel safe and secure: while nature is being destroyed, inequalities stemming from power imbalances of all kinds—in terms of gender, class, country of origin, age, and so on—have been exacerbated. The dynamics that lead to social exclusion are accelerating, at a terrifying rate.

Only a small minority of men, and even fewer women, can live their lives as if they face no physical constrictions, and as if they have no responsibility to other people. Even so, the hegemonic economy, politics, and culture are organized as if those same individuals are, in fact, the universal subject. Economic, financial, legislative, political, ethical, and religious systems have been created to fit perfectly with that fantasy, that is, the fantasy of independence from Earth and our bodies. The dominant imaginaries do not help us see that we are facing catastrophe, and neither do they suggest ways of avoiding it. The processes of socialization build suicidal subjectivities.

The twentieth-century historian Fernand Braudel highlights the close bond between a given social regime and the type of people required to make it work.[2] Capitalism, and its accompanying culture and social organization, can be maintained only if the masses are complicit, if people are made to see things as capitalism sees them, making them yearn for the things it can give them. They must also internalize the notions of progress, wealth, property, justice, freedom, and hierarchy, all of which are crucial for the continuation of the regime.

Therefore, it is imperative that we scrutinize and understand the foundations upon which our culture is built, and we must identify the dogmas, myths, and beliefs that condition how we interpret and react to all that surrounds us.

Analyzing how humankind has embroiled itself in this war on life, and pinpointing which ideas have led it there, is important if we are to plot out the urgently needed transition to other ways of doing things. Changing course—so that we start to live as if a war on life really has been declared—means finding a way to penetrate the imaginaries that most people use to understand and act in the world. Essentially, it means diving directly into all that which is "believed to be true."[3]

Rethinking all the mental blueprints and representations that we use to understand and act in the world is crucial if we are to reposition ourselves as a species. We must form different kinds of relations so that we can rebuild what was lost and invent that which never happened.

The following discussion focuses on two of the main reasons why, in my opinion, humankind is hurtling toward anthropological collapse. We shall consider the ontological breakdown that falsely separates Western societies from nature and bodies as well as certain fictions that arise from ideas about conventional economics, that is to say, the falsehoods we perceive as absolute truths. These are not the only beliefs that can be harmful to human beings and societies—fictions based on notions of tech worship and androcentrism also need to be revised—but these beliefs are particularly relevant here, because they make it harder for people to see themselves as eco- and interdependent, thus obscuring their awareness of the essence of human life itself.

We Exist in Vulnerable Bodies, on a Planet with Physical Limits

We humans are just one of many species that inhabit this planet, and, as with all of them, we take exactly what we need to stay alive: food, water, shelter, energy, minerals, and so on. That's what I mean when I say we are radically ecodependent beings.

When considering the place of the human species in nature, we immediately arrive at the problem of ecological limits. Nonrenewable matter is limited by how much of it already exists (as is the case for minerals and fossil fuels), and anything seemingly renewable also has limits, based on how quickly it can regenerate. The water cycle, the oxygen in the atmosphere, the phosphorus and nitrogen in the soil—all depend on complex sequences that work at a pace nothing like the one imposed, for example, by the farming industry. Also, the planet's natural carbon sinks break down the generated waste by means of biogeochemical processes, which, today, appear to be reaching saturation point.

Nine planetary boundaries affect these biophysical processes, all of which are fundamental to ensuring the continuation of nature's processes at large. These nine limits, which are interdependent, set out a framework within which human life can continue with relative certainty.[4] Overstepping these boundaries takes us into unknown territory where, after certain thresholds, large-scale and high-speed changes could come about, leading to different natural conditions that are less favorable to the human species.

The boundaries in question relate to climate change, the rate of biodiversity loss, the nitrogen and phosphorus cycles, stratospheric ozone depletion, ocean acidification, freshwater use, land-system change, aerosol contamination, and the chemical pollution of land and water.

Of these nine boundaries, the first four have already been surpassed. Today, we are actually living beyond the limits. At a global level, we are no longer living off the riches that nature is able to regenerate: instead, the reserves that allow for such regeneration are being diminished.[5]

Alongside the fact that we live within nature, we humans also exist within our vulnerable, dependent, and finite bodies. Accepting human corporeality leads us to an awareness of the immanence of each human life and the necessary interdependence among people. From birth until death, we depend physically and emotionally on other people and all the work they do for us. Throughout our lives, and particularly at certain points of the life cycle, we survive only because other people devote their time and energy to looking after our bodies.

Throughout history, women have been in charge of this ongoing, cyclical, and vital task. As such, men were liberated from it, shirking this responsibility and enjoying a great deal of free time for other, more leisurely, and often more public activities. Although some have ascribed this responsibility to women's supposedly inherent caring nature, this arrangement is not just a case of straightforward altruism: women's lives are invariably "circumscribed by obligated labour performed on the basis of duty, love, violence or fear of loss of economic support."[6]

The invisibility of interdependence, the devaluation of maintaining social connections, and the subordination of empathy and caregiving logics in favor of reason and economic utility are key tenets of patriarchal societies: "The greater the devaluation, in the social discourse, of relationships and emotions, the more patriarchal the society."[7]

Dualisms That Legitimize the Culture of Violent Control over Nature and Bodies

The Western model was built upon the idea of Man's control over nature and Man's control over women. One of the most effective tactics in establishing this culture of domination was to implement a model based on dual thinking. This binary approach, which was rooted in classical Greco-Roman culture, was prevalent in the construction of modernity, and it played a key role in shaping the sensibilities of the Enlightenment-era subject.

Dual thinking interprets the world as composed of binary opposites that separate and divide reality: nature versus culture, reason versus emotion, science versus traditional forms of knowledge, public versus domestic, and so on. But the quirk of this Western vision is that hardly any mutual interaction exists between these supposed opposites, nor any complementarity, and that, furthermore, these proposed dichotomies are in fact hierarchical. Within each pair of opposites, one is seen as superior to the other. Culture beats nature; the mind is superior to the body; reason is above emotion. In the end, the term deemed superior is proclaimed the universal one, and it thereby represents the whole. The other term in the pair, the inferior one, thus becomes the simple absence or lack of the absolute term, until it is ultimately made invisible.[8]

Feminist thinking considers how these pairs relate to one another and also how they are furthermore assigned to each gender—again, in a binary way. On one side is man, along with culture, the mind, reason, and a public presence; on the other side is woman, perceived as essentially linked to nature and the body, "subjugated" by her own emotions, and "naturally" responsible for the domestic sphere. Without the need to formulate any direct equivalences between these binaries, nonexplicit semantics emerge, whereby the supposedly superior terms all become associated with each other and vice versa, leading to the construction of two separate worlds.[9]

To build a culture of emancipation, of noncontrol and nonviolence, we need to thoroughly revise some of the myths that this dichotomous way of understanding the world has instilled in our cultural framework.

The First Myth of the Ideology of Control: Man Is Nature's Master

Despite our irrevocable dependence on nature, in Western societies human beings have put up a symbolic wall that cuts them off from the rest of the living world, creating a true ontological rift between human life and the planet it exists upon.[10] Our culture explores and understands nature from a position of exteriority, superiority, and instrumentality.

In the seventeenth century, Isaac Newton "discovered" the mechanical and predictable character of nature. The utter complexity of the universe was reduced to the logic of a vast machine, and the science that arose during modernity seemed to conclude that nature was stupid.[11] Thus science came to be seen as a system for controlling and dominating this submissive automaton. Francis Bacon had earlier linked knowledge to power, and he highlighted its utilitarian side by claiming that nature may be "commanded and subdued" by scientific advances. Similarly, René Descartes, in 1637, claimed that acquiring further knowledge of the laws of mathematics that order nature would allow human beings to manipulate the living world according to their whims. For him, animals and plants are also machines that work by reacting to external stimuli.

Following the "discovery" of the mechanical simplicity of the living world, people no longer saw nature as something magical—as supernatural and unfathomable—a perception that had endured until the end of the Middle Ages. Instead, in the modern era, people began to see nature as an automaton, an obstacle to be overcome, to be dominated from the outside.[12] Galileo Galilei too agreed with this idea of human progress as the rejection of natural materiality. As the physical chemist Ilya Prigogine and philosopher of science Isabelle Stengers note, it would seem that "the more that nature is belittled, more glorified is he who escapes from it."[13]

Understanding nature and the body as automata is what triggers the "elimination of magic from the world."[14] Nature is stripped of its divine character, of its unpredictable and mysterious condition. It is no longer a complex, living organism but rather a clock governed by a mathematical mechanism that the scientist must endeavor to comprehend. Nature is reduced to a measurable web, ordered by geometric and mathematical laws.

If nature is thus simple and predictable, then the illusion of transcendence—of getting closer to God—is achieved by separating oneself from it, and by using one's reason to subdue any and all matter that can be dominated. Over time, as scientific and technological advances allowed for more and more of nature's phenomena to be controlled, the result was a heightened sense of power and greater emotional detachment for humankind.[15] Individuals' relationship with nature came to be established by means of ideas and abstract concepts rather than experience.

Later, particularly in the twentieth century, science moved on from these initial visions of modern physics. It found that nature is, in fact, a complex system, somewhat closer to the medieval intuitions that were based on a firsthand and emotional approach to it. Nature contains cause-and-effect relationships, but also feedback loops and synergies. Its logic features both fixed rules and randomness. Life flits between conservation and change, between structure and surprise.[16] While today nobody would claim that nature works like a vast machine, many technoscientific applications still operate as if this is believed to be the case. Our planet has become a great laboratory, subjected to an enormous range of experiments designed to boost the profits of various economic sectors.[17]

Today's collective imaginary remains riddled with the notion of being able to control nature. Due to this worrying ecological illiteracy, a large part of global society and many of its institutions still treat rivers as waterpipes and animals as factories of protein and fat. Most citizens do not consider themselves part of nature, and they believe that science and technology will be able to reverse all the damage they are doing. A great many have absolute faith in technology, and they therefore believe, noncritically, that science will invent something to replace the materials and fossil fuels that the economic metabolism is rapidly depleting, or that some technical innovation will come along to restore the planet's biocapacity.

The idea of progress is often linked to breaking through what is perceived to be a limit. Control over life itself, of which we are part, is embodied in our obsession with eliminating the obstacles that get in the way of our desires. Any "accident of geography" or physical limit that prevents this from happening is deemed a challenge to overcome. But what we do not see, when crossing such boundaries, is the destruction, depletion, and deterioration of that which we need in order to survive.

The Second Myth of the Ideology of Control: The Delocalized Being

In addition to reducing the world to a series of binaries, dual thinking establishes a dichotomous relationship between mind and body, the latter of which is considered the natural and less valuable side of one's being.

We even find evidence of the devaluation of the body in classical Greece. For Plato, *logos* is what brings order to the world, while the body and materiality are essentially chaotic. Ever since this philosophical conception separating the "mind" and the "body," a rupture has existed between the world of ideas and corporeality.

The cultural rift between man on the one side and nature and the body on the other is founded upon political organization. In Athenian democracy, women became associated with domestic production and reproductive sexuality, and enslaved subjects were those who interacted with nature in order to produce what was needed to sustain life—and yet carrying out these functions was still not enough for them to attain the status of citizen.

Modern philosophy delved even deeper into the dichotomous vision that separates mind and body. Descartes considered the body to be an array of limbs, a collection of particles that obey uniform laws of physics and are set into motion at God's will. For him, the human essence is something that resides in the mind and its ability to reason. The body, according to this view, is just an accidental condition that holds what is truly human: the mind, and its ability to think. Thus, there is an ontological division that divorces the body from the person. The body is literally dehumanized. It is nothing more than a string of mechanically arranged particles that, just like nature, can be controlled. Ultimately, it is only the ability to reason that bestows this machine-body with humanness.

Modern man's lack of any emotional link with nature or his own "exploitable" body is thus explained. The control and subjugation of all that is deemed to be simple, mechanical, and predictable is thereby "rationalized." Placing the feminine (dichotomously separated from the masculine) on the same side as nature and the body is a way of justifying the subjugation and control of women. The rational human being, detached from nature, from others, and from his own body, becomes the definitive abstract subject of history.

The body is the metaphor for the individual's own localization. It is the realm of the being, and, like nature itself, it is finite. But capitalist culture, in its crusade against physical limits, also rebels against human time frames, and it treats the body like any other commodity that "must always be brand new and in perfect condition."[18] This culture encourages contempt and fear of old age and sickness, and it strives to ensure death is terrifying. As we ignore the body's vulnerability, we construct a deranged illusion of immortality.

In human terms, the body is where culture and time are inscribed.[19] As human beings, we are nothing more than a body, in its various dimensions: materiality, appearance, aesthetics, body language, movement, sensoriality, emotionality, perception, intuition, and cognition. The body should not be understood as only a biological or a sociological category; it is rather an intersection between the physical, the symbolic, and the sociological. The body contains not only the identity and the material conditions of existence but also that which we call agency—that is, individual and collective praxis.[20]

Accepting the body's finiteness, its vulnerability and needs, is crucial for understanding the interdependent essence of our species, as well as for setting out reciprocity, cooperation, connections, and relationships as indispensable conditions for humankind. This dependence, which is inherent to the human condition, is systematically ignored, just like the invisible many who look after vulnerable bodies.

Life cannot be reproduced if no one cares for other bodies. This is why, although caregiving is an invisible and unspoken task, capitalism and patriarchy join forces to oblige women to carry it out, in the private space of the home. In this sense, feminist sociologist Maria Mies and ecofeminist Vandana Shiva make the case that both seeds and women's bodies, as holders of the capacity for regeneration, make up some of the last remaining colonies in the eyes of the patriarchy.[21]

The Great Transformation: The Economy against the Earth and Bodies

Within this context of the dichotomous worldviews that came to separate Man from nature and the body, significant changes came about—the results of applying modern scientific postulates to economics as well as the creation of the fiction of a self-regulating economy. These changes not only influenced economic science but also affected social organization, the idea of the person, and collective imaginaries.

The early twentieth-century economic historian Karl Polanyi calls this shift "the great transformation." He highlights how the rise of the new economic sciences triggered a mechanism with the sole motivation of making profit. The result "was comparable in effectiveness only to the most violent outbursts of religious fervor in history."[22]

Conventional economics, now hegemonic, is a direct descendant of this approach. It is worth highlighting some of its fictions in order to piece together the knowledge that might help us reorient it and allow us to comprehend the dominating subjectivity it has constructed.

When the Notion of Production Covers Up the Destruction of Material Bases

For the physiocrats of the eighteenth century, production meant all that which nature regenerates cyclically, with the aid of human labor. Production was, for example, agriculture. A planted seed bears fruit thanks to sunlight, water, the nutrients in the soil, and the work of farmers. Fishing, as long as the regeneration rates in the fishing waters were respected, was also considered production, as was the exploitation of forests.[23]

Therefore, production meant boosting nature's riches without diminishing the physical base that allowed for their cyclical regeneration. In the physiocrats' view, consumption and economic growth made sense only as long as they were based on this notion of organic production and if nature's capacity for reproduction could be conserved.

Since this first conceptualization of the notion of production, which is now the hegemonic one, a shift of huge cultural significance has occurred.

The first step in this transformation was the downgrading of the concept of "value" to the concept of "price." That is, whereby something has economic value only if it can be expressed in monetary units, with the importance of "use value" replacing that of "exchange value." Production thus became any process in which an increase in value occurs, measured in monetary terms. As such, materials like iron, fossil fuels, and copper started to be "produced," though this incorrect use of the term was a front for the mere profitable reselling of preexisting finite riches.[24] Production became confused with simple extraction, ignoring the idea of limits, and thus establishing the myth that it is possible to "produce," on an industrial scale and at will, everything we need to stay alive.

Even genuinely renewable types of production, such as, historically, those derived from farming and fishing, have gradually become unsustainable and harmful to ecosystems due to the ramping up of production rates.[25] As a result, traditional agriculture, based on solar energy, photosynthesis, and human labor, turned into industrial production, which requires the extraction of finite resources like oil and minerals, often brought in from faraway places.

This transformation would not have been possible without vast technological deployment. These advances took the modernity-era dream (i.e., of control over nature) and turned it into a reality—albeit temporarily and thanks to the availability of cheap energy. The combination of capitalism and technoscience has managed to channel the global flows of energy and material reserves toward the capitalist economic metabolism.

The step down from "value" to "price" meant that the complexities of natural regeneration, as well as the human tasks that do not fit into the commercial model, accordingly became overlooked and excluded from the realm of economic study. Both became invisible and divested of all importance.

In essence, this downgrading is what led society and the economy to believe that land and work can always be replaced by capital. And little wonder that such an idea colonized people's minds, because technology has undoubtedly allowed some places to exceed their maximum-load capacity at the expense of other territories' resources. The mistake is to assume that crossing the limits in this way can be sustained over time and can spread to all territories (without even expanding on the fact that this is based on an unequal and unjust relational framework).

Capital can replace land and work only so long as there exist places to buy cheap energy and materials and a semi-enslaved workforce. We have gone from living in an empty world to a full world,[26] and there are now fewer and fewer places left to pillage. And the insurmountable physical limits show that once material reserves have been exhausted and natural processes altered beyond repair, it's too late: what has been destroyed cannot be regenerated (at least not in human-scale time frames), no matter how much you pay.

This transformation in the idea of production influences the cultural plane greatly. When production is solely measured in terms of profit, the economy and society are not bothered about the nature of what is being produced, and we end up being unable to distinguish between the manufacturing of cluster bombs and the cultivation of wheat. Both of these productions are measured in money, but in terms of their social utility, one destroys life whereas the other nourishes it.

If we look only at the side that creates value in the market (i.e., the price of what is bought and sold) and we do not take into account any negative externalities, then our sole aim is for the production of any given commodity to increase as much as possible, regardless of whether this is socially desirable or not. This is true even if a rise in profits has direct negative knock-on effects. Conventional economics has barely any tools to measure this kind of deterioration, and it celebrates all those types of production that generate economic gains, even if, along the way, the present and future of people and ecosystems are left in tatters.

This is how the sacred myth of growth is built—that is, the belief that any economic growth, considered separately from nature and the work that sustains it, is inherently positive, and that growth is the only possible way for life to go on.

The need for the economy to grow ends up justifying the snatching away of workers' rights, the destruction of land, the obliteration of public services, and the proliferation of penal code reforms. Anything and everything is worth sacrificing if it brings about economic growth, which is the more important aim. And this is so deeply ingrained in our mindsets that the dissenting voices are in the minority; that is, we can now barely hear those who denounce the risk of pursuing economic growth as an aim in itself, without wondering what the cost is, what the motivation is, and who takes the spoils.

Thinking exclusively within the abstract universe of monetary values has cut the umbilical cord that used to connect nature and the economy.[27] We have reached the absurd point of using, in absolute terms, a whole set of indicators according to which truly essential goods and services are not considered riches. This is unlike destruction itself, which counts as wealth under this system: selling weapons or polluting a river can make money, while peace or the conservation of nature might not have much bearing on economic indicators.

To build an economy that suits human beings, production needs to be linked to the maintenance of life and the well-being of people.[28] Some productions are socially necessary, whereas others are socially undesirable. Distinguishing between the two is crucial, and monetary indicators make it impossible to discern between work that satisfies human needs and work that drains finite resources without satisfying any needs at all.

Current societies lay down concrete, build walls, and fly over lands at speed; they wear short sleeves in the winter and get chilly in the summer. They think that money can buy eternal comfort and luxury, and that technology—the fruit of human intellect and reason—can "create" all that which keeps people alive. This is a dangerous concept of progress: one that turns people into admirers of the very civilization that is destroying them.

When the Idea of Work Is Downgraded to Employment

The rise of industry and the process of dispossessing the rural working classes led to the birth of the proletariat, a huge mass of people with no means of production and who, in order to survive, were forced to sell their labor to the owners of these means of production.

Work became what people did in the commercial sphere in exchange for wages, and all tasks carried out in the domestic production space (i.e., those that guarantee reproduction and caregiving) became disregarded. This is despite the fact they are, of course, still essential, both for ensuring survival itself and for actually producing the "commodity" that is the workforce.[29]

From this point on, a new dichotomy was established: the domain of work, which takes place in the economy's public and visible space, became separated from the domain of reproduction, which is not usually reflected in the monetary world, and which is considered less important than the logics and demands of a hypertrophied economy.

The new economy transformed work and the land into commodities and treated them as if they had been produced in order to be sold. The sheer scope of this "great transformation"—as good at stockpiling and making profit as it is dangerous to human communities—can be understood by recalling that "labor is simply the activity of human beings, [and] land is subdivided nature."[30] The creation of both the labor market and a notion of work as falsely cut off from the rest of society was "an act of vivisection performed on the body of society," which in turn became "an accessory of the economic system."[31]

The new notion of work meant that the body had to be in a suitable condition to enact the consistency and automatism demanded by the discipline of capitalist production.[32] That is, the body become a work machine. But the regeneration and reproduction of bodies is not the responsibility of the economy, and so these tasks are consigned to the domestic sphere instead. There, away from the public gaze, women are forced to take on these tasks, which are devalued, despite being fundamental to a decent life as well as to the ongoing reproduction of capitalist production.[33]

Economic theory posits the existence of a kind of abstract subject, the *Homo economicus*: namely, those beings who go to the markets every day to compete, ferociously, against others, in order to feed their own egos. It would seem that only other areas of society (i.e., the ones outside the supposedly self-regulating economy, cut off from the rest of life) are where fairness and mutual support are to be encouraged. But, paradoxically, the commercial space, where reciprocity and limits are not taken into consideration, is that which orders time and space. The relations of ecodependence and interdependence are thus subordinate to the logic of economic utility, which does not prioritize people's well-being but rather the maximization of profits.

No wonder, then, that the result of this form of material organization is the conflict between civilization and life.

Toward a Culture That Is Conscious of Limits and Vulnerability

Rebuilding a fair and sustainable economic metabolism, as well as a different form of social organization in keeping with it, is complex, and changing imaginaries so extensively saturated with symbols and representations from an androcentric, capitalist, and tech-worshipping society is just as difficult, though equally essential. This change will not come about through providing systematic and rational information alone; rather, it requires the mobilization of emotions, perceptions, and practices that can help shed light on new subjectivities. It calls for a process that is both political and artistic.

The urbanologist Ramón Fernández Durán used to say that, for him, a decent society ought to be fair, ecological, antipatriarchal, and happy. I share this view, and I believe that reaching such a utopia will happen only by adhering to certain nonnegotiable conditions that forcibly subvert the aforementioned myths and fictions, that is to say, the falsehoods upon which the cultural narrative of our societies is built.

The first of these conditions is the unavoidable reduction in the economy's material sphere. This is not really up for debate as an idea; it is a factual baseline. The planet's physical limits demand it. Material degrowth will either come about nicely (that is, in a planned, fair way) or not so nicely (abruptly, unjustly, violently).

If we accept that we must comply with the planet's limits, then we must of course also accept that societies will necessarily have to be more austere in their use of materials and their generation of waste. They must use renewable, clean energies and operate more locally in order to close the cycles and conserve diversity. They will also have to slow down, considerably.[34]

The second condition is related to interdependence. The concept of dependence is often associated with raising children, looking after the sick, or assisting those with a disability. However, as we have seen, dependence is not something specific to certain parts of the population, but, rather, as feminist economist Cristina Carrasco notes, "it is the representation of our vulnerability; it is something inherent to the human condition, just like birth and death."[35]

Accepting interdependence (which is necessary for the existence of humankind) in nonpatriarchal societies means that the society as a whole has to take responsibility for well-being and social reproduction. The ideals of equality and social justice can only ever make sense in societies where caregiving tasks are not determined by sex, gender, race, or class.[36] The notion of work thus needs to be broadened, since caregiving should be a basic and indispensable human task, one that creates genuine wealth that can satisfy human needs in a fair and sustainable way. That is, work will have to be about relating with nature and other people and acquiring the means to be able to live decently, and, as such, it will no longer be falsely cut off from the rest of life. As labor scholar Laura Mora Cabello de Alba points out, Taoist philosophy sums up this idea perfectly and beautifully, insomuch as work is considered "the capacity of being."[37]

A third condition is about the distribution of wealth. If we have a planet with limited resources, which are already partially destroyed and dwindling, then the only chance for justice is to divvy up the riches. Fighting against poverty means going after the hoarding of wealth. Reconverting the economy, under this logic, involves answering three questions that arise in feminist economics: What are everybody's needs and how can they be met? What productions are required to meet these needs? What are the socially necessary jobs for these productions?

The final condition stems from the will to build societies that are actually worth living in. The great challenge is learning how to lead a good life with fewer materials and less energy, in such a way that well-being can become universal, for all.

Breaking the symbolic links that associate today's consumerist society with quality of life cannot be put off any longer. Along this journey, as political poet Jorge Riechmann says, "we do not have any metaphysically guaranteed values, but we do have human coexistence, beauty, eroticism, day-to-day pleasures, [and] being there for each other in the face of illness and death."[38]

Placing Life at the Center of Thought and Experience

Reviving perceptions, bringing back a sense of ecodependence and interdependence as a hallmark of the human experience, and destroying the idols of progress linked to growth—these are long overdue and urgent tasks, and necessary if we are to overturn the cultural hegemony that pervades capitalism.

The greatest challenge is convincing people to want this transition to happen. There are no shortcuts, and the work must be done collectively, in institutions, support networks, and civic organizations. This is about educating people, a task that must be carried out almost door to door and using a range of methods. If a change is to come about, we need to highlight the myths and fictions and compose a different cultural narrative more in tune with the essence of human life. This requires science and information, but also art, poetry, and passion.

We are life—in our case, animal life—and becoming conscious of this is one of the first steps toward rethinking the world in ecological terms. This is about comprehending, valuing, and loving the planet's different lifeforms and acknowledging that we are part of a network made up of the climate, water, plants, and air.

Putting life at the center of experience also means being conscious of birth, growth, and death. It means learning to respect nonhuman animals and recognizing how we are both similar to and different from them; it means figuring out the complex and dynamic relationships of ecosystems, which do not work like machines.

Comprehending life also means accepting its rhythms. Slow growth, small alterations, the nuances of day-to-day life: this is how we reach sustainable ways of living, as opposed to the quickfire rhythms and sudden changes so common in our urban and digital surroundings.

Recognizing Interdependence: Building Communities and Collective Power

Placing life at the center means understanding the value of reciprocity and mutual support. Interdependence is a key practical experience when it comes to valuing life and rebuilding societies. As such, if well-being is to become the objective of the social metabolism, then certain nonnegotiable steps must be taken, such as speaking out against those people (mostly adult men) who force other people (generally adult women) to look after them, when they could in fact do this work themselves; learning about the existence of transnational chains of care, always run by women; and demanding the reorganization and fair distribution of this work.

Encouraging the kind of thinking that can help form relationships of mutual support between human beings and Earth means coming up with alternative frameworks based on the ethics of reciprocity, radical democracy, and cooperation. That way, everybody will be included, in terms of their rights as well as their duties.

Caregiving is a complex form of reciprocity, and it should form part of the socialization process. People need to be educated in the culture of "taking responsibility for the other" as a fundamental starting point—this would provide them with a care-centered motivation and outlook, so that they prioritize the ongoing sustainability of human life, lived to the full.

It is mostly in the home where we acquire a sex-based identity, a name, a language, and the rules and technical skills that allow us to become human, or, rather, culturally transformed nature.[39] It is only by receiving this care that we become autonomous, while also dependent—we are transformed into someone who interacts with other human beings in increasingly complex networks of relational interdependence. From this point of view, being human entails being concerned for other people.

Relations of interdependence exist in the realm of material relations, but also within that of affect and emotion. The emotional side is often omitted from disciplines such as economic analysis, but it is irremediably linked with the material side of caregiving and it clearly influences the perceptions and subjectivities of well-being in people's day-to-day lives. The primatologist and ethologist Frans de Waal notes:

> *Except for a tiny percentage of humans—known as psychopaths—no one is emotionally immune to another's situation. The fundamental yet rarely asked question is: Why did natural selection design our brains so that we're in tune with our fellow human beings, feeling distress at their distress and pleasure at their pleasure?*[40]

Empathy, which is strongly stimulated in reciprocal relations, can bridge the gap between selfishness and altruism, since it makes us feel bad about others' hardships. It is based on proximity, similarity, and closeness, and, when it was combined with the overarching aim of social harmony, it evolved in small-scale societies that sought equality and solidarity. The development of empathy—helping us toward a culture of "taking responsibility" for the land and other people—is, in my opinion, the driving force that might help us bring about the right kind of politics and economics for tackling more-than-predictable ecosocial collapse.

Collective organization has created and still creates new possibilities for intervening in the world and exerting power, a power that has been expropriated from many human groups. Today, one socially necessary job is to reweave the fabric of community.

Considering the political aspect of emotions is also important. Within social movements, we have great conceptual wealth and we move freely within the realm of the rational, but we are lacking in regard to the symbolic and we do not connect well with emotions. There can be no revolution without passion, without a love for life and people. Investing time and energy in such an unequal struggle—where there are so many doubts about the outcome—is only possible if you live with feeling, with your head *and* your heart.

We humans cannot be indifferent to others if we want to build a so-called society or community. That is the essence of the social contract and of the possibility of constructing a counter-hegemonic form of power. That is the crux of the civilizing work that needs to be done.

Some Final Considerations: Building Secure Spaces in the Face of Global Risk

In our societies, the home and our nearby community make up the networks that give us most of our safety and security. Building up security is the first and most important reason for social life. The more vulnerable a species is, the larger its aggregations.[41] But, paradoxically, the more individualized a person is—possible only *because of* interdependent society—the lesser their need to feel connected with the community in order to feel subjectively safe. This supports the feeling of independence that many men have, and it constitutes the fantasy of individuality.[42]

The immanence of individual human nature is always framed in radical uncertainty, and, in the face of this, societies have developed knowledge, institutions, and practices to provide the minimal level of security so that people feel safe and sound. In current societies, the sensation of feeling exposed is increasing at a rapid rate: homelessness, job insecurity, the climate crisis, exclusion, violence against women, terrorism, on and on. The extent to which societies are willing to tackle the dangers of depleting resources and the changes in nature's self-organization, as well as the risks of obstructing and incapacitating the ability for day-to-day life to be reproduced, is very much linked with hegemonic visions of political and economic power, which are patriarchal and profit focused. It is also linked with the environmental and biological illiteracy of most people, who have interiorized an unviable idea of progress, well-being, and wealth—the perfect mindset for sustaining the current dominant system.

The rhetoric of prioritizing security is based on the dominant discourse regarding national defense, reinforcing borders, and the criminalization of those who are different. I believe that an ecofeminist material approach would help in rethinking what it means to be safe, what a protective and welcoming society is like, and how we can build safe spaces. The key is to respect limits and the vulnerability of living things. In this sense, economist Kate Raworth makes an interesting point: we human beings have a minimum foundation of needs, and if they are met, we are guaranteed a decent life.[43] However, there also exists an environmental ceiling that we cannot reasonably break through if we want to avoid serious danger. Between this environmental ceiling (marked by the nine planetary limits as described above) and the minimum foundation of needs (housing, food, care, safety, and participation), there is a space in which it is possible to build a secure life for all. If we cross all the boundaries, and given the increasing inequalities in all aspects of domination—class, gender, ethnicity—then we can see that the task at hand, at least on the theoretical and conceptual planes, is clearly enormous.

If we agree that we need an ecological identity based not on the expropriation of the natural world (the body and the land) but rather on a connection with it, then the aim becomes to reorient the social metabolism in such a way that we can avoid—or at least adapt to—the destructive consequences of the current model. This would entail striving for an anthropological vision that positions natural and human physical limits and immanence as inherent features of human existence.

This outlook is beautifully expressed in Cristina Carrasco and Enric Tello's proposal to reformulate the first article of the Declaration of Human Rights. Their version is based on the perspective of care, and I have taken the liberty of making a few additions, based on the viewpoint of ecological limits.

This first article, formulated in 1948, says:

All human beings are born free and equal in dignity and rights. They are endowed with reason and conscience and should act towards one another in a spirit of brotherhood.

To include relations of ecodependence and interdependence, which address (among other disciplines) the environmental and feminist economies, Tello and Carrasco suggest that the first article should rather look something like this:

> *All human beings are born from a mother's womb and they eventually become equal in dignity and rights thanks to the immense and dedicated tasks of attention, care, and day-to-day work, from one generation to the next, which should be shared by both men and women as a fundamental civilizing action for our species. Thanks to this work, people can become endowed with the reason and conscience that allows them to act in a spirit of kinship toward others, being aware that they inhabit a planet with physical limits, a planet shared with all other living things in the world and which they are obliged to conserve.*[44]

This is the enormous but beautiful challenge we face. There is no doubt that everybody is necessary to this task—our diverse knowledges, our inspirations, and our commitment. We'll get there, together.

This is a translation of "Sujetos arraigados en la tierra y en los cuerpos – Hacia una antropología que reconozca los límites y la vulnerabilidad," published in *Petróleo* (*et al.* series), ed. Pablo Martínez (Barcelona: MACBA-Arcàdia, 2018), 77–112.

Translated from Spanish by George Hutton.

NOTES

1 Santiago Alba Rico and Carlos Fernández-Liria, *El naufragio del hombre* (Hondarribia, Spain: Hiru, 2010).

2 Fernand Braudel, *La Dynamique du Capitalisme* (Paris: Flammarion, 1985).

3 Almudena Hernando, "Teoría arqueológica y crisis social," *Complutum* 23, no. 2 (2012): 128.

4 Johan Rockström et al., "Planetary Boundaries: Exploring the Safe Operating Space for Humanity," *Ecology and Society* 14, no. 2 (2009).

5 Rockström et al., "Planetary Boundaries."

6 Mary Mellor, *Feminism and Ecology* (New York: New York University Press, 1997), 189.

7 Hernando, "Teoría arqueológica y crisis social," 136.

8 Celia Amorós, *Hacia una crítica de la razón patriarcal* (Barcelona: Anthropos, 1985).

9 Amorós, *Hacia una crítica de la razón patriarcal.*

10 Jorge Riechmann, *La habitación de Pascal* (Madrid: Los Libros de la Catarata, 2009).

11 Ilya Prigogine and Isabelle Stengers, *La nueva alianza: metamorfosis de la ciencia* (Madrid: Alianza Editorial, 2004).

12 Silvia Federici, *Caliban and the Witch* (New York: Autonomedia, 2004).

13 Prigogine and Stengers, *La nueva alianza*, 78.

14 Max Weber, *The Protestant Ethic and the Spirit of Capitalism* (London: George Allen & Unwin, 1930).

15 Hernando, "Teoría arqueológica y crisis social," 133.

16 Stuart Kauffman, *Investigations* (Oxford: Oxford University Press, 2000).

17 Yayo Herrero, Fernando Cembranos, and Marta Pascual, eds., *Cambiar las gafas para mirar el mundo. Hacia una cultura de la sostenibilidad* (Madrid: Libros en Acción, 2011).

18 Rico and Fernández-Liria, *El naufragio del hombre*, 65.

19 Rico and Fernández-Liria, *El naufragio del hombre*, 65.

20 María Luz Esteban, "Cuerpos y políticas feministas: el feminismo como cuerpo," in *Cuerpos políticos y agencia. Reflexiones feministas sobre cuerpo, trabajo y colonialidad*, ed. Cristina Villalba and Nacho Álvarez (Granada: Universidad de Granada, 2011).

21 Maria Mies and Vandana Shiva, *Ecofeminism* (Halifax, NS: Fernwood, 1993).

22 Karl Polanyi, *The Great Transformation: The Political and Economic Origins of Our Time* (1944; repr. Boston: Beacon, 2001).

23 José Manuel Naredo, *Raíces económicas del deterioro ecológico y social. Más allá de los dogmas* (Madrid: Siglo XXI, 2006).

24 Naredo, *Raíces económicas del deterioro ecológico y social.*

25 Naredo, *Raíces económicas del deterioro ecológico y social.*

26 Herman E. Daly, John B. Cobb, and Clifford W. Cobb, *For the Common Good: Redirecting the Economy toward Community, the Environment, and a Sustainable Future* (Boston: Beacon, 1989).

27 Naredo, *Raíces económicas del deterioro ecológico y social.*

28 Amaia Pérez Orozco, *Perspectivas feministas en torno a la economía: el caso de los cuidados* (Madrid: Consejo Económico y Social, 2006).

29 Cristina Carrasco, "Mujeres, sostenibilidad y deuda social," *Revista de Educación*, no. 1 (2009).

30 Polanyi, *The Great Transformation.*

31 Polanyi, *The Great Transformation*, 181, 126.

32 Federici, *Caliban and the Witch.*

33 Carrasco, "Mujeres, sostenibilidad y deuda social."

34 Jorge Riechmann, *Biomímesis. Ensayos sobre imitación de la naturaleza, ecosocialismo y autocontención* (Madrid: Los Libros de la Catarata, 2005).

35 Carrasco, "Mujeres, sostenibilidad y deuda social," 179.

36 Carrasco, "Mujeres, sostenibilidad y deuda social," 180.

37 Laura Mora Cabello de Alba, "El trabajo con sentido en proceso constituyente," *Papeles*, no. 122 (2013).

38 Riechmann, *Biomímesis*, 116.

39 Mellor, *Feminism and Ecology*.

40 Frans de Waal, *The Age of Empathy: Nature's Lessons for a Kinder Society* (New York: Random House, 2009), 43.

41 De Waal, *The Age of Empathy*, 21.

42 Almudena Hernando, *La fantasía de la individualidad* (Madrid: Katz Editores, 2013).

43 Kate Raworth, "A Safe and Just Space for Humanity: Can We Live within the Doughnut?," *Oxfam International*, February 13, 2012, https://www.oxfam.org/en/research/safe-and-just-space-humanity.

44 Amended quotation from Cristina Carrasco and Enric Tello, "Apuntes para una vida sostenible," in *Sostenibilitats. Polítiques públiques des del feminisme i l'ecologisme*, ed. Maria Freixanet (Bellaterra, Spain: Institut de Ciències Polítiques i Socials de la Universitat Autònoma de Barcelona, 2012).

Margherita Isola

Guerrilla Drugstore

(2021)

GUERRILLA DRUGSTORE

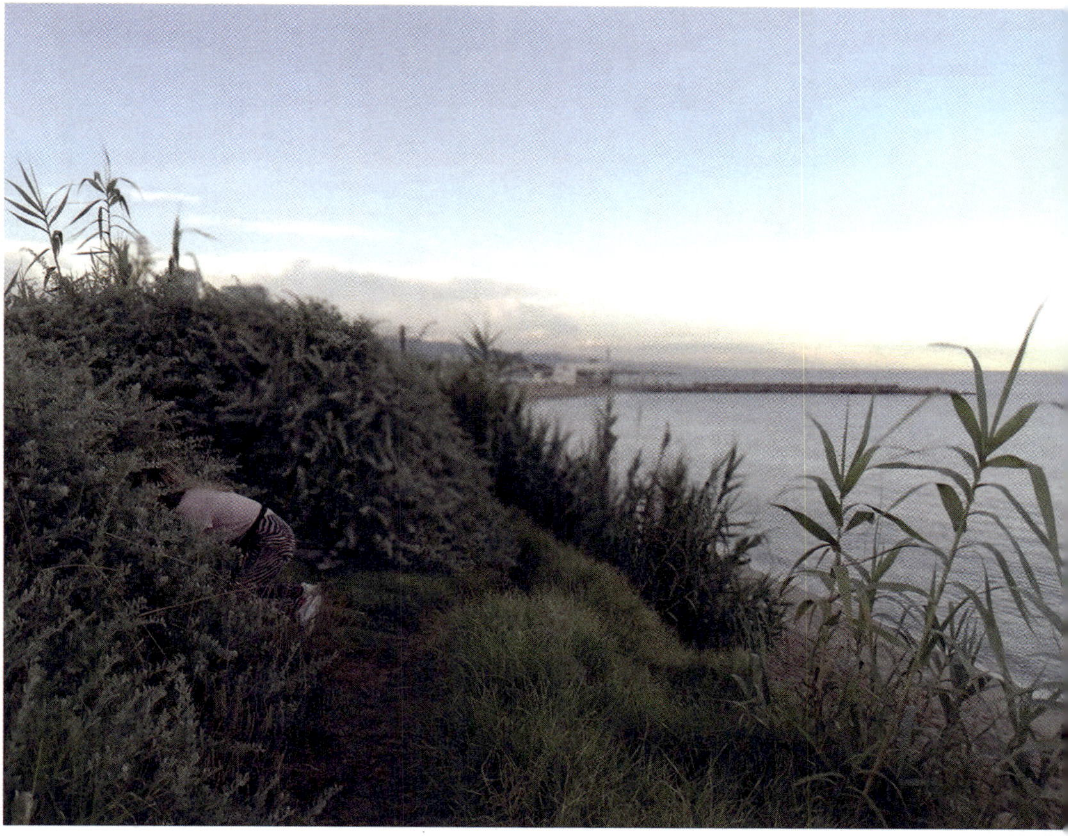

CONEXIÓN CURA

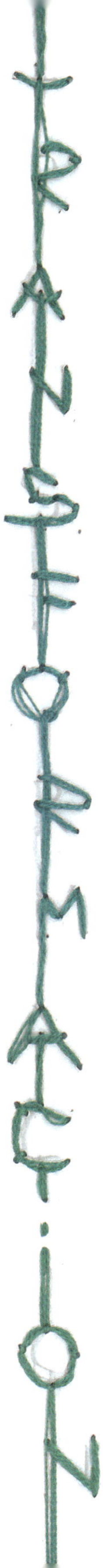
TRANSFORMACION

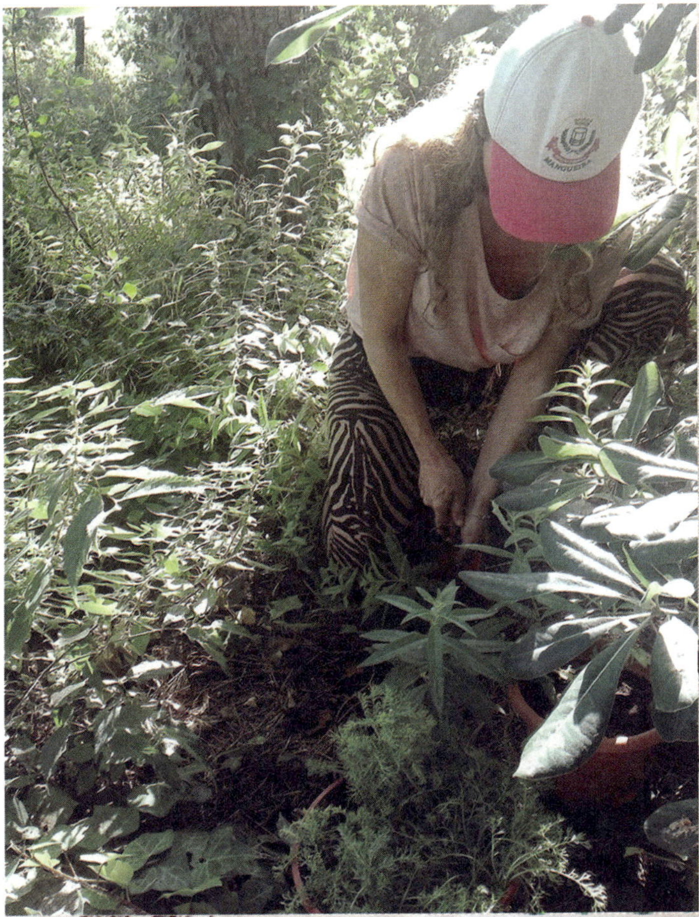

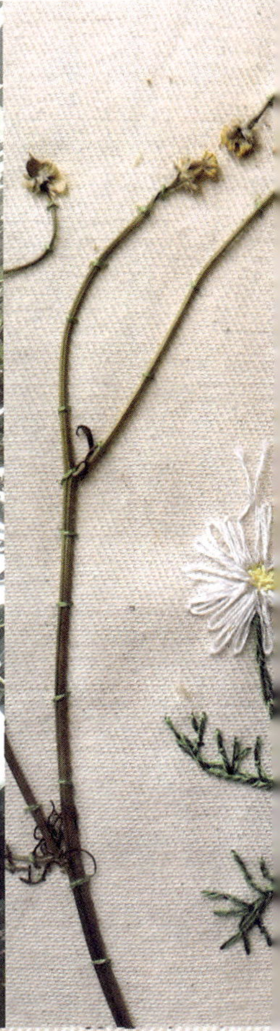

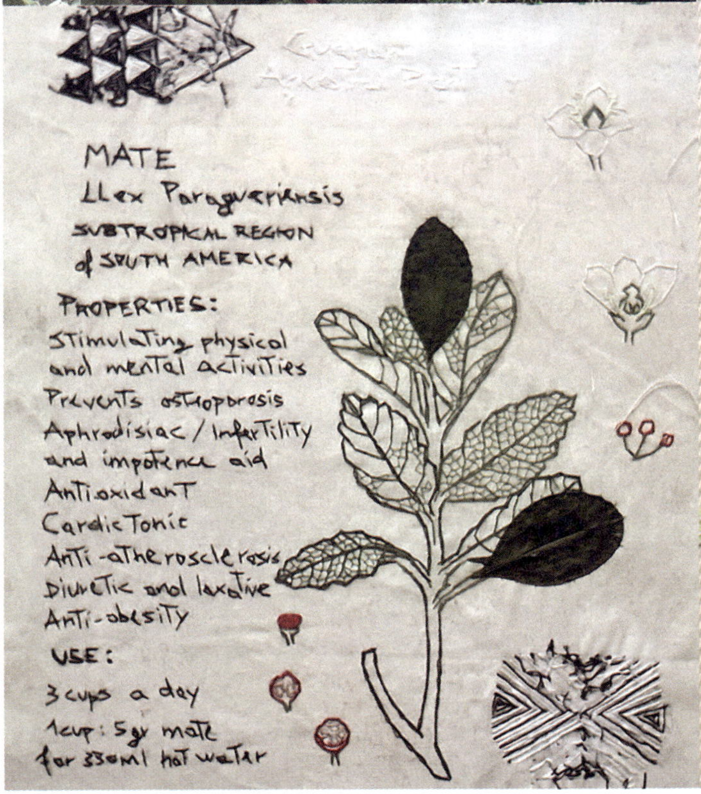
MATE
Llex Paraguariensis
SUBTROPICAL REGION
of SOUTH AMERICA
PROPERTIES:
Stimulating physical
and mental activities
Prevents osteoporosis
Aphrodisiac / Infertility
and impotence aid
Antioxidant
Cardiac Tonic
Anti-atherosclerosis
Diuretic and laxative
Anti-obesity
USE:
3 cups a day
1 cup : 5gr mate
for 330ml hot water

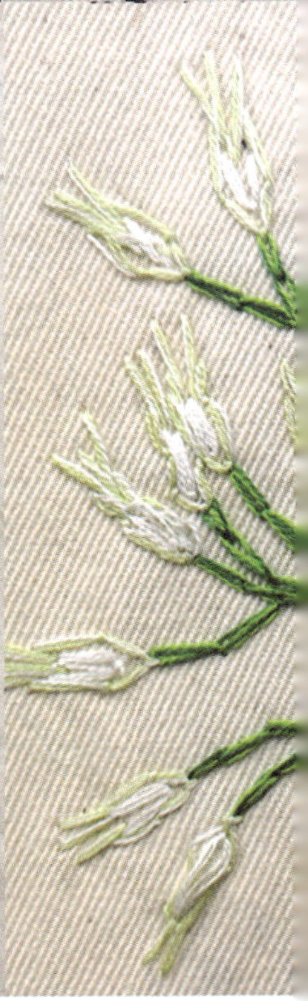

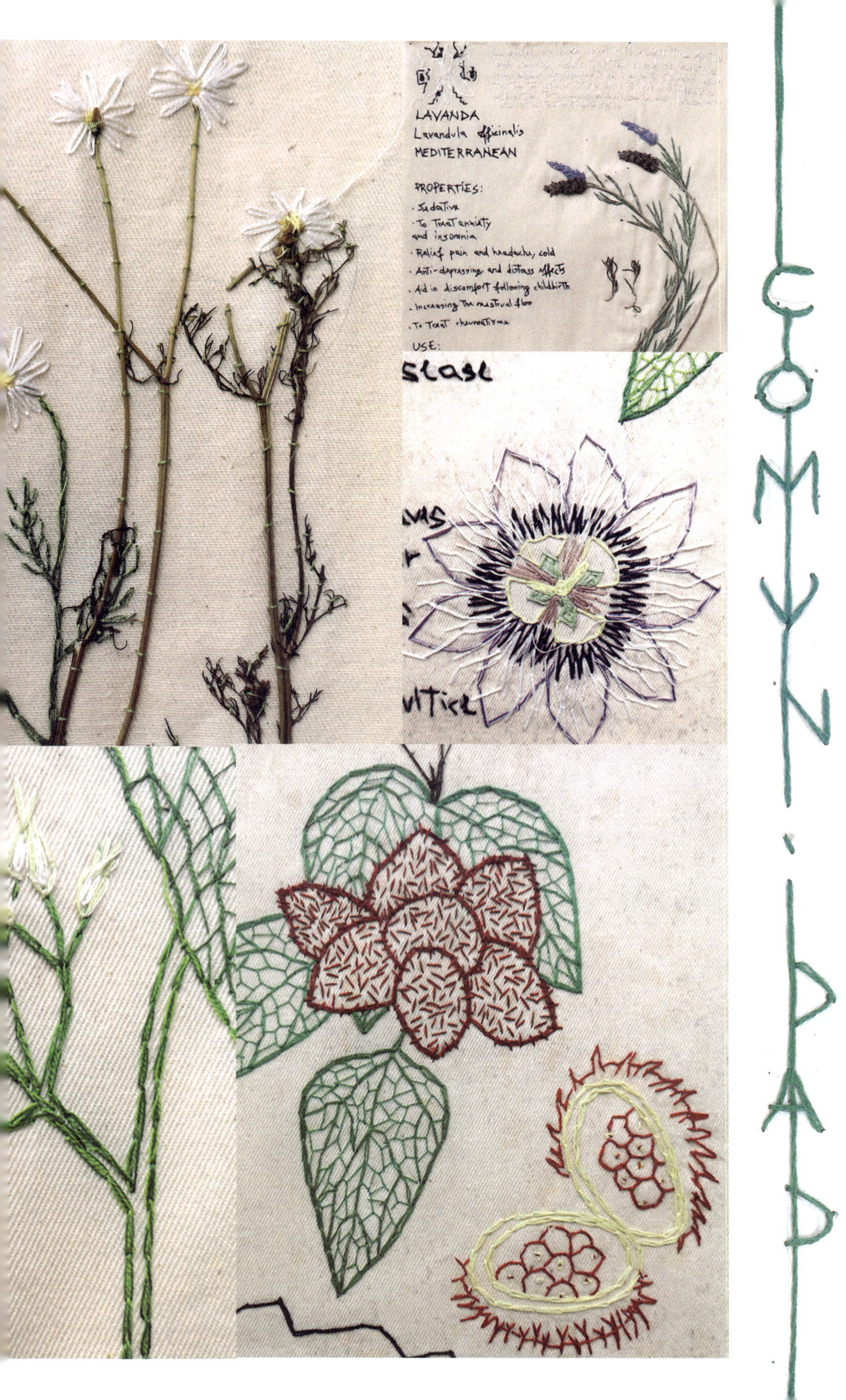
LAVANDA
Lavandula officinalis
MEDITERRANEAN
PROPERTIES:
· Sedativa
· To Treat anxiety and insomnia
· Relief pain and headache, cold
· Anti-depressing and distress effects
· Aid in discomfort following childbirth
- Increasing the menstrual flow
· To Treat rheumatisms
USE:
COMUNIDAD

LISTEN

Dear Julia,

Thank you for accepting my invitation
and taking care of this sacred plant,
which was raped
and which is still being violated to this day.
Incredible as it may seem,
I planted its seeds at the spring equinox,
on my terrace, in the middle of the lockdown.
I planted these seeds, so small that they seemed to be nothing,
in the worst conditions,
but completely hopeful.
The seeds were given to me by the Mujeres do Gau,
a wonderful collective of retired women
who run a garden on the outskirts of São Paulo.
I packed a sacred twig from the South in my suitcase
and took it to Barcelona.
I waited a few weeks and
out of the darkness of the earth this little plant was born.
The tobacco you're going to take care of is part of the remedies of
Guerrilla Drugstore,
a street pharmacy of medicinal plants that were once
suppressed,
capitalized,
forgotten,
and made invisible,
which is being born in Barcelona to expand outward.
Most of the pharmacy's remedies are cultivated by taking up land in the city,
but in the case of tobacco, it is grown indoors,
managed through a home-based care network
of which you are part.

As a caregiver
you receive the plant on the day of the summer solstice,
under a totally favorable sky,
with a partial eclipse of the sun and a new moon.
Please note that it is a plant that loves heat and humidity.
Plenty of water, but well filtered so that no deposits remain.
The direct sun of the European climate dries its leaves too much,
so you can humidify them regularly
by creating a homemade tropical microclimate.
Each caregiver can continue to weave
the tobacco's web of connection,
by distributing new plants to other beings
who can take care of them
and be nurtured by them.
Part of the tobacco kit is a musical piece composed by Younes Zarhoni.
"Tabac Tarab."
A song for the spirit of the plant,
because, as Bob Marley said
—all songs come from the Gods.
As our dear Karen said, it is an invitation to listen
and feel the energy of the plants,
of this one and others.
To feel them is a gift firstly for us,
because to do so,
we need to feel and listen to ourselves deep inside,
and in this connection of listening, caring, and interdependence
it is possible to create other forms of life.
Let's make this happen.
Please, savor the listening.

https://guerrilladrugstore.bandcamp.com/releases

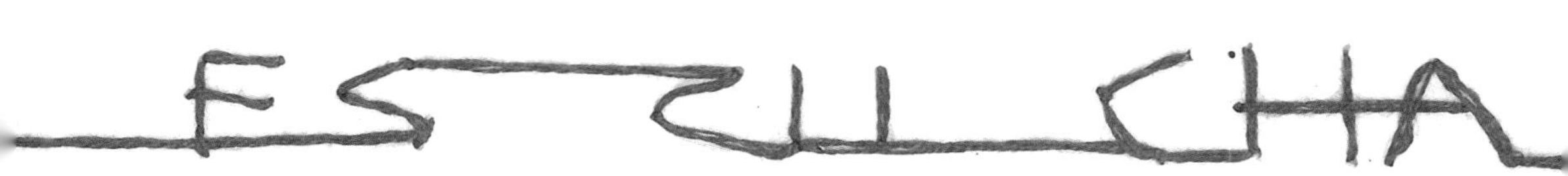

Sandi Hilal & Alessandro Petti (DAAR)

in conversation with WHW

Tree Schools

The Tree School is a gathering place for groups and individuals interested in learning from each other and in sharing common urgencies based on lived experiences. Developed by Sandi Hilal and Alessandro Petti, who work under the name DAAR–Decolonizing Architecture Art Research, the Tree School can last for days, months, or years, depending on the participants' interests. It is a space for conviviality and the joy of learning together. Learning under the shade of a tree is a common practice found in many cultures around the world. The tree is a living being with its own particular story and mythologies. Its connection with other plants offers a physical and metaphorical space for sharing knowledge.

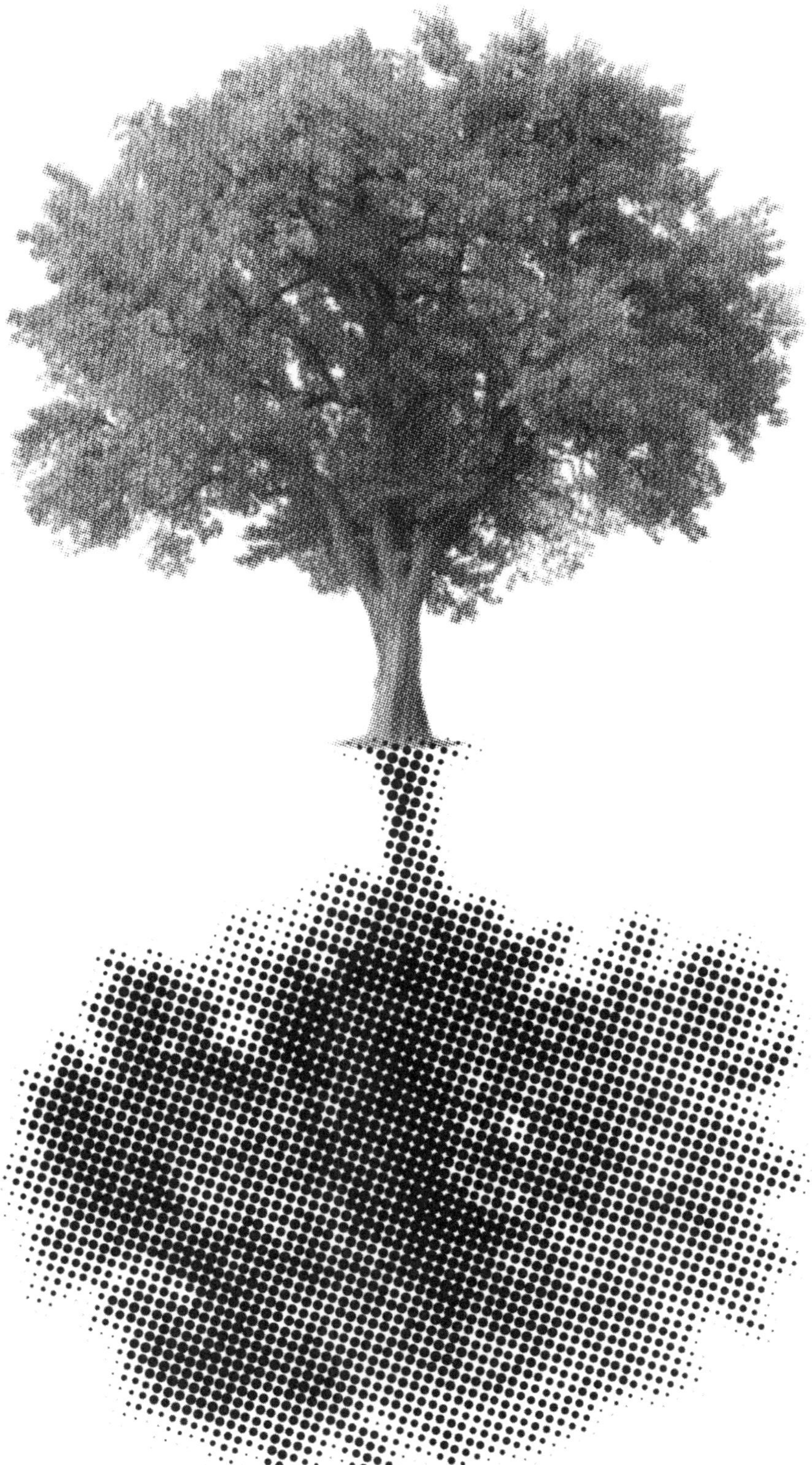

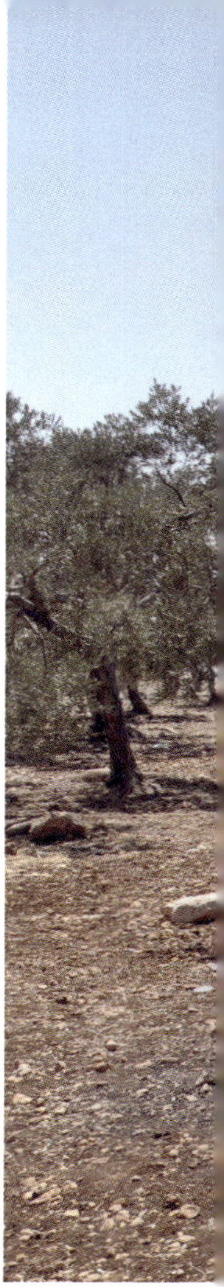

WHAT, HOW & FOR WHOM / WHW: Before we get to the Tree School—the idea behind it, its development, and its iterations—tell us about DAAR and how it started.

DAAR: DAAR is an art collective, and the name has a twofold meaning. On the one hand, it stands for "decolonizing architecture, art, and research." Our artistic practice is situated at the intersection of these fields, and we experiment by trying to inhabit these different worlds and bring them together. In doing so, we strive to create learning environments through our practice.

But the name DAAR also derives from the Arabic word for "home" (دار, *dār*), since our practice originated in our own domestic space. We are partners in both life and work, and through our practice—as a family and with extended family—we look into everyday practices of life, to try to better comprehend and understand them, in order to improve life itself. So we thought that perhaps there was no better place to start a discourse not yet present in public than the domestic space. It is indeed the crux of our approach: to operate in the domestic and influence the public realm, rather than the other way around.

Another important aspect of our practice is that it is always done in collaboration, and usually built around a series of relations. These relations form between people, places, and research and exist between architecture, politics, and the arts.

Before you came to Sweden—where you have lived and worked for four years now—you were in Palestine. How did that segment of your life shape your practice?

When we arrived to Palestine in 2002—which was a return for Sandi, since she lived in Beit Sahour until she was seventeen—we realized not much discussion was happening around decolonization in general, let alone decolonizing knowledge and architecture. So we began looking into the Israeli colonization and Israeli architecture in order to find strategies to subvert these predetermined spatial relations. But moving to Palestine was crucial for us to

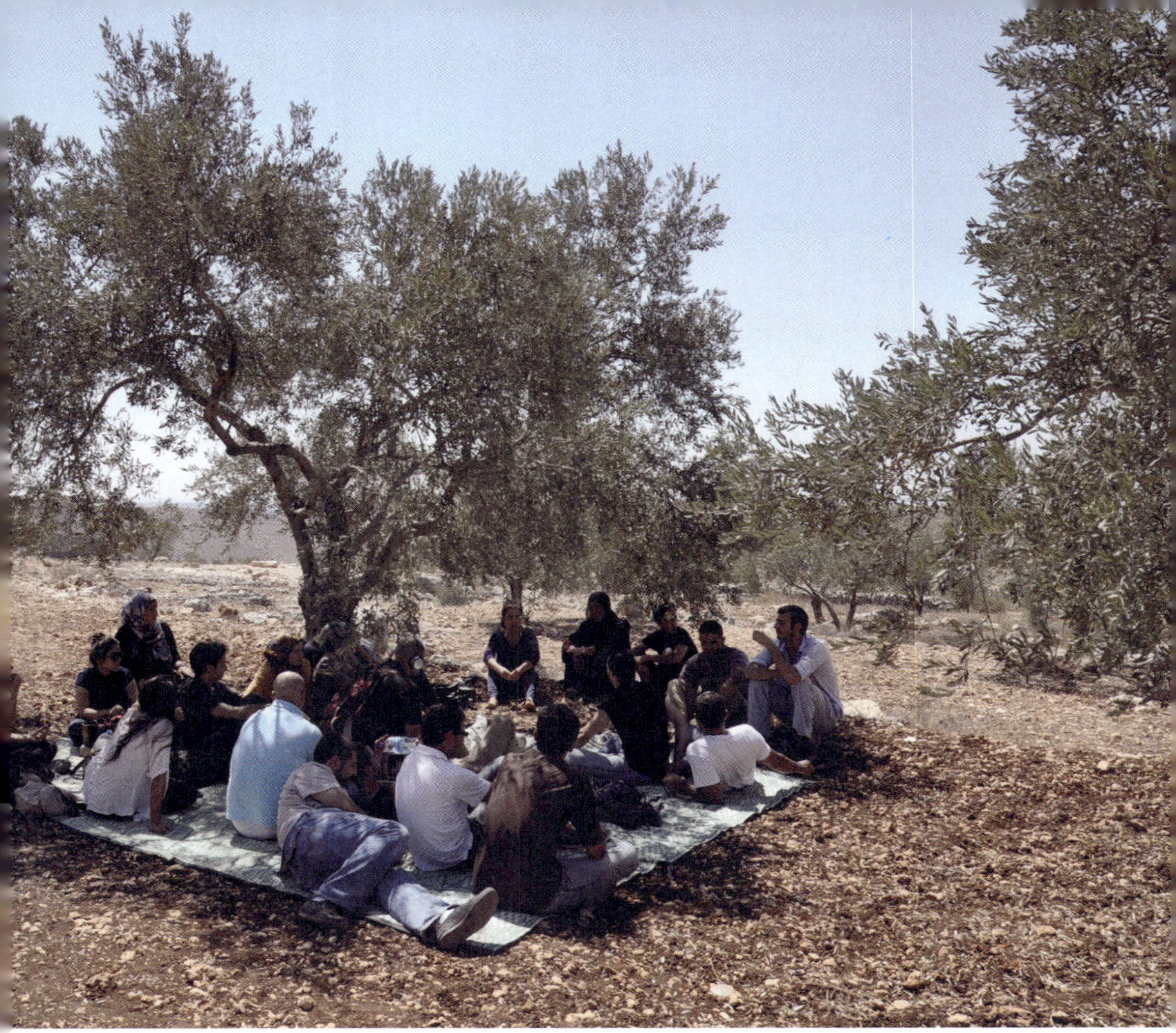

Campus in Camps, Dheisheh refugee camp, Bethlehem, Palestine, 2013
PHOTO: DAAR archive

consider how to build a self-organized learning environment in a place where not too many formal educational institutions exist. It is this desire and interest in the process of learning that brought us to different places and different experiences. We went to refugee camps and started to think about how to decolonize knowledge, how to understand these loaded concepts such as “the right of return,” “migration,” and “refugees.” Being a refugee carries a certain political subjectivity—being in need of aid, being confined, being without a home. But what we also saw is that refugee camps have so many things to teach us: the way refugees self-organize and build their lives beyond the state. They have managed to create different concepts of what a “neighbor” is and what “being together” means and to build collectivity beyond the state.

Were your life in Palestine, your interactions in the communities, and your observations of refugee camps the origins of the Tree School?

In a way. Palestinian refugee camps were established in 1948 as a consequence of the Nakba (Arabic for "the catastrophe"). They were established to provide shelter for the hundreds of thousands of Palestinians who were exiled and had to flee their homes, located in what today is Israel. Over the past seventy-plus years, these camps have developed into dense, semiautonomous, urban environments that are no longer simply recipients of humanitarian aid but rather active political spaces.[1] In 2012, DAAR established an experimental educational program, called Campus in Camps, in Dheisheh Refugee Camp in the West Bank that engaged young participants in new forms of visual and cultural representation of Palestinian refugee camps. After three years of spatial interventions[2] and the creation of a common vocabulary,[3] we felt the need to expand the conversation to people and sites that share similar urgencies.

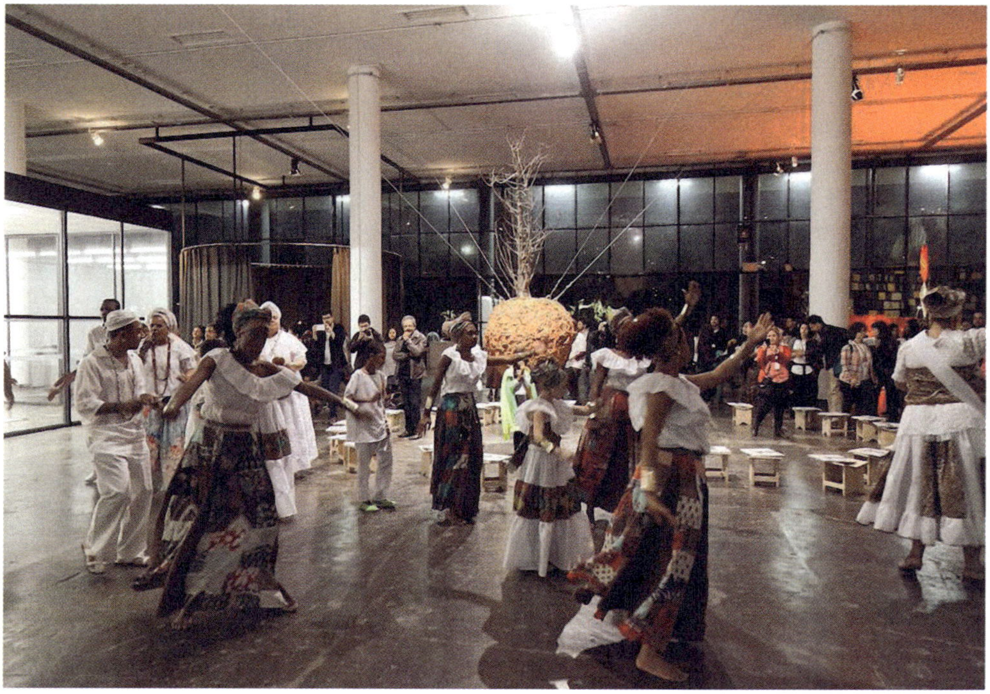

The Tree School at the São Paulo Biennial, Brazil, 2014
PHOTO: DAAR archive

We started thinking about what kinds of tools, platforms, or devices would be necessary to engage in discussions in different locations without losing the political commitment or neglecting the sites themselves. We reflected on the minimal elements necessary to create a learning environment. That is where the Tree School, as both a metaphorical and a material environment, emerged: to build a school, it's enough to gather under the shade of a tree!

The first Tree School was established in Bahia, in southwest Brazil, in 2014, on the occasion of the São Paulo Biennial. In collaboration with the São Paulo-based art collective Grupo Contrafilé, and in dialogue with T.C. Silva, a musician from the Brazilian *quilombos*, and members of the Landless Workers Movement, we established a series of gatherings that revolved around analogies and differences between two exceptional spaces: Palestinian refugee camps and Brazilian *quilombos*. Similar to Palestinian refugee camps, *quilombos* were communities established by the displaced—enslaved Africans and their descendants who fled their oppressors as an active form of resistance. Later, these communities became spaces of refuge for many other groups in Brazil as well. Our shared interest in these spaces and communities provided a key for reflecting on and understanding the relationships between community, territory, and politics beyond the idea of the nation-state.

It was important for us to try to establish these conversations among places that usually do not have the chance to communicate with each other. Global channels of communications are usually established for economic reasons—often through Europe or "the West"—and so we tried to bring into conversation sites that usually do not have much contact despite the fact that they have a lot in common.

Beyond taking place beneath a leafy green canopy, what makes something into a Tree School?

A tree is a living being that reminds us of our modernist disruptions—our ruptures with nature. Especially people living in urban areas seem to have lost their sense of relation to and knowledge of nature.

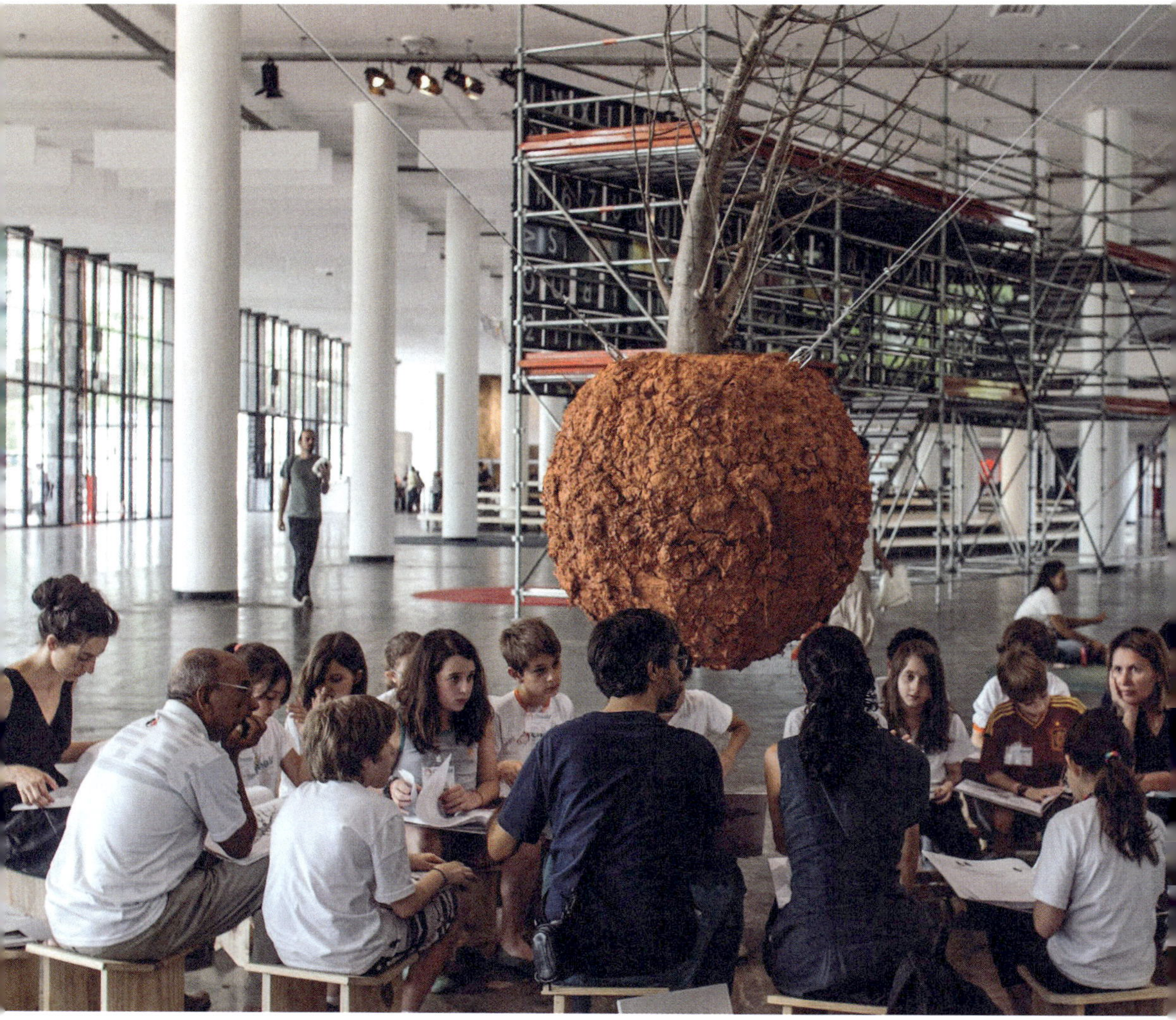

The Tree School at the São Paulo Biennial, Brazil, 2014
PHOTO: DAAR archive

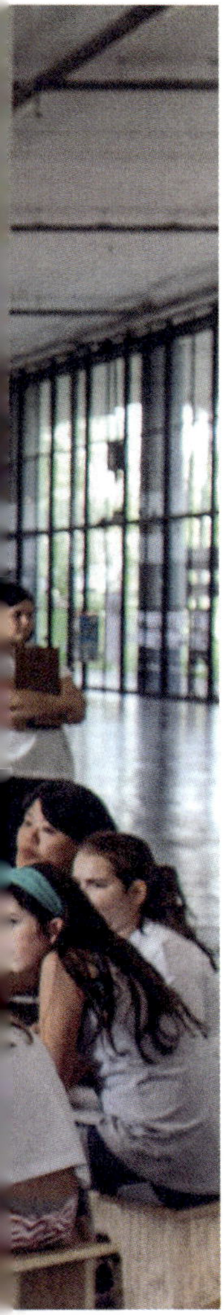

While at a Tree School, our life becomes an important source of knowledge. It's not about books or quoting philosophers. The Tree School is the opposite of what we learned to do in traditional schools. Instead, we look at who we are, who our parents and grandparents were, how we go about our daily lives. The trees and other nature that surround us remind us that being together as human beings and exchanging and sharing knowledge—thinking together—is already enough to have a school. To build a school, we need nothing more than the shade of a tree and people willing to be together and learn together. This creates one of the best learning environments, because everyone is there because they want to be there and to learn from each other. Because we understand that the lives of the other people around us are an important source of knowledge. At a Tree School, people value each other and exchange ideas.

The Tree School departs with almost no program, because it's about a spontaneous, organic way of being together, of letting each other explore, of not have expectations beforehand, not having to prepare. Rather, it's about letting things go and letting them grow slowly, by being with one another in this mutual learning process.

For the Tree School in Bahia, you chose to site it under a baobab tree. In a region with such vast biodiversity, why did you choose that particular species of tree?

Yes, the baobab became a gathering space for *quilombo* residents, schoolchildren, students, and visitors to the São Paulo Biennial. The baobab tree is at the center of many stories and myths. During the Tree School in Bahia, we heard one narrated by the activist Eugênio Lima.

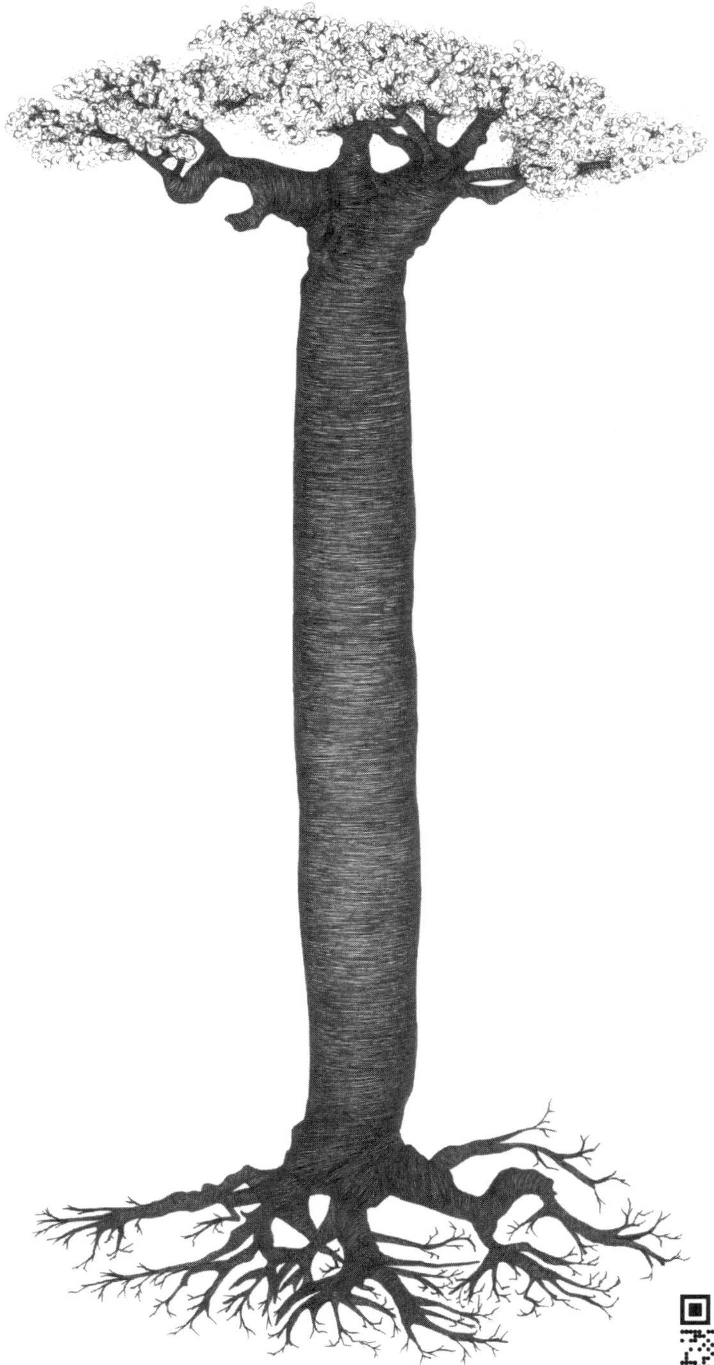

From Campus in Camps and Grupo Contrafilé, *The Tree School* (2014), published on the occasion of the 31st Bienal de São Paolo

the baobab creation

Many are the myths about the baobab. Originally from Africa, it is one of the world's oldest trees.The adult baobab is the tree with the thickest trunk, sometimes reaching up to twenty meters in diameter. Baobabs are living witnesses of history, guardians of the memories of the world. They may live up to six thousand years and grow up to thirty meters tall. In their gigantic stalk, they can store up to one hundred and twenty thousand liters of water. This is why they are also known as the "bottle tree". In many parts of Africa, they are sacred.

The elders say there are no young baobabs; they are all born old. The baobab I know is a young-old-kid, and while I sat against its trunk, it confirmed the story I had heard about the upside-down tree:

At the dawn of life, the Creator made everything in the world. First he created a baobab and only then did he continue making everything else. Next to the baobab there was a pool of still water. Sometimes its surface was as flat as a mirror. The baobab stared at itself in that water mirror. It stared at itself and complained: "Well, maybe my hair could have more flowers, maybe I could have bigger leaves." So the baobab decided to complain to the Creator, who listened carefully.

Whenever the baobab took a breath and interrupted its complaining, the Creator commented: "You are a beautiful tree. I love you, but let me go, for I must finish my work. You were the first being to be created and therefore you possess the best features among all creatures."

Still the baobab begged him: "Please, make me better here, make me better there ..."

But the Creator, who had to make people and all the other creatures of Africa, left him alone. So the baobab followed him everywhere he went, wandering to and fro (and this is why the tree exists all over Africa).

The baobab looked at everything that had been created and continued begging for improvements: "Creator, make that tree over there a little better! Creator, that river is too dry, can't you put more water in it? Creator, is that mountain high enough?"

Of all beings, the only one that was never satisfied was precisely the one the Creator thought was so wonderful, the one that didn't resemble any other, the first to be created! One day the Creator became very, very angry, for he didn't have time to do anything else. He was furious. So he turned to the baobab and said: "Stop bothering me! Stop complaining and stay quiet!"

But the baobab didn't stay quiet.

So the Creator grabbed it, pulled it out of the ground and planted it again. But, this time, upside down, with its head in the ground, so it would remain silent. This explains why today the baobab looks so strange, as if its roots were on its head ... The baobab is just an upside-down tree!

And still today it is said that its skyward-pointing branches resemble arms that continue complaining and begging the Creator for improvements to the planet.

They also say that those who sit under the baobab may listen to its stories.

Eugênio Lima

At the end of the biennial, a baobab tree-planting ceremony was held at the Tainã Cultural House, a political space for cultural and educational production in Campinas, which is part of Rede Mocambos (the Mocambos Network), a workshop based around connecting rural communities.

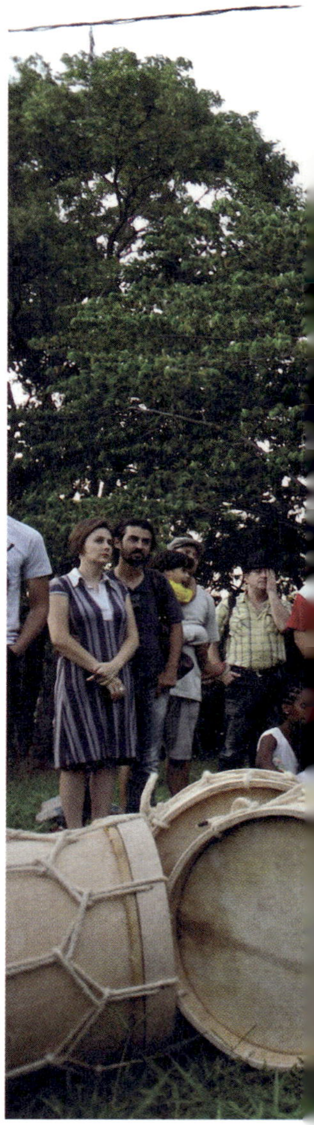

"One of the largest *quilombos* in Brazil, Quilombo dos Palmares, dated back to 1630. It lasted almost a hundred years before it was destroyed. There were almost 30,000 people living there, and it came to be known as the first democratic republic in the Americas. The *quilombo* is born out of the phenomenon of people becoming refugees and autonomously finding and choosing a place of their own. Nowadays in Brazil, there are at least three thousand communities remaining from the original *quilombos*. Most of them are located in rural areas. These are huge territories and they hold possibilities for sustainable living, because there is only collective land and no private property."

—T. C. Silva, musician and co-founder of Tainã Cultural House

In the winter of 2015, the Tree School traveled to Serralves Museum in Porto, Portugal, where we hosted gatherings around art and participatory education with activists, educators, and cultural producers.

Can you describe more how you "detached" the Tree School from one place? What aspects did you consider when moving it from its original location, in Palestine, to Brazil—and then to Portugal and beyond?

We realized the Tree School is not a model that can be replicated exactly the same way in different contexts. In fact, this was something we resisted. It is important to consider the Tree School as a sort

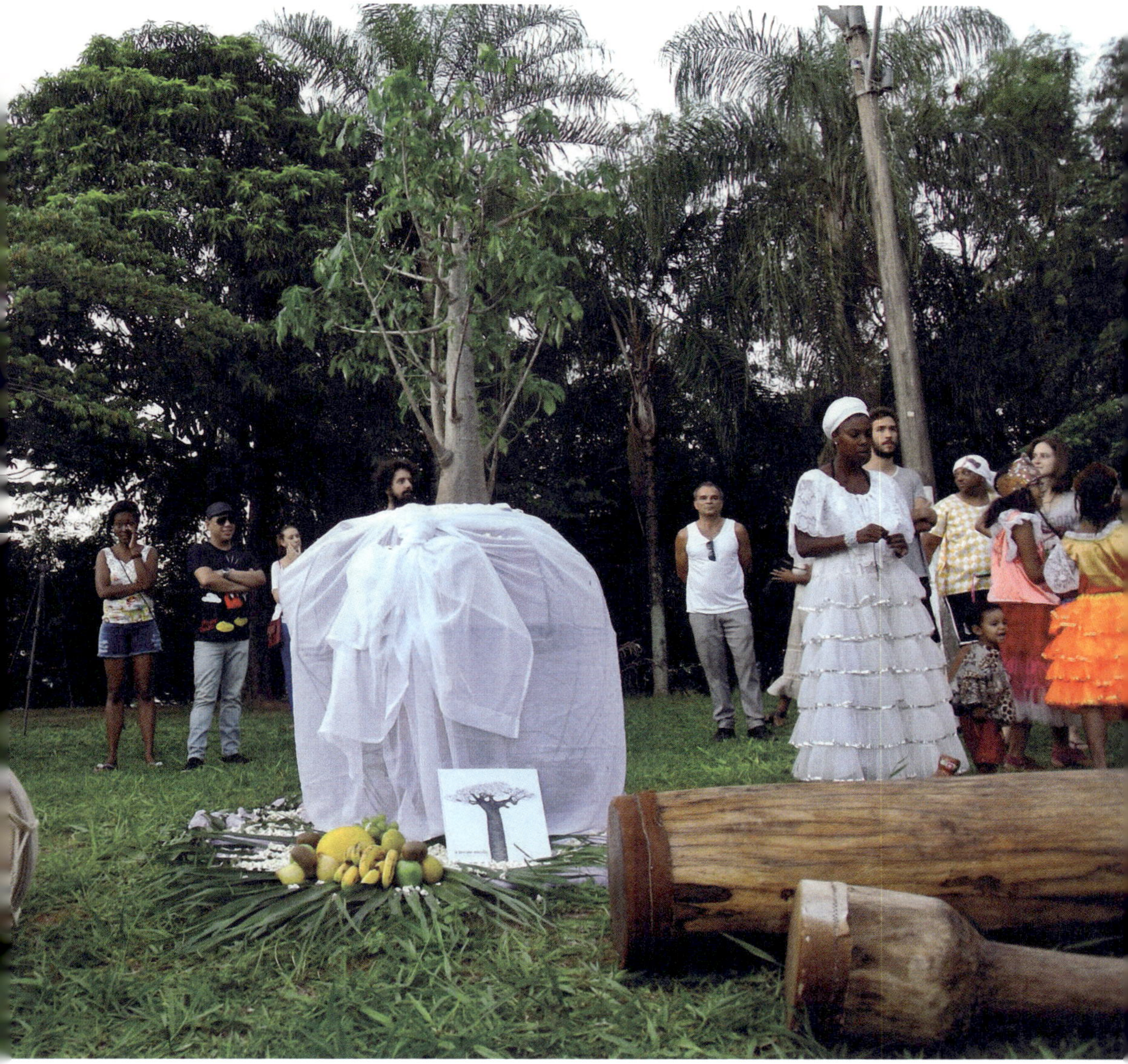

Tainã Culture House, São Paulo, Brazil 2015
PHOTO: DAAR archive

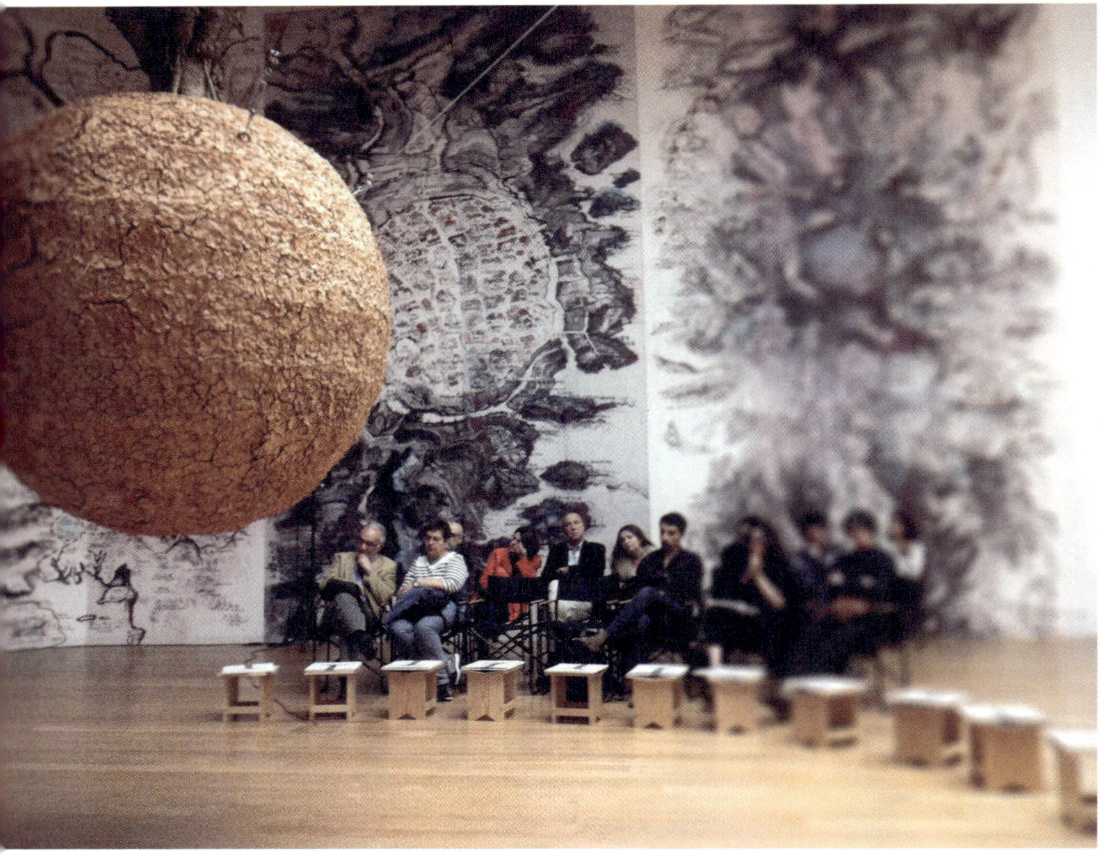

Serralves Museum, Porto, Portugal, 2015–16
Courtesy Sandi Hilal, Alessandro Petti, and Grupo Contrafilé

of entry point, as a way to set up the context. The Tree School works only if there is exchange, and so it requires being open to the essential ways in which each context it appears in informs it.

After the Tree School in Bahia, we asked ourselves if it would be possible to bring the Tree School with us wherever we went. In the summer of 2015, at the invitation of Akademie der Künste der Welt (Academy of the Arts of the World) in Cologne, Germany, we organized a series of gatherings at Hiroshima-Nagasaki-Park in that city.

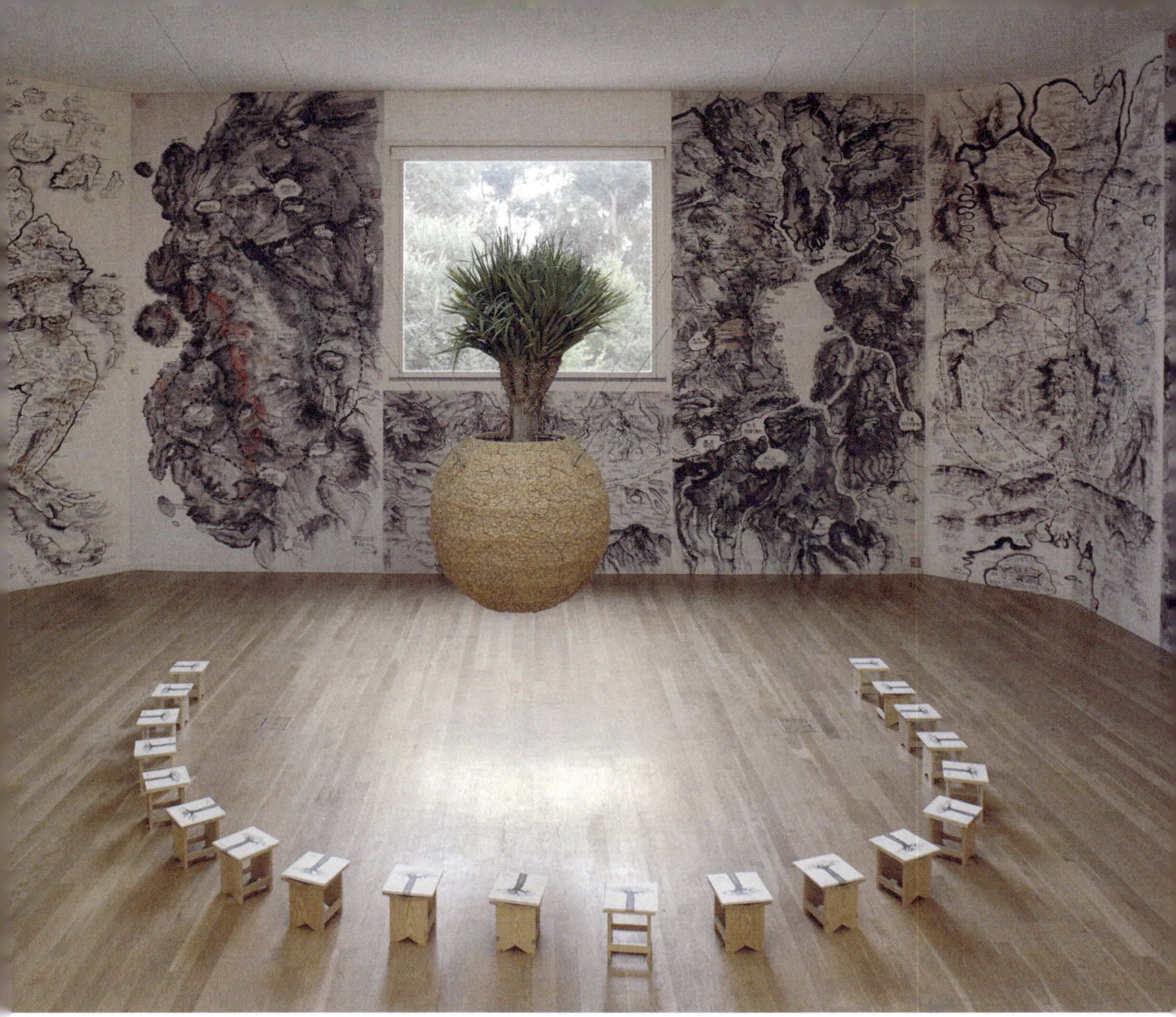

"What struck me most, sitting under the Tree School at Hiroshima-Nagasaki-Park, was that many different things were happening simultaneously throughout the public park: people were chatting, playing music, playing football, reading, enjoying the sun. This gave the place its own specific tone and a sense of belonging for all the different people. The Tree School attracted the curiosity of many, and some even came to our circle to listen to our discussion. This welcoming atmosphere led me to consider the importance of public spaces and to further imagine how to cultivate these multiplicities of activities in our common spaces in the camp."

—Isshaq Al-Barbary, Campus in Camps participant

In January 2015, DAAR was invited to bring the Tree School to Tepoztlán, near Cuernavaca, Mexico, just south of Mexico City, by Estudio SITAC and Alumnos47. Here, the Tree School offered educators from different parts of Mexico the space to reflect on their pedagogical practices in a workshop inspired by the teachings of the theologian and philosopher Ivan Illich, who in 1965 established the Centro Intercultural de Documentación (Intercultural Documentation Center), an informal university in Cuernavaca that attracted a diverse group of intellectuals and knowledge-seekers from around the world. The Tree School lasted for a few days, during which a close group of participants took the space and time to critically reflect on their practices; to take distance from their respective sites of intervention; and to reflect collectively upon the role of radical pedagogies in the transformation of society.

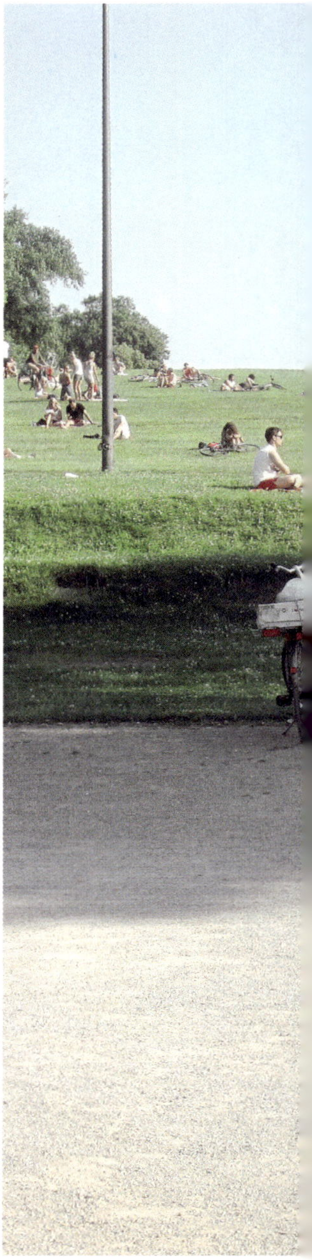

You often transgress these figures of "host" and "guest" that are prevalent in educational settings. Teachers act as hosts—perhaps even as curators—in that they choose the topics and materials and organize the learning process. Students are then invited to take part in this experience as guests, as visitors; they aren't offered much involvement in the creation process. With the Tree School, though, you try to overcome this dichotomy.

Each Tree School invites the participants to decide for themselves what is most relevant in terms of discussion content, as well as how these conversations should happen, in what format. This is also how the Tree School differs from formal educational models, which have the tendency to establish themselves in repeatable, and thus static, formats. We are all probably familiar with the stress the educational system imposes on us as learners—with the frustrations that stay with us and

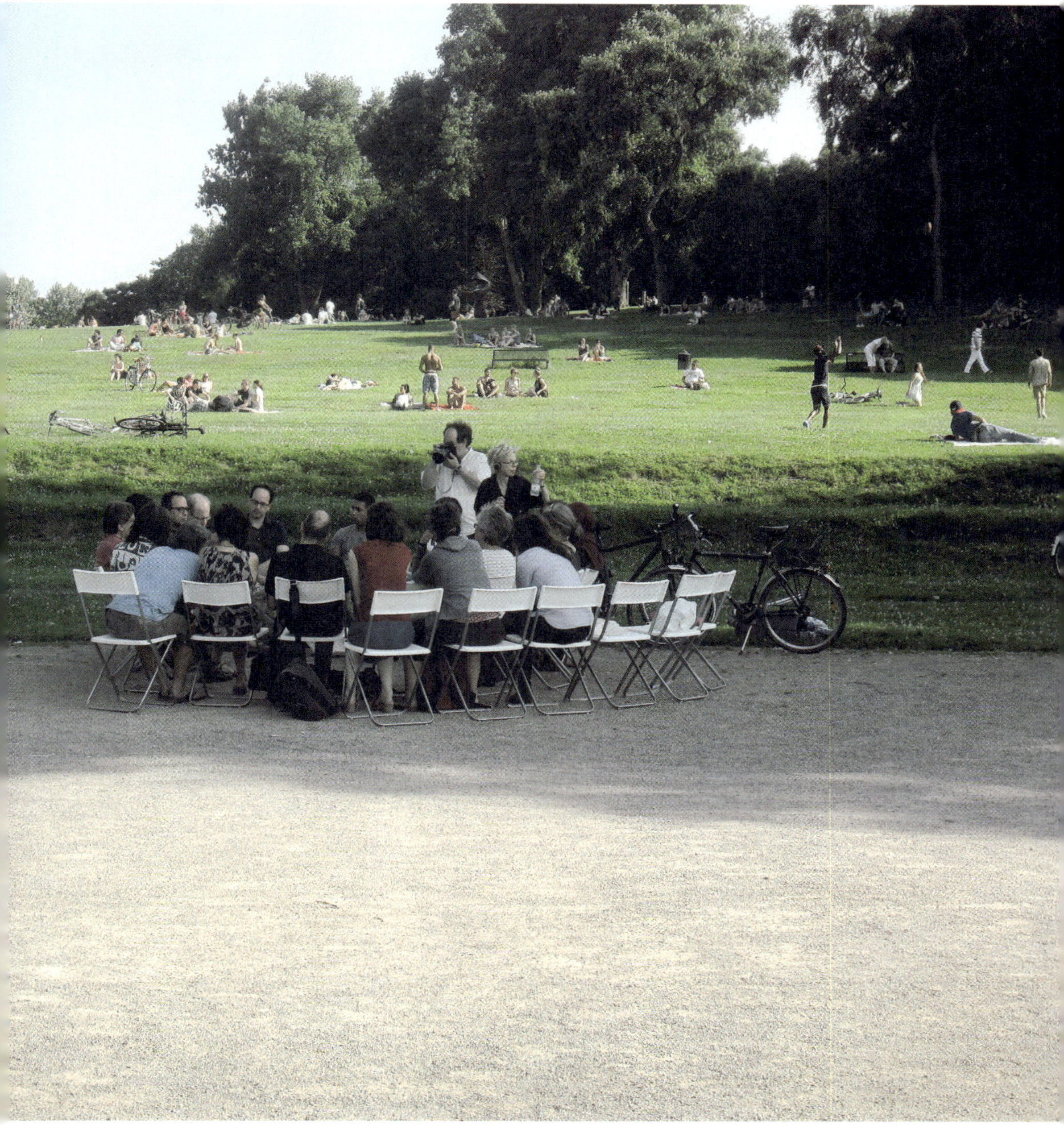

The Tree School at Hiroshima-Nagasaki-Park in Cologne, Germany, 2015
PHOTO: DAAR archive

impact our lives for many years. If the learning system boils down to being graded and grading others, and when learning outcomes are related merely to grades, this only perpetuates hierarchies in the educational system.

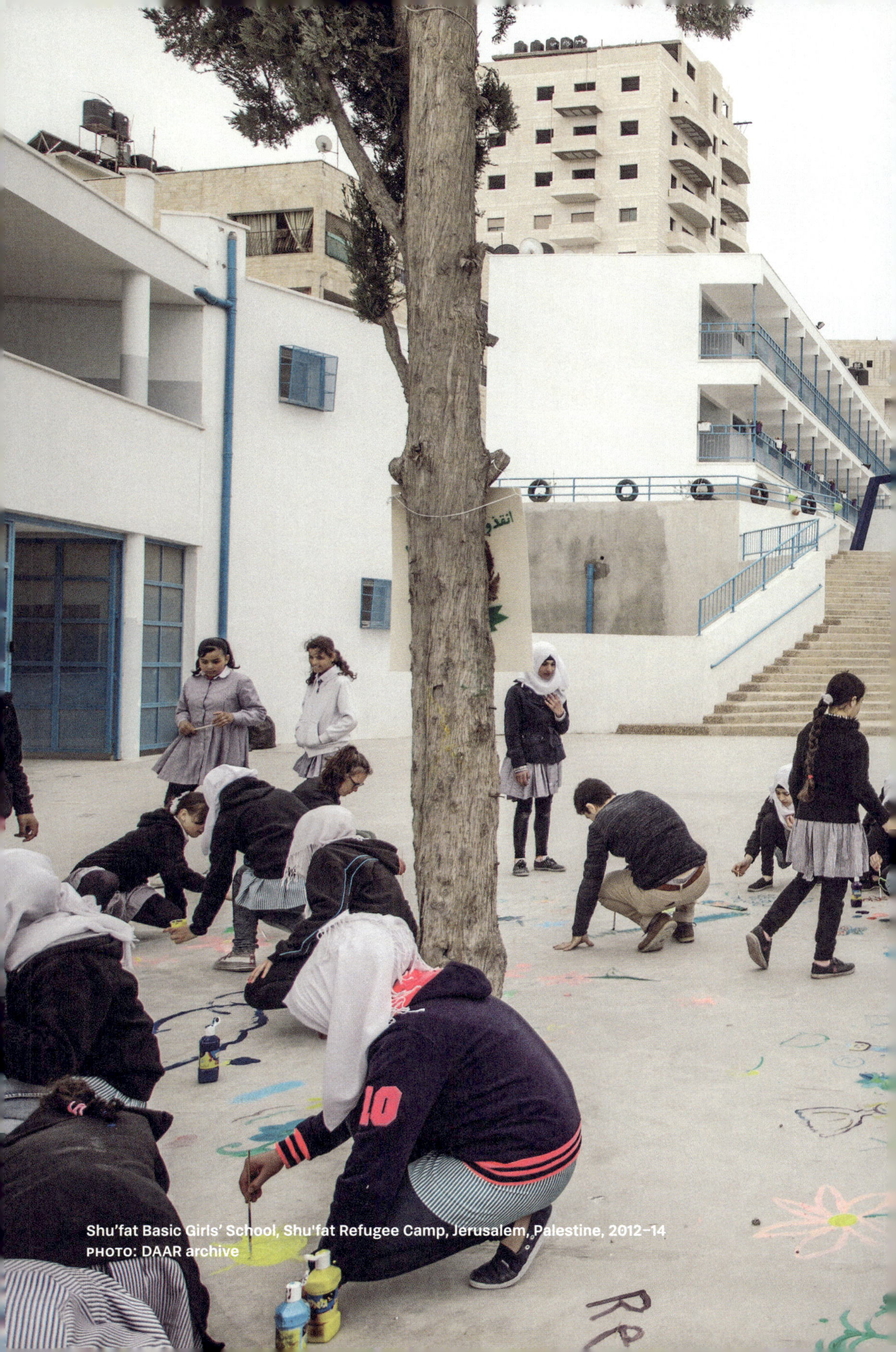

Shu'fat Basic Girls' School, Shu'fat Refugee Camp, Jerusalem, Palestine, 2012–14
PHOTO: DAAR archive

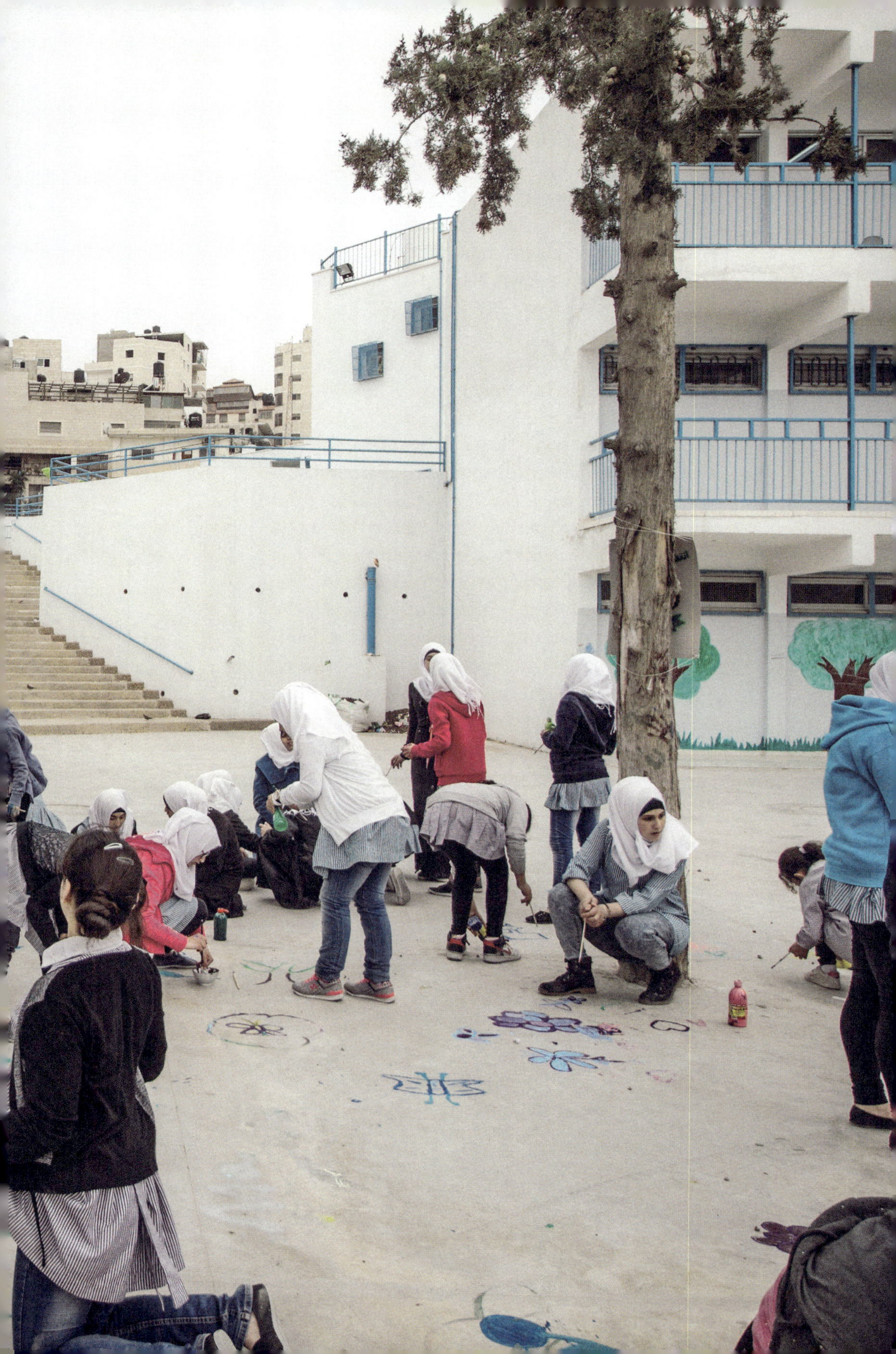

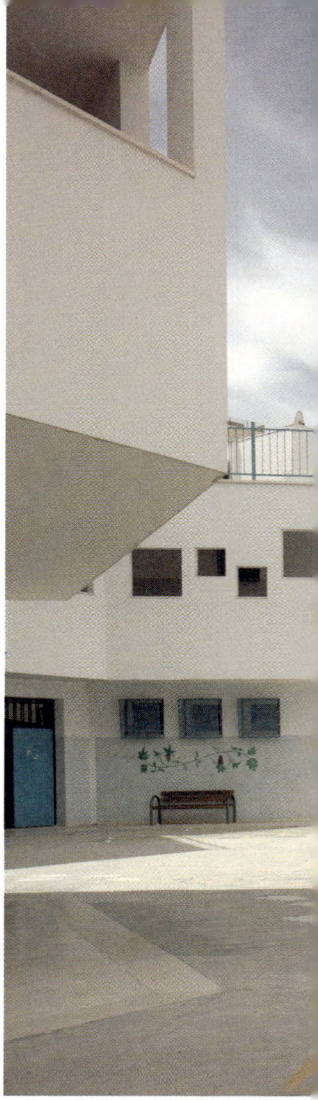

The origin of the word "school" is the Greek word *scholē*, which means "leisure" or "play." So, then, in any moment when you are at school and you are not playing, you are not really at school anymore. Thus it is a sort of "serious playfulness" that is crucial for transgressing hierarchies between teacher and students, host and guests.

In standard educational settings, knowledge rarely has anything to do with your everyday life. With the Tree School, we believe that the learning needs to adapt to the situations and needs of the learners—to actually be very close to the knowledge grounded in people's experiences. The Tree School stems from the belief that each participant is a source of knowledge. Each one of us went through experiences, which formed knowledges that we are interested in. This is what we hope to explore with each iteration of the Tree School: to share our experiences with one another, and, through that, to create collectivity. Thinking together is very important. Whereas educational systems tend to individualize and segregate by age, the learning at the Tree School is transgenerational and fosters conversations through which ideas can freely emerge.

A lot of your work as DAAR has taken place in refugee camps, not just with the Tree School but also with projects such as Campus in Camps (2012–15), Shu'fat School for Girls (2012–14), and the Concrete Tent (2014–15). You overturn the image often associated with camps as something temporary, soon to be dismantled, and mainly linked to suffering, by pointing out that these exceptional places are sources of valuable knowledges.

Refugee camps harbor knowledges and social structures that are often not recognized, not even by the communities themselves. But we feel there is a lot to learn from how people in refugee camps organize their lives beyond the idea of the nation-state, despite all the suffering they have experienced and the fact they have been forced into that situation—into a place where the notions of "private" and "public" are absolutely irrelevant.

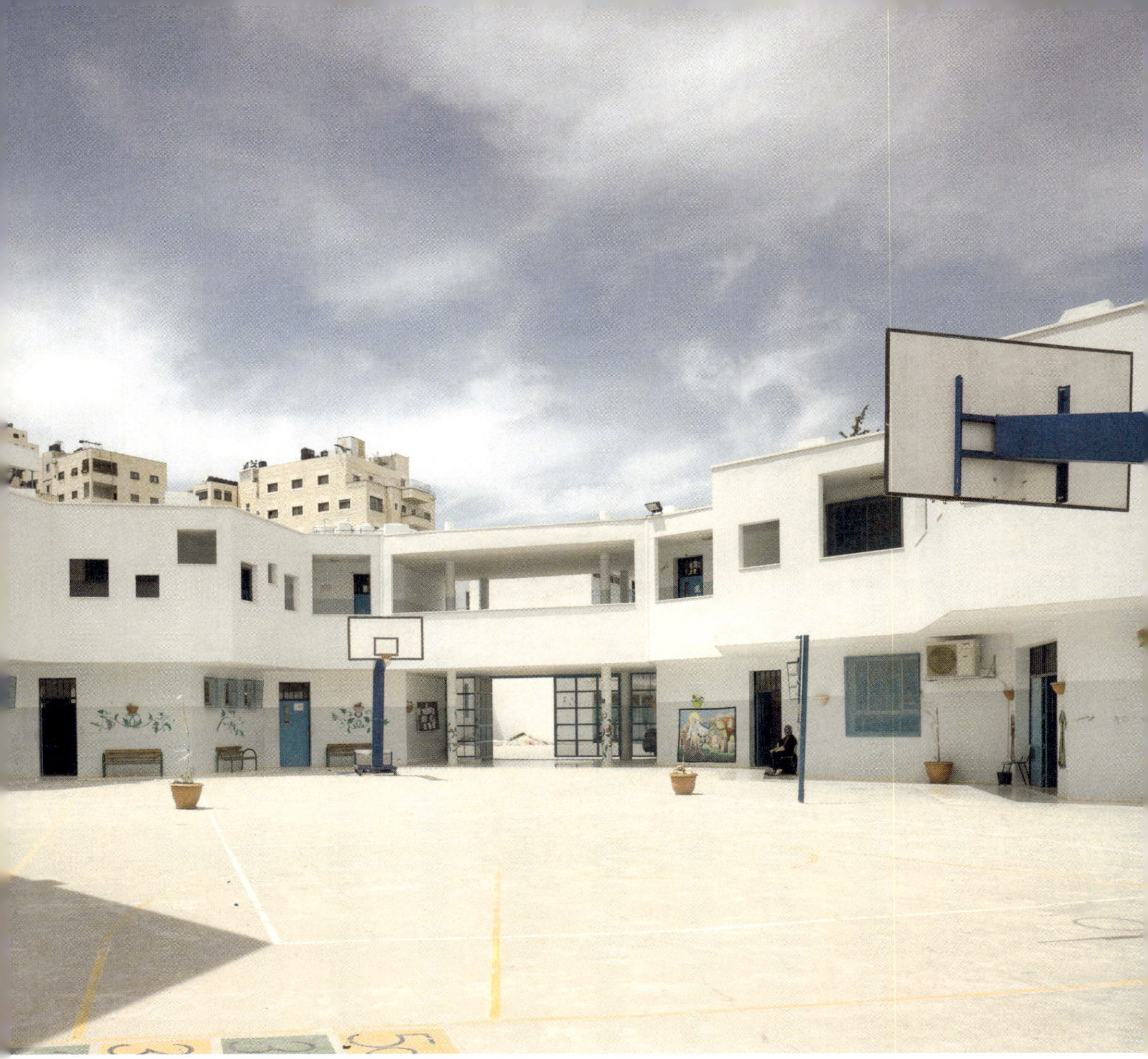

Shu'fat Refugee Camp, Jerusalem, Palestine
PHOTO: Luca Capuano, 2016

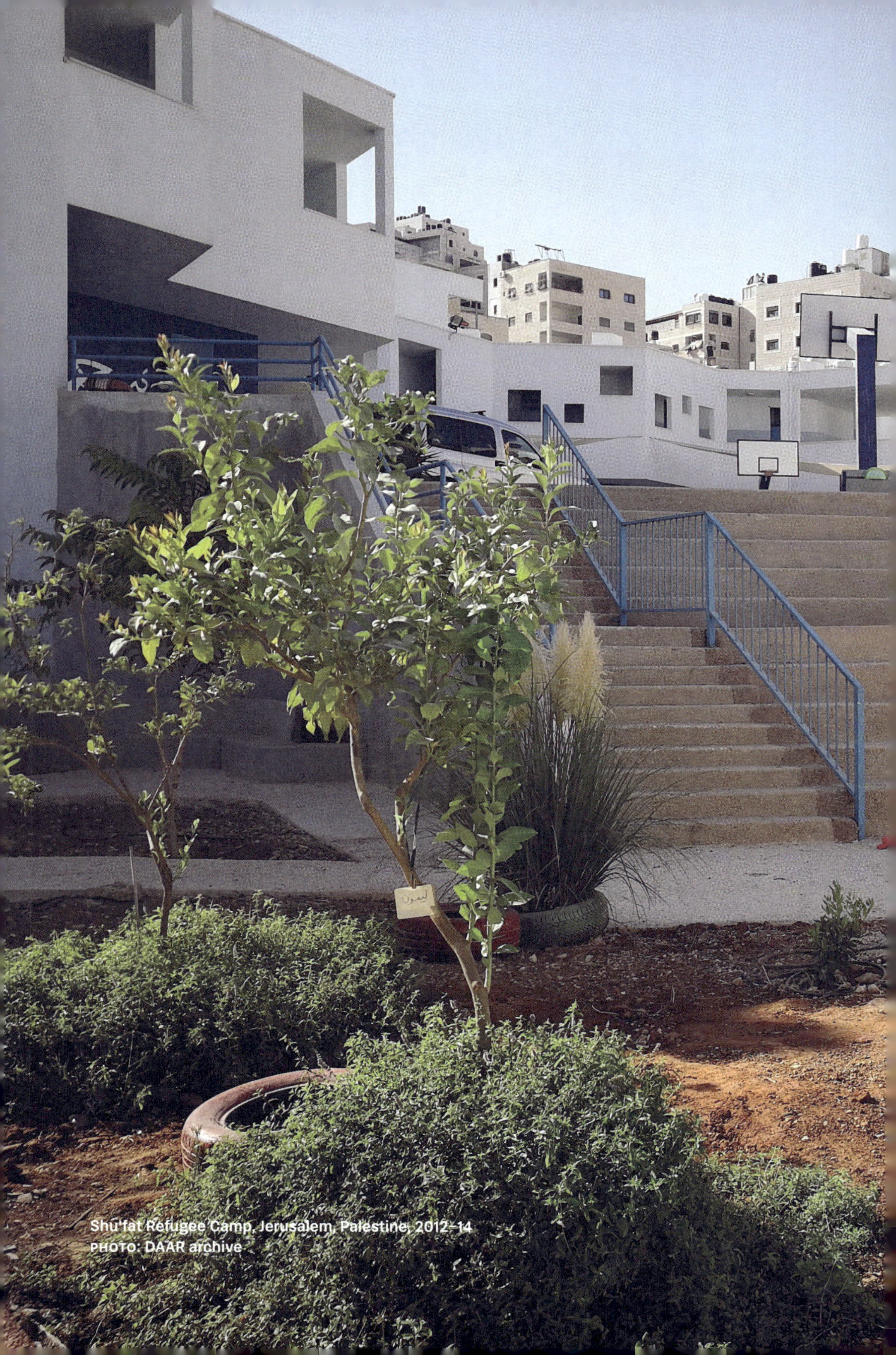

Shu'fat Refugee Camp, Jerusalem, Palestine, 2012–14
PHOTO: DAAR archive

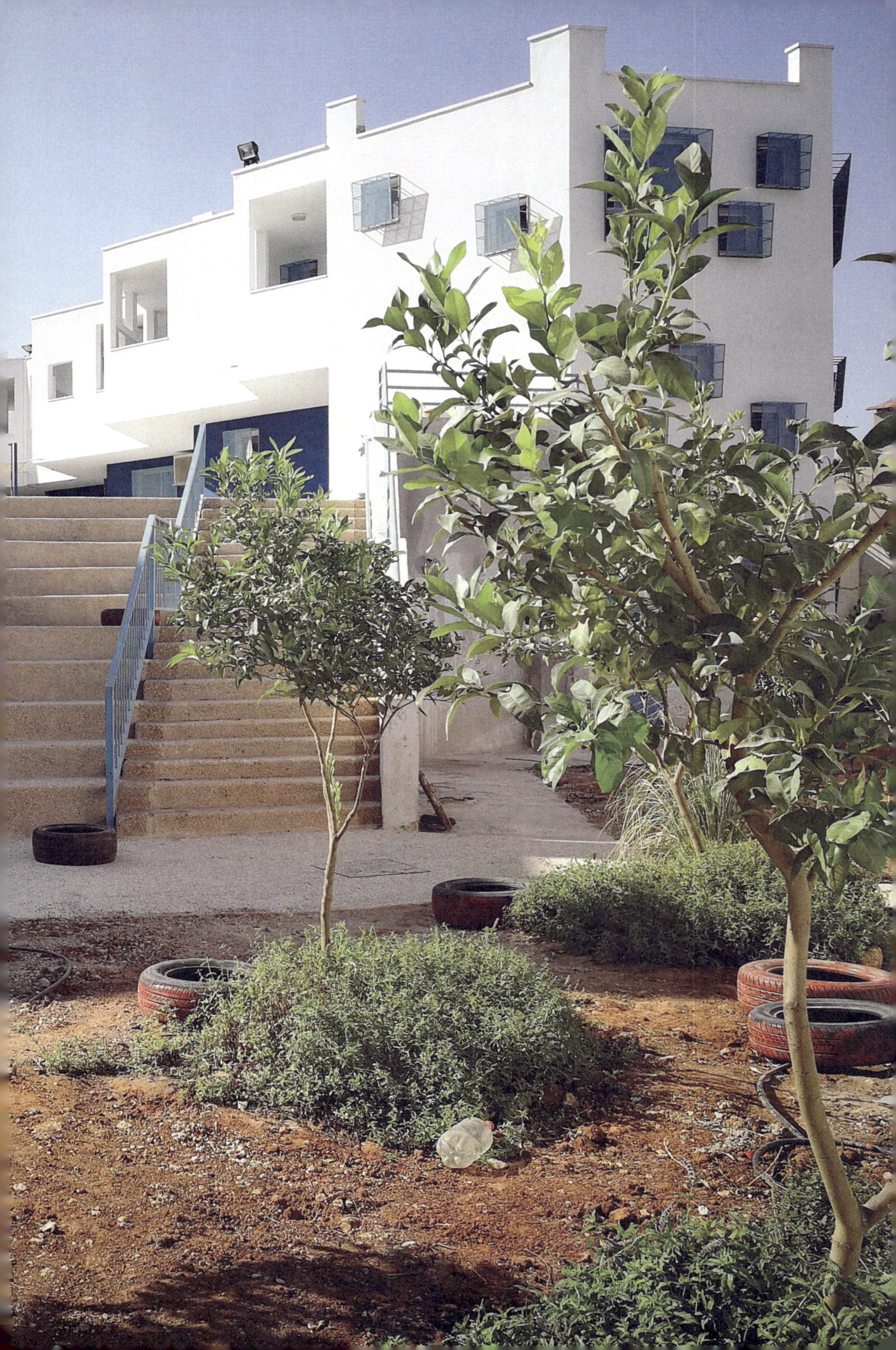

School in Exile

[download the pdf]

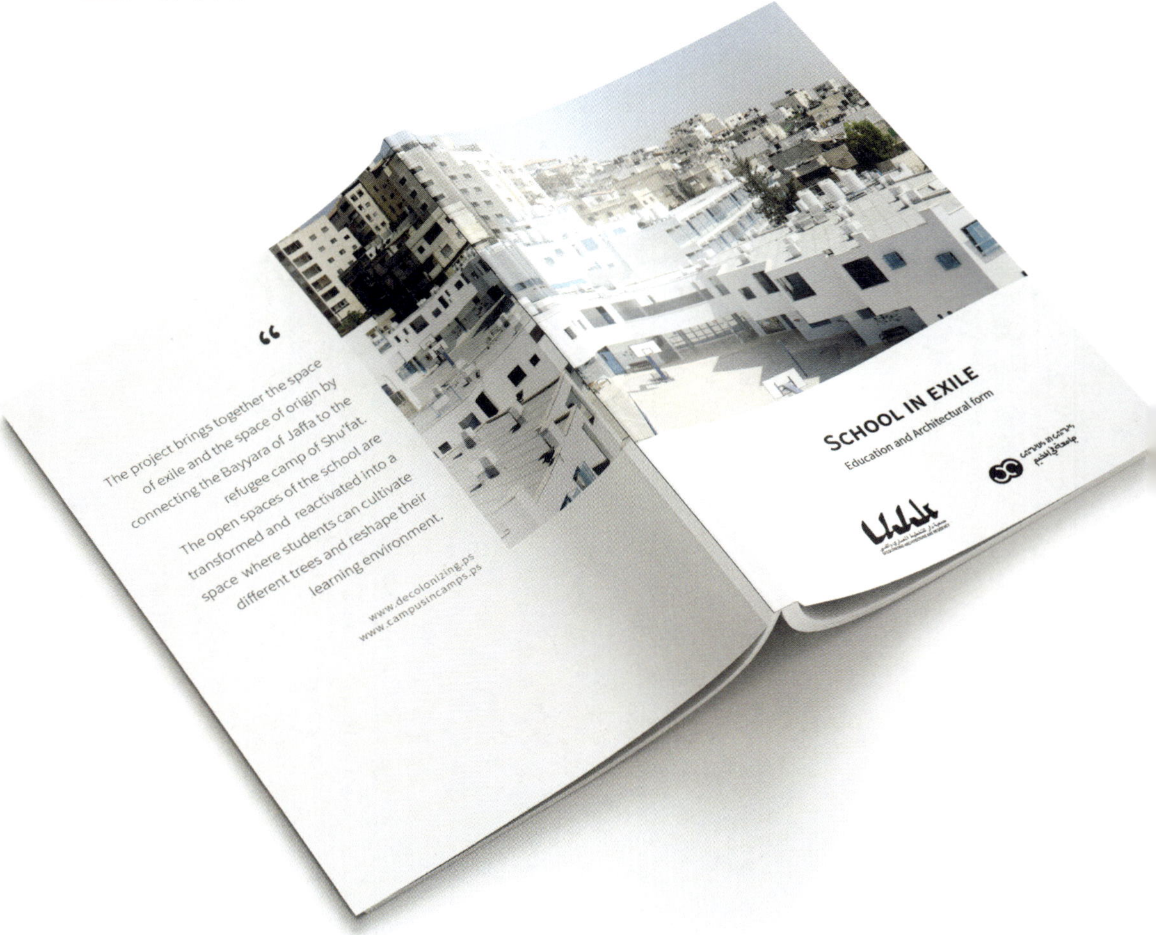

Notes on Participation

[download the pdf]

In the spring of 2015, we had the rare occasion to design a school in a refugee camp in Jerusalem based on the Tree School principles. Since 2002, Shu'fat Camp has been enclosed by walls and fences built by the Israeli government, trapped in a legal void neither inside nor outside Jerusalem's borders. We asked ourselves whether any intervention at all was possible in such a distorted and unstable political environment.

Recognizing that Shu'fat Camp is a spatial expression of a particular relation to another place—the place of origin—the school, instead of dismissing this relation, inhabited this tension and contradiction by mirroring the indoor classroom in an outdoor green classroom. The outdoor classroom recalls a particular type of open green space that was once common in Palestine, called *bayyaraat* (from the Arabic for "wells"), which resembled agricultural land comprising citrus plantations, gardens, and a small number of buildings. The outdoor school at Shu'fat transformed and reactivated a space where students could cultivate different trees and reshape their learning environment.

Each iteration of the Tree School is so specific to site and place. What other Tree Schools have you run around the world, and how did they respond to place and community?

In the fall of 2019, we were invited to Hong Kong by Asia Art Archive, a nonprofit organization with a library and archive on contemporary Asian art. Over the course of two weeks, we met with artists, educators, community organizers, and students of different ages to speak about care, community, and the role of artists in shaping education outside of institutional settings. We transformed a house in Shek O, a fishing community on Hong Kong Island, into an informal gathering space for groups and individuals to discuss the formation of learning environments. The rooftop school offered the group a reminder of the historical rooftop schools that have emerged in Hong Kong when people have taken refuge there during times of political unrest. Unfortunately, due to the combined effect of the protests and government restrictions under the COVID-19 pandemic, we were unable to activate our intended series of Tree School experiments across the city of Hong Kong, in collaboration with teachers and students from local schools.

Then, in March 2021, within the framework of "Tree Story," an exhibition at Monash University Museum of Art in Caulfield, Australia, which brought together creative practices from around the world to create a "forest of ideas" relating to critical environmental and sustainability issues, the Tree School took the form of yarning circles and discussions. Due to the ongoing COVID-19 pandemic restrictions, we could not travel to Australia. This limitation pushed us to think about how the Tree School could be activated without our physical presence. In dialogue with the curators of "Tree Story" and artist and educator Moorina Bonini, we decided the solution was to involve Monash University faculty members and students in a program of both planned and unplanned activities. In this case, the Tree School—emerging as an informal educational space within the formal educational structure of the university—offered professors and students the possibility to experiment with different forms of collective learning.

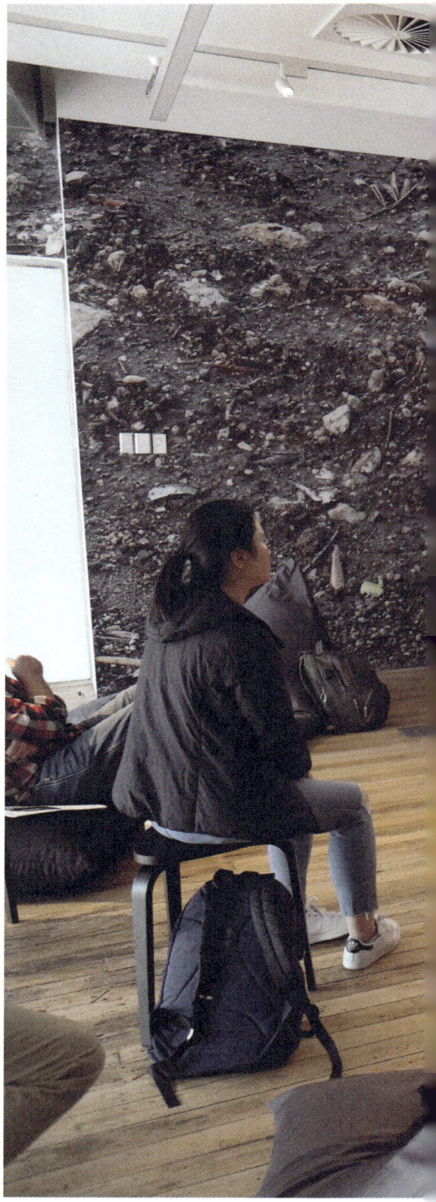

Continuing as part of that March 2021 iteration, the Tree School also took place—like in Bahia—under an actual tree of great significance. In dialogue with N'arweet Dr. Carolyn Briggs AM and Dr. Brian Martin of the Wominjeka Djeembana Indigenous Research Lab at Monash University, the Tree School was established under a Boon Wurrung tree, which with its very presence alludes to the foundation, strength, and resilience of the Boon Wurrung people and culture. The conversations and yarning circles that took place around this tree were informed by it, foregrounding ideas of caring for the country and learning from trees and storytelling.

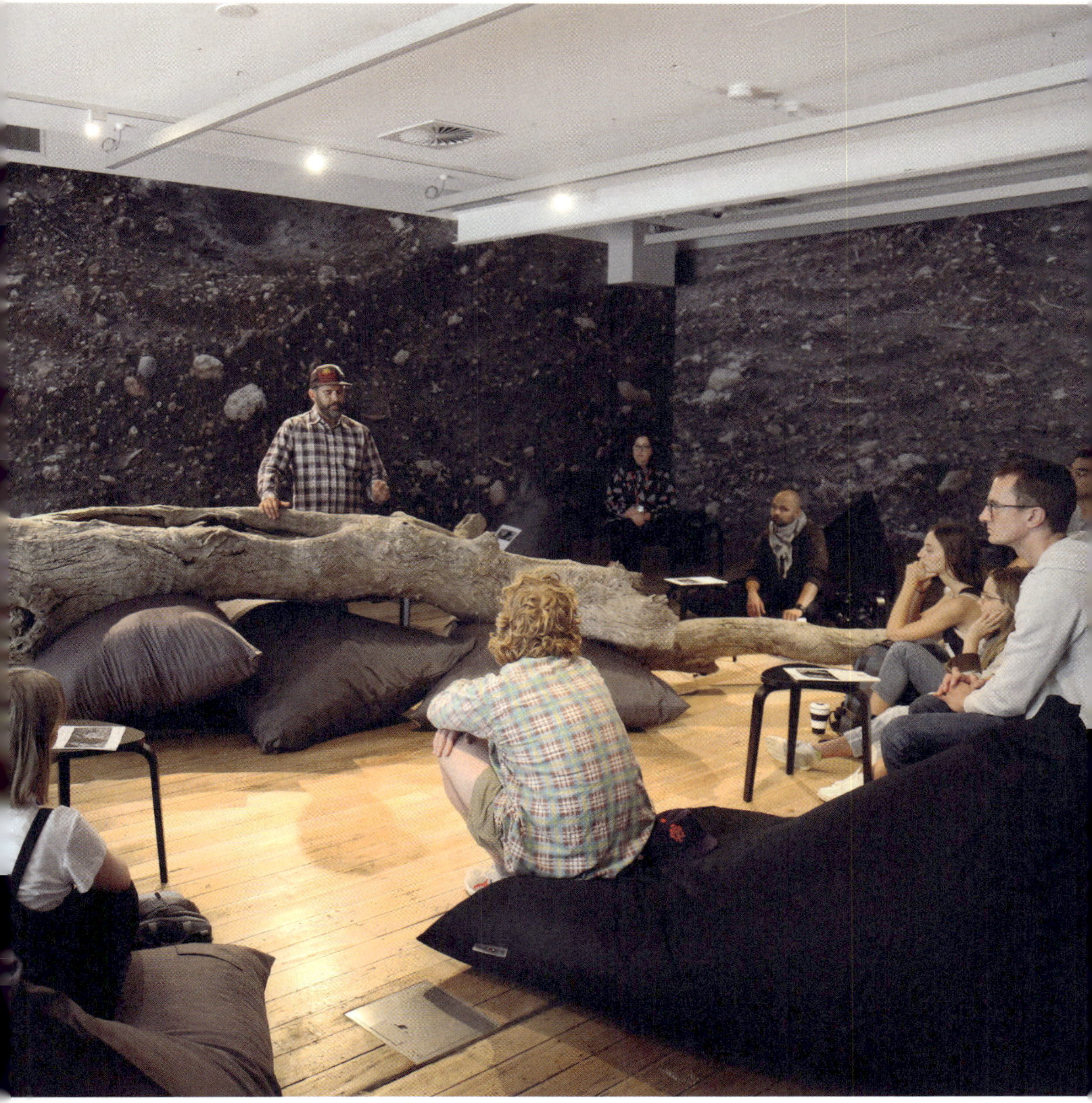

The Tree School at MADA Gallery, as part of the "Tree Story" exhibition at Monash University Museum of Art (MUMA), Melbourne, Australia, 2021
PHOTO: MUMA

The Boon Wurrung Tree (video)

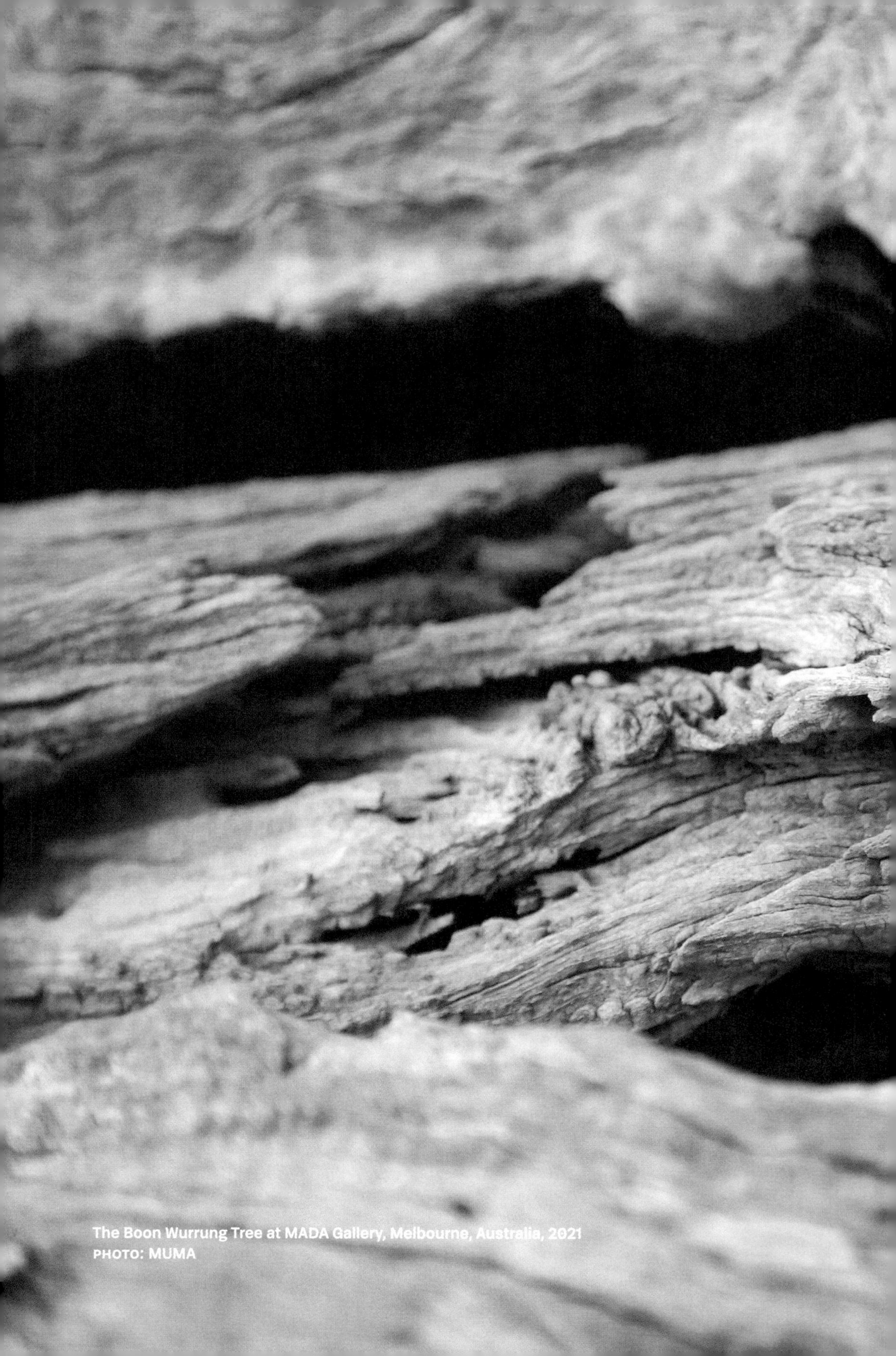

The Boon Wurrung Tree at MADA Gallery, Melbourne, Australia, 2021
PHOTO: MUMA

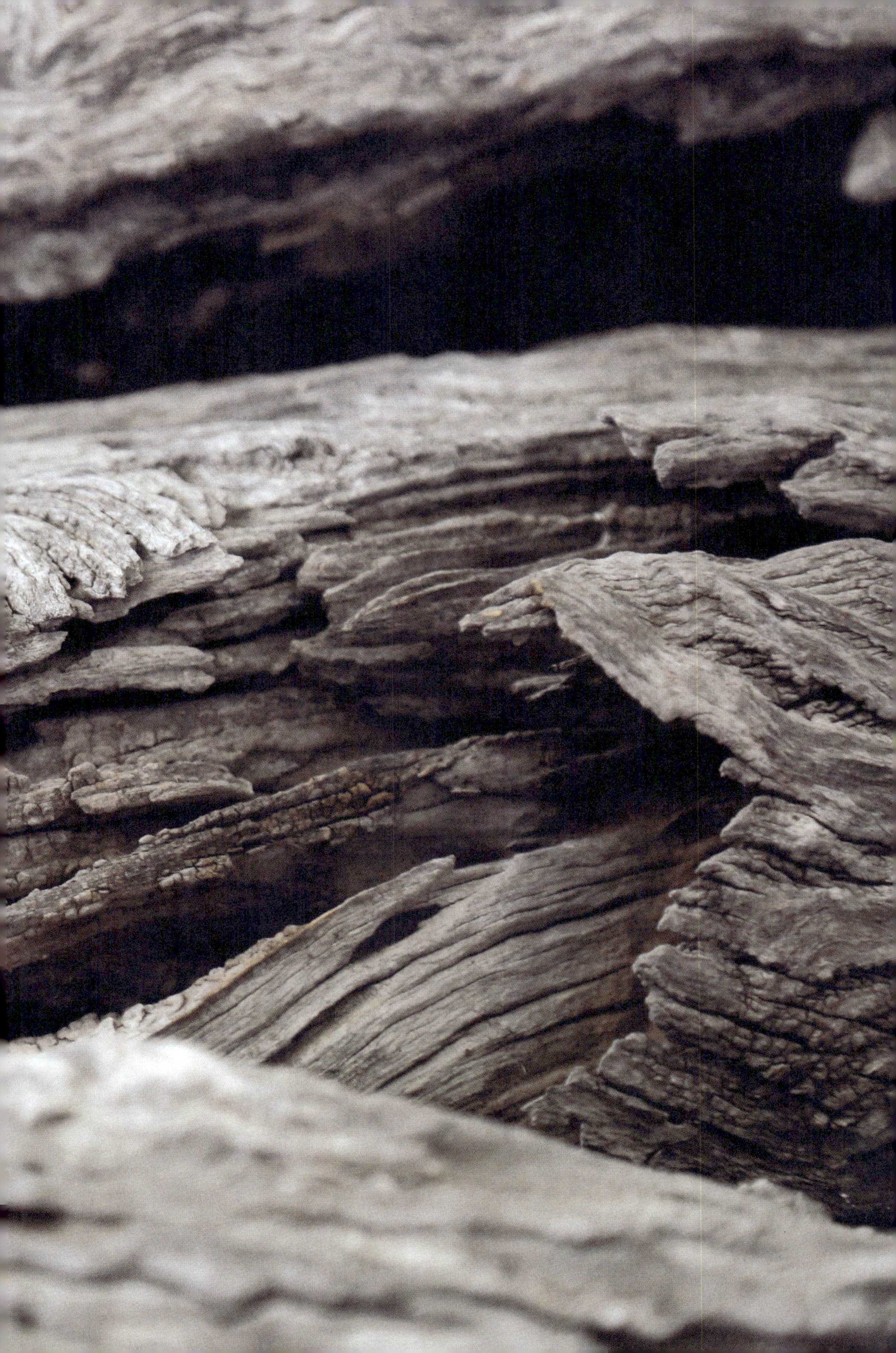

For WHW Akademija, an independent study program we've run since 2018, we wanted to organize a Tree School with you in Zagreb in 2020—but then the pandemic happened. After many months of intense online work, we were finally able to gather together in person during the subsequent edition of WHW Akademija, with the Zagreb Tree School finally taking place in July 2021. The strange necessity produced by the pandemic—for togetherness, but also for seclusion, for getting away—made us appreciate all the more the fact that the Tree School provided us with a temporary distance from our everyday routines.

The Tree School with WHW Akademija students and invited guests took place in the forest of Sljeme, close to Zagreb, between July 12 and 16, 2021. After more than a year of isolation due to COVID-19 restrictions, the Tree School indeed provided a welcome opportunity for collective gathering. The students had the opportunity to share their work in informal conversations among themselves and with invited guests. The forest inspired the sharing of stories linked to political resistance and ancestral legends. Moreover, due to the nature of WHW Akademija and the project *Education from Below*, which the 2021 Tree School was part of, the group reflected on how independent and informal learning environments might influence formal educational institutions. In this iteration, we also started thinking about how to include pedagogy within art practices.

For these conversations, we invited the large group of participants to displace themselves from their usual environments. This is a strategy we have learned through practicing the Tree School: when we visit the outdoor school site with the group, we are taking them out of their normal context. This is why some said they would prefer meeting in a café—meeting in the forest was an unusual situation for them. But this displacement puts everyone on par: everyone is a guest in this new situation.

We used this opportunity to think together about the urgency of decolonizing

The Tree School at WHW Akademija, Sljeme, Croatia, 2021
PHOTO: Damir Žižić

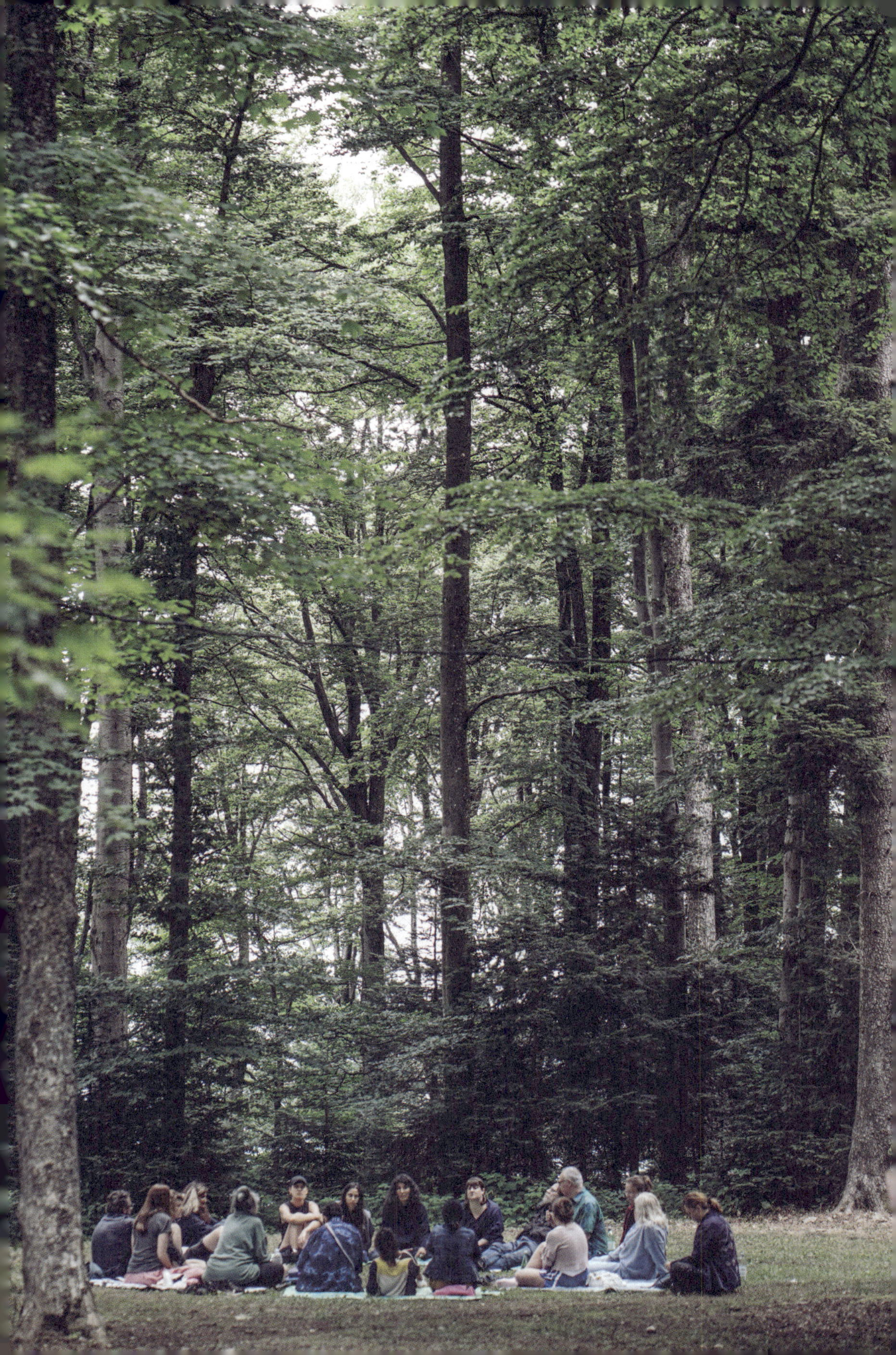

knowledge, of thinking and rethinking our practices and their role within creating a pedagogical platform. What transpired is a collective realization that building alliances by learning from each other, connecting with each other, and understanding each other as part of a larger movement is absolutely necessary. This strengthened our commitment to working and collaborating with others in our practice.

Let's discuss methodology for a moment. You have been experimenting with different formats for the Tree School. Some have lasted for months, and others just a few weeks or even a few days. And, every time, it is different—a different learning experience, a different set of knowledges. But what is it that all iterations have in common? Is there such a thing as a "Tree School methodology"?

In all these different Tree School experiences, we have been asked many times to extract a methodology. But—fearing that the Tree School will then transform itself into an educational model to be repeated everywhere in the same way, and in order to preserve its informal, joyful, communal, and spontaneous spirit—we prefer to instead share what we call the "Tree School ingredients" rather than attempting to convey a methodology. "Ingredient" comes from a Latin word meaning "entering into" (*ingredi*, from in-, "into," and *gradi*, "walk"), and an ingredient is of course a component part of any combination, recipe, or mixture. Therefore, Tree School ingredients acquire different meanings, tastes, and intensity according to how the participants put them in relation to each other and according to how they "enter into" relation with a specific location.

Tree School Ingredients

● Unpredictability

The Tree School is a temporary space that emerges out of trusting the knowledge of each participant, leading to unpredictable and unknown conversations. Being unpredictable does not mean being disorganized or careless; it is a way of learning to be open to the unknown and being exposed and honest. ►

● Unlearning

There is no preset curriculum, program, or readings. What is at stake with the Tree School is the possibility of unlearning and relearning. What constitutes knowledge? How do we unlearn modernist and colonial conceptions? How can we regain the right to learn from experiences and not only from books? ►

● Rituals

Instead of prepackaged activities, the Tree School is organized around rituals that create a safe place for sharing emotions, feelings, and spirituality. The unpredictability and unplanning requires setting group rituals so that participants can join the unplanned collective in thinking and connecting to each other. ▲

● Al-Atabeh

The *al-atabeh*, in Arabic, is the space that connects the entrance of the house with its immediate surroundings. It is in that space where a person feels they belong to both the house and the outside, the unknown. It also describes a space of transformation and movement from one place to another. The Tree School aims to create that space of both safely belonging and navigating the unknown. It offers a space to be safely critical toward our own knowledge in connection with others who feel the need to do the same. Seeking knowledge at the *al-atabeh* and being critical does not mean that we are leaving behind the house and our local knowledge, and yet we also do not want to be confined within the walls of our own knowledge. Being at the *al-atabeh* is being in a safe place that allows you to transform your life experiences and be critical without leaving home behind. ►

● Cooking

Cooking and eating together is one of the most immediate exchanges of knowledge. Sometimes we might find it challenging to be open to other cultures—but we open up immediately for each other's different ways of cooking and eating. Together, these two practices constitute the foundation of the Tree School. ▼

● Conversations

At the Tree School, we understand conversation as the primary source of knowledge production and interaction. Conversations are ways to formulate thoughts and elaborate them collectively. ▲

● Ritrovo

In Italian, *ritrovo* means getting together with the joy of being with one another as friends. By gathering under the tree together, participants of the Tree School share individual memories that form the foundation of the school as a joyful space for learning. ►

● Dislocation

The act of dislocation is fundamental to the Tree School. It can alter who is the local and who is the outsider, who is the host and who is the guest. Dislocating is an act that enables the Tree School's participants to quickly build common foundations for learning from each other that are not located in one place but rather have different locations that interact with each other. ►

What are the overlaps between the Tree School and your artistic practice? What avenues will the Tree School explore in the future?

After being invited to activate the Tree School in different contexts—Hong Kong, Dubai, South America, Europe—now seems to be the time to try to bring all these different groups together. This semi-post-pandemic situation, in late 2021, is also a peculiar moment: artistic practices, curators and artists, are starting to reflect on the crisis, on the increased isolation due to the pandemic. The shuttering of exhibition spaces—sometimes reducing artistic practice only to object-based experiences—reinforced the idea that creating learning environments can itself become an artistic practice. A way of inhabiting a world that has become so difficult to inhabit.

What is both interesting and necessary is that artists show up on the frontlines—that they're working to reopen the spaces of education and to invite big institutions to rethink their role. For our part, DAAR must try to bring together all these experiences from different parts of the world, in order to build strong alliances based precisely on those differences and also the analogies that these remote places share. Exploring how people gather beyond state-run institutions is an urgent issue, and the Tree School can be a vehicle for creating learning environments beyond formal educational and state institutions.

This interview was initially conducted by WHW Akademija team members Martina Kontošić and Ana Kovačić during Tree School for WHW Akademija in Zagreb and continued digitally with the book's editorial team.

NOTES

1 See, for instance, Refugee Heritage: https://refugeeheritage.org/.

2 See www.campusincamps.ps/skill/initiatives.

3 See www.campusincamps.ps/skill/collective-dictionary.

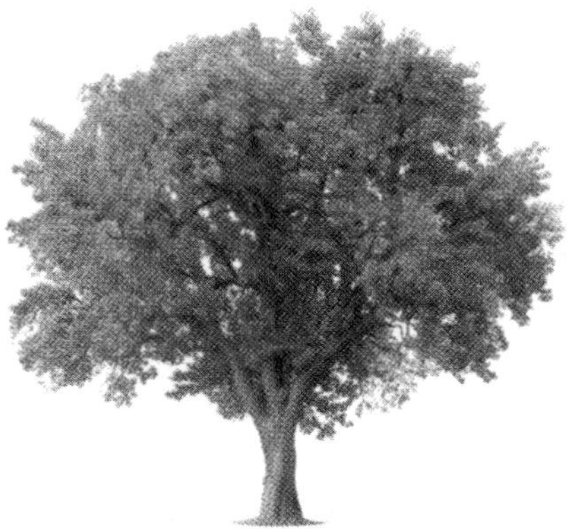

Participants, mentors, and the organizational team of the third edition of WHW Akademija gathered on Sljeme mountain near Zagreb beween July 12 and 16, 2021, as a part of the Tree School organized by Sandi Hilal and Alessandro Petti (DAAR). In a simple yet invaluable act of being together over three full days, the process of sharing experiences and knowledge created an atmosphere of collectivity.

Tree School Attendees

WHW Akademija participants: Luna Acosta • Eva Ďurovec • Teuta Gatolin • Lama El Khatib • Yulia Krivich • Ghita Skali • Raluca Țurcanașu

Professorial team: Marwa Arsanios • Alex Baczyński-Jenkins and Kasia Wlaszczyk (Kem) • Vlatka Horvat • Pablo Martínez • Aude Christel Mgba • Dan Perjovschi

Guests: Charles Esche • Emily Pethick

Organizers: Sandi Hilal and Alessandro Petti (DAAR) • WHW collective and team members

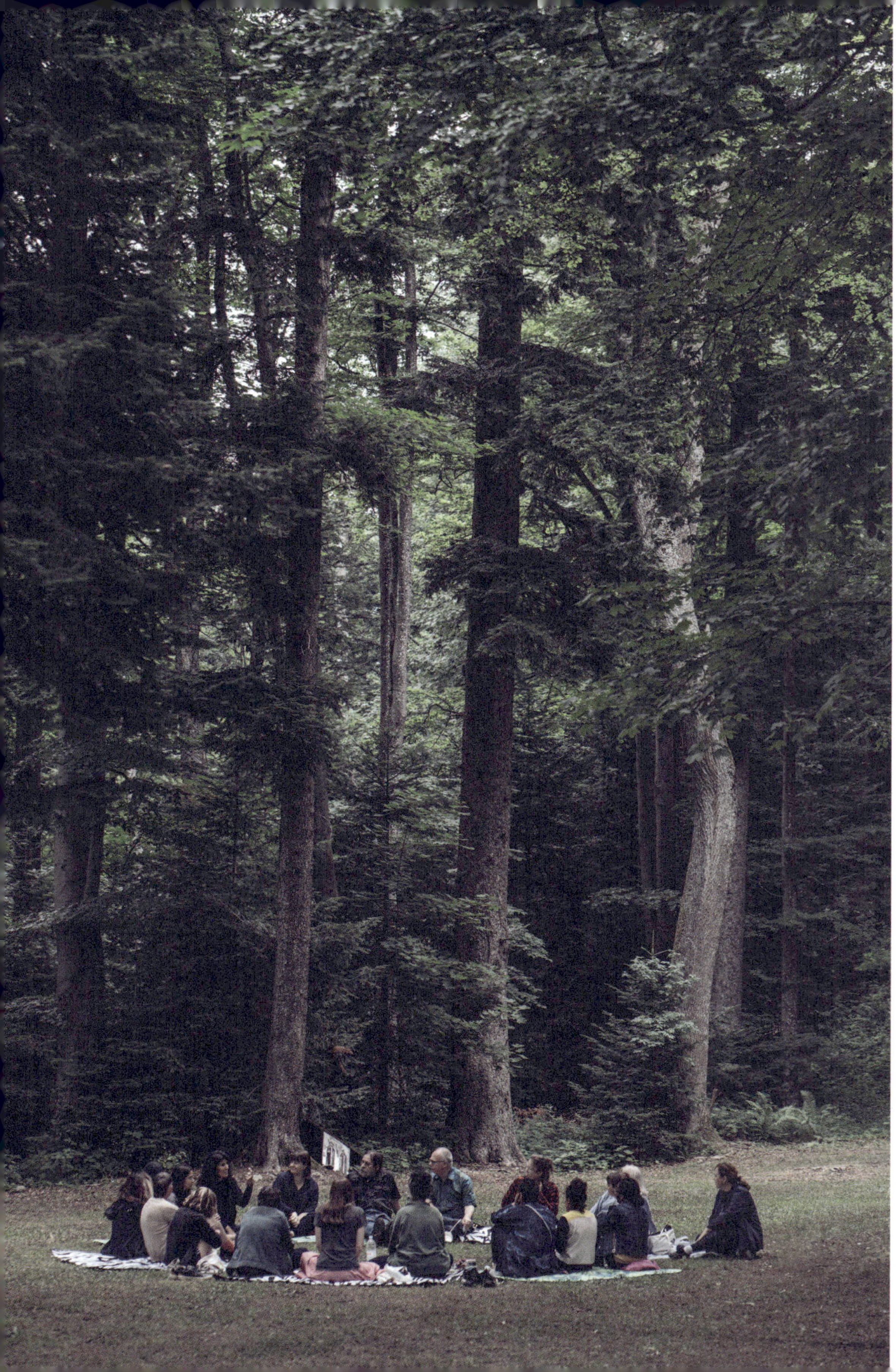

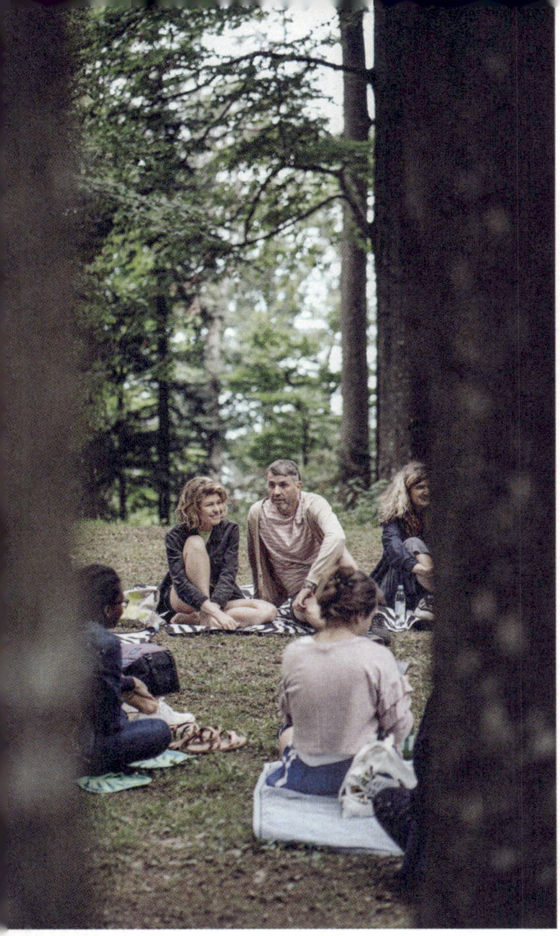
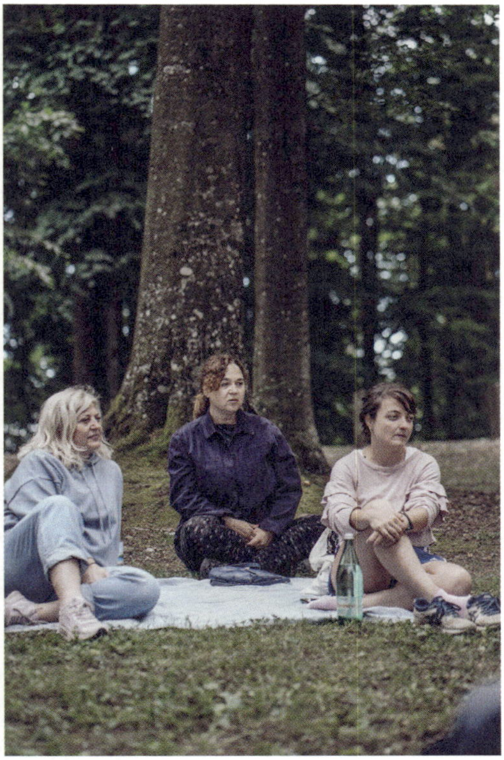
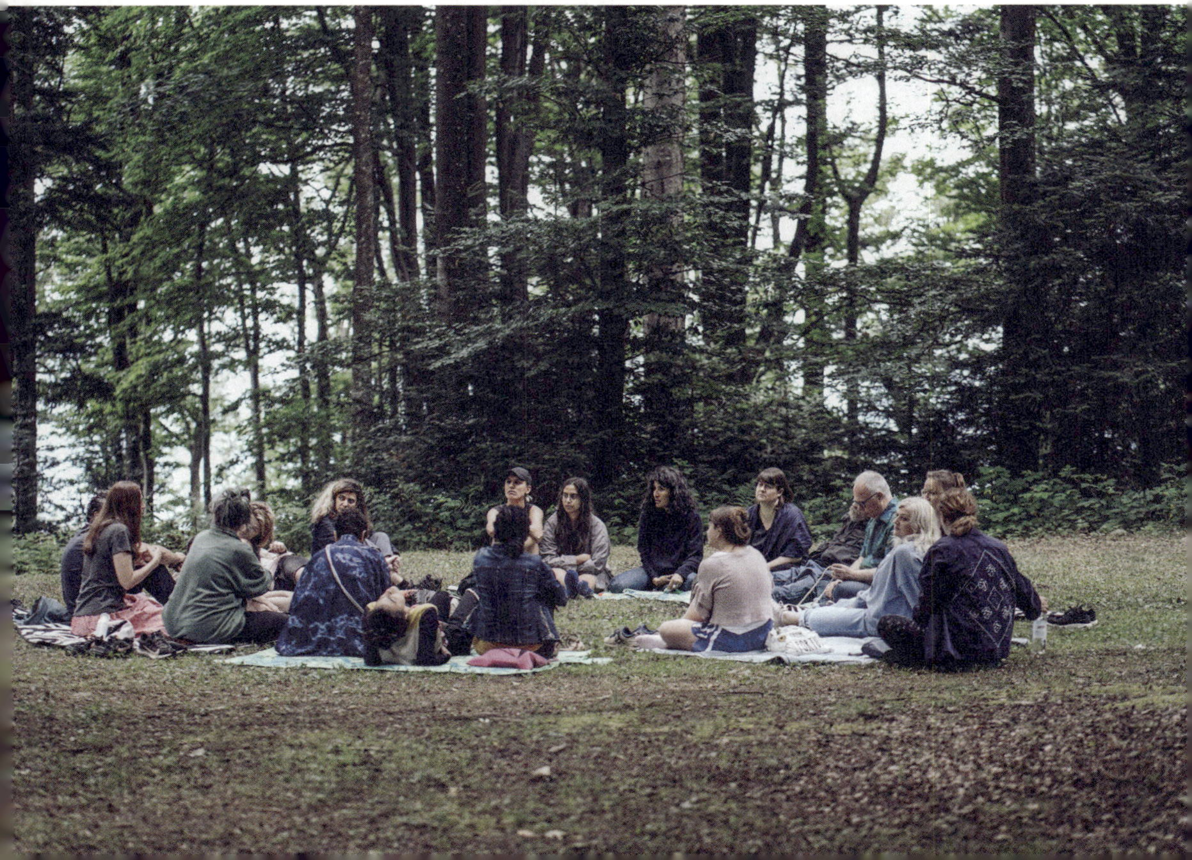

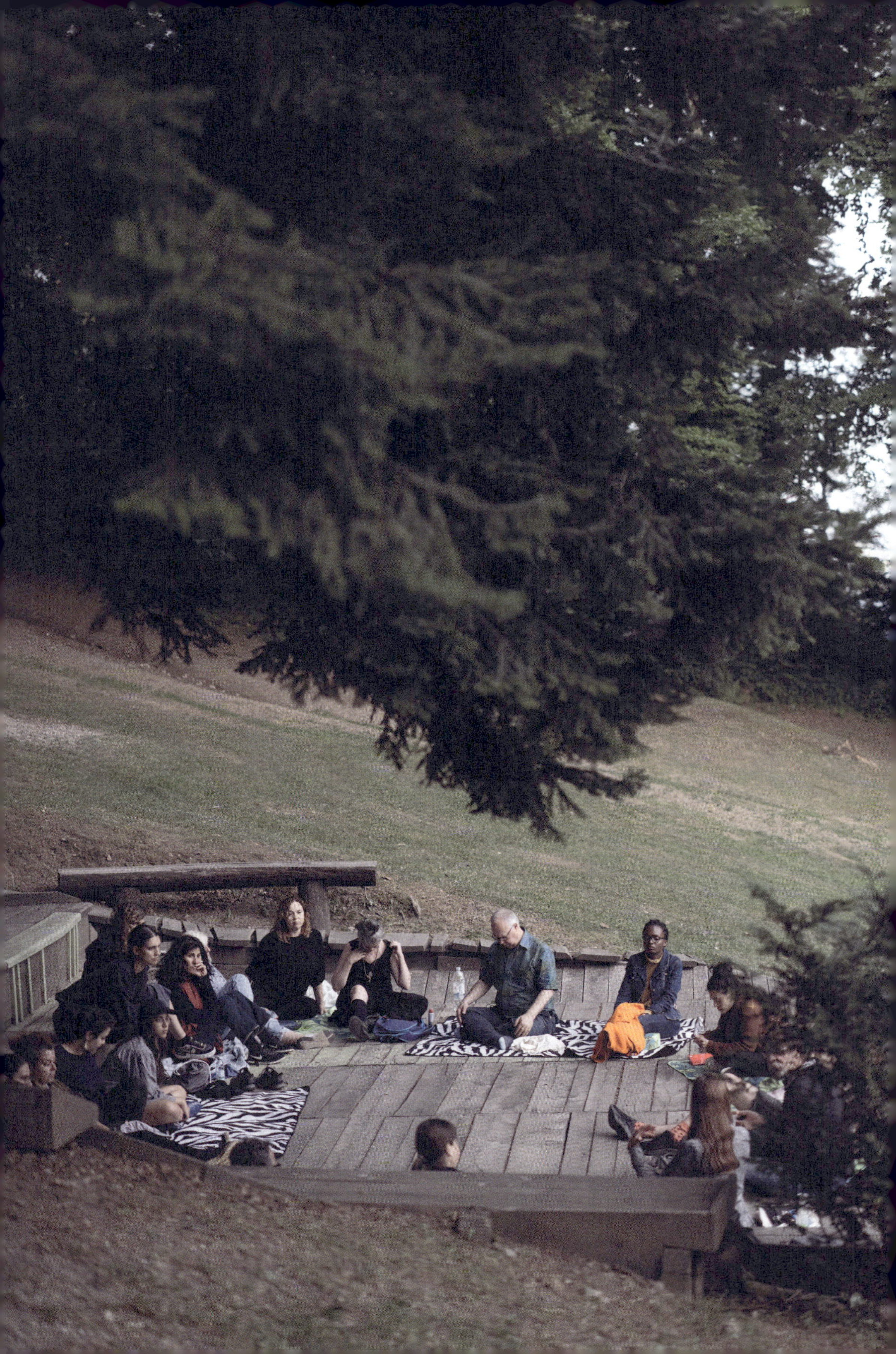

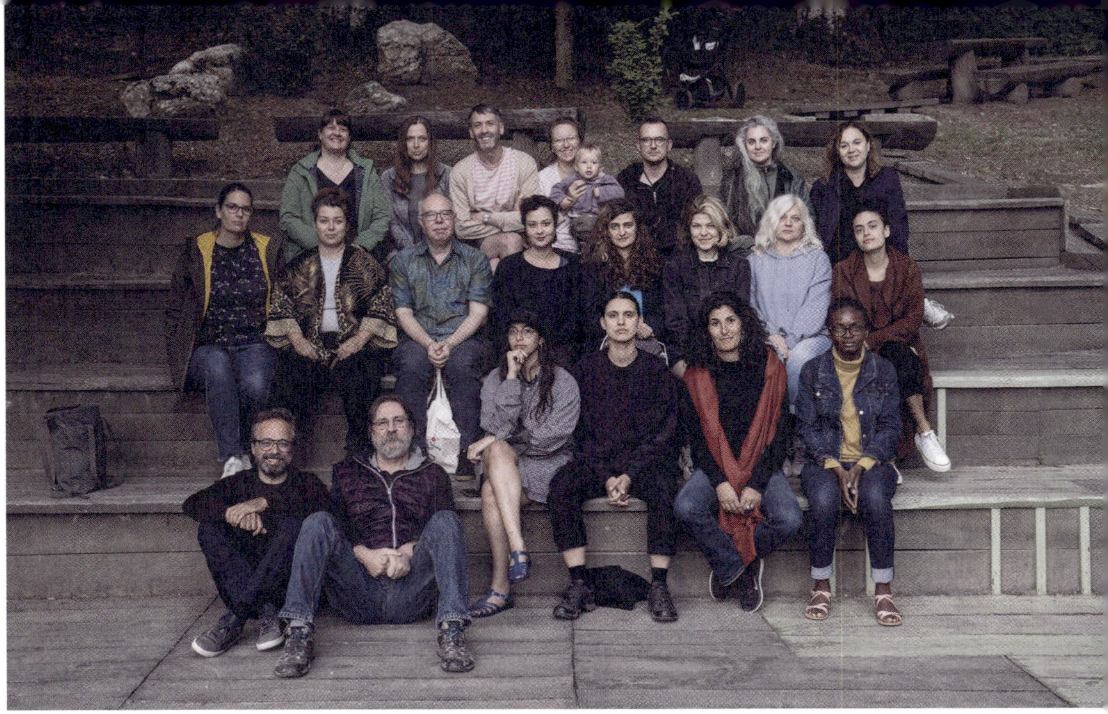

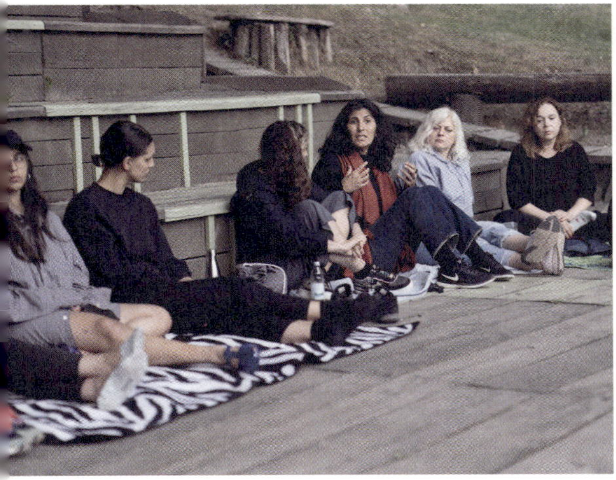

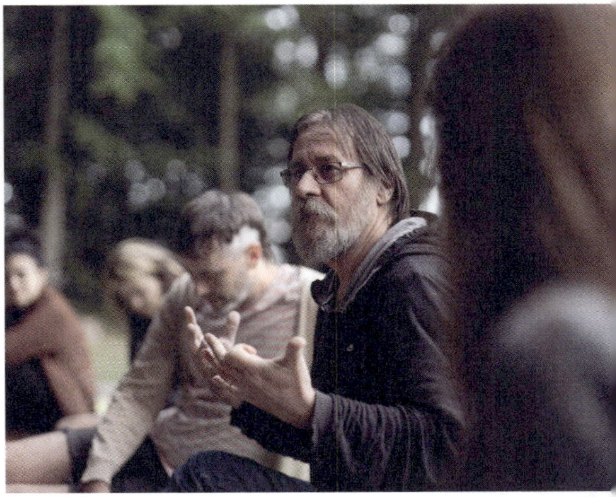

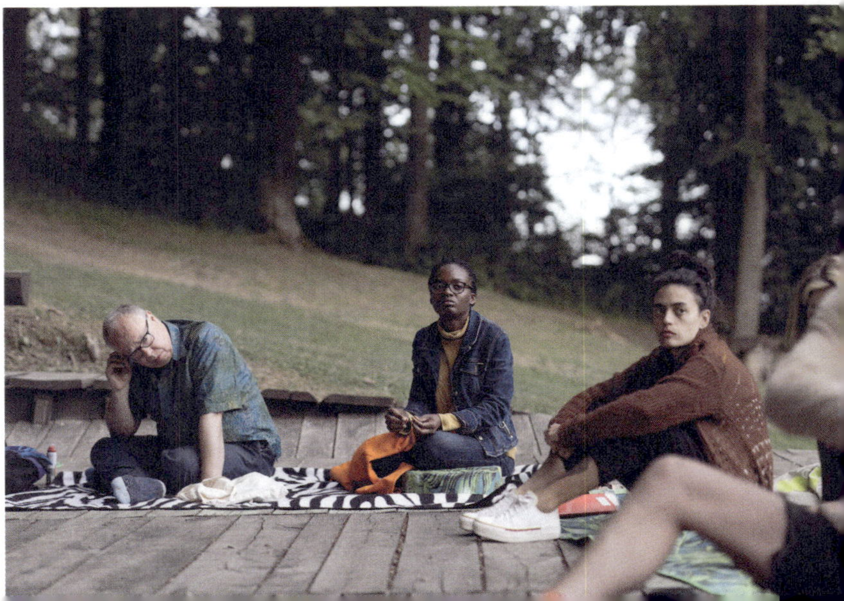

The Tree School at WHW Akademija, Sljeme, Croatia, 2021
PHOTOS: Damir Žižić

Luna Acosta

Sociometabolism

(2021)

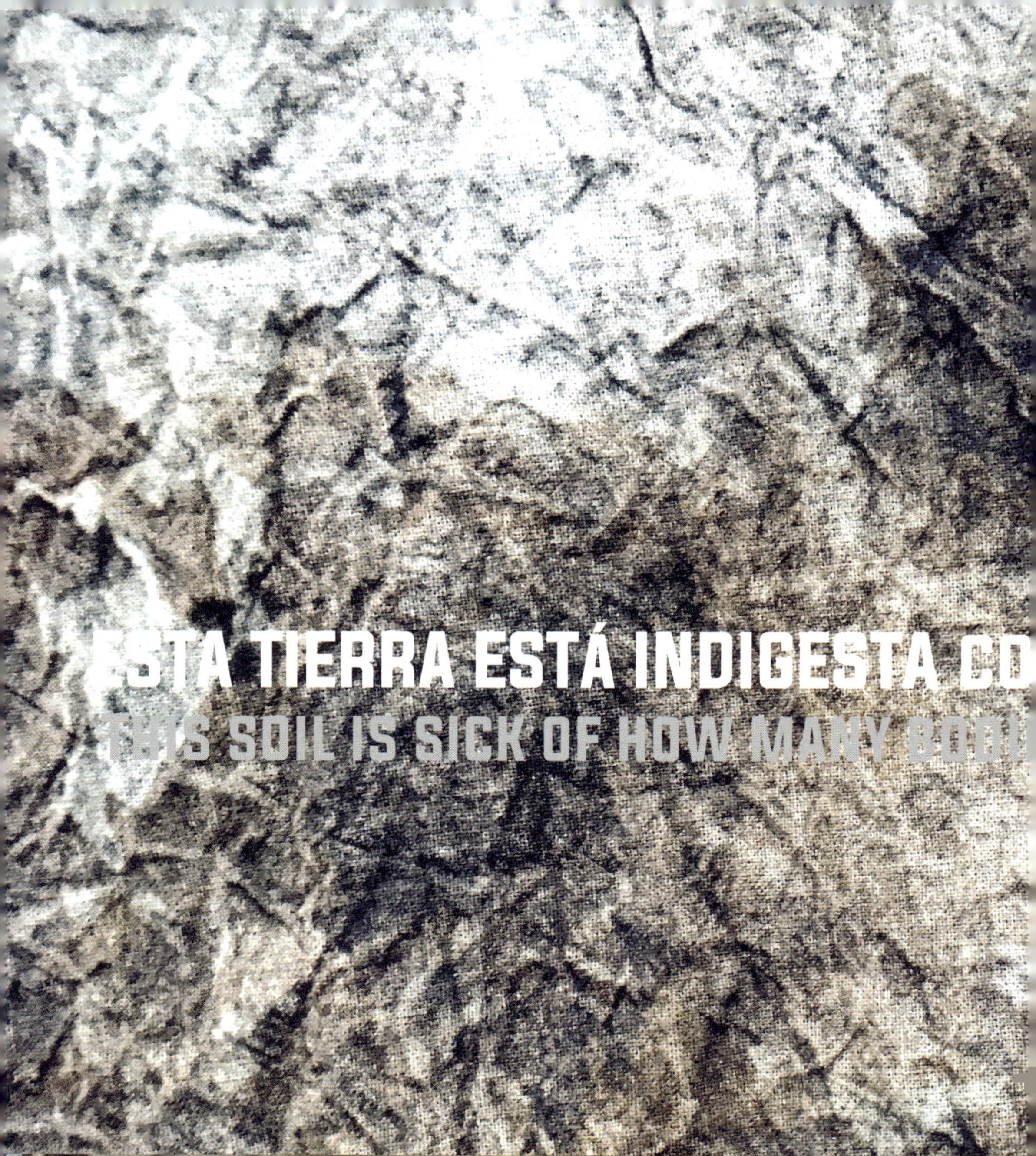
ESTA TIERRA ESTÁ INDIGESTA
THIS SOIL IS SICK OF HOW MANY

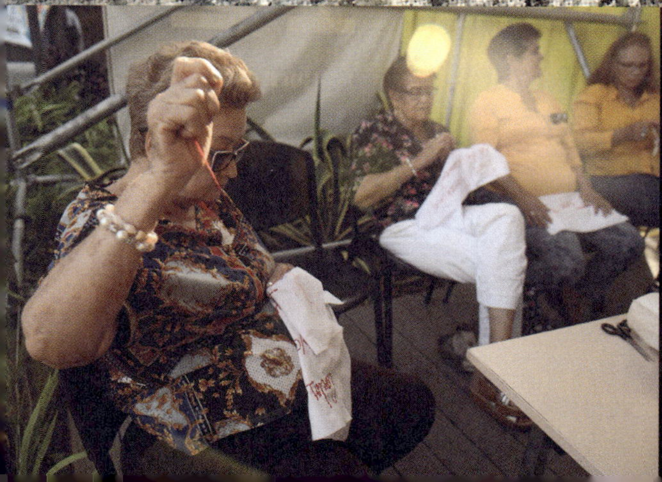

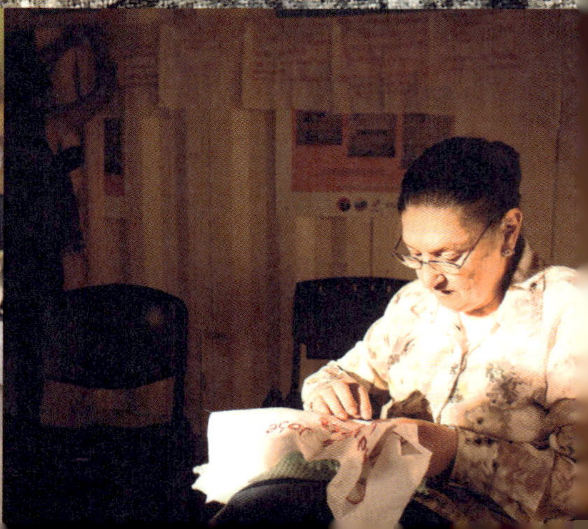

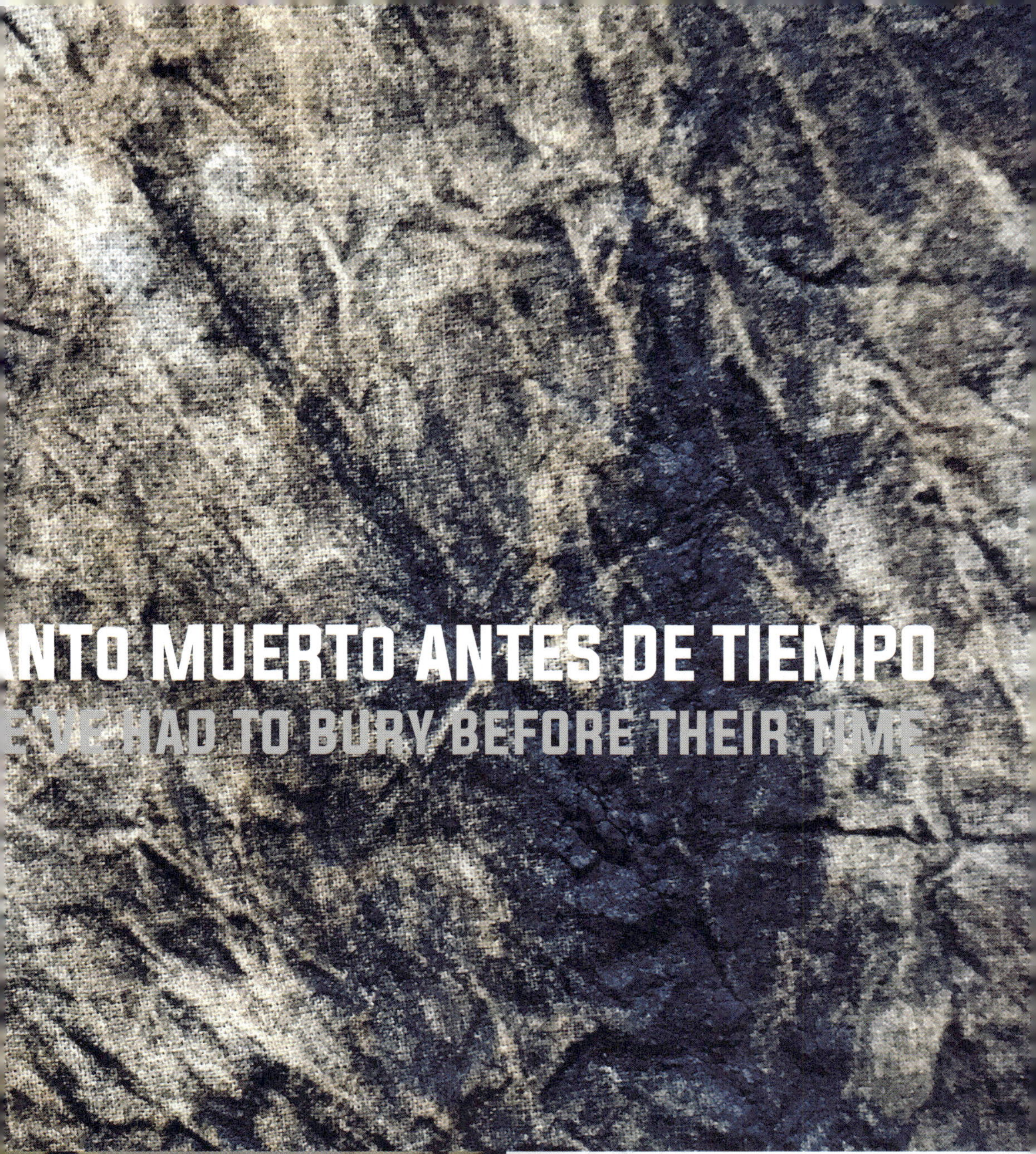
ANTO MUERTO ANTES DE TIEMPO
E'VE HAD TO BURY BEFORE THEIR TIME

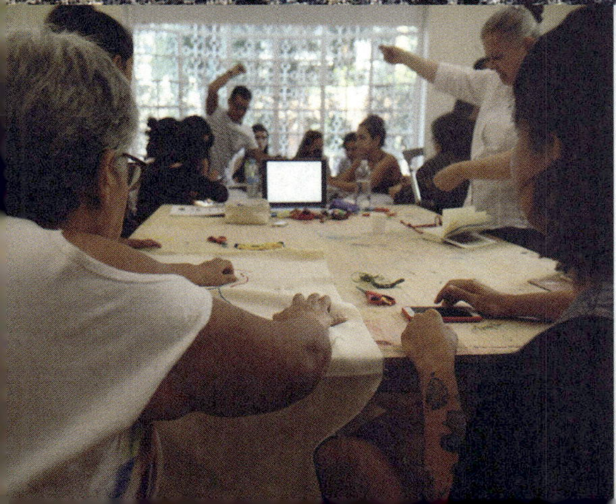

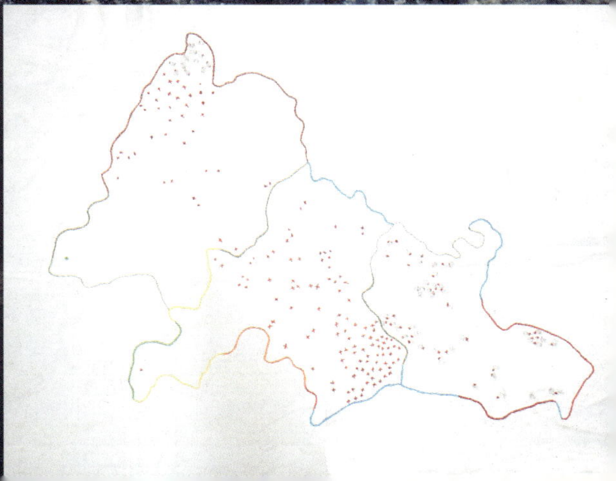

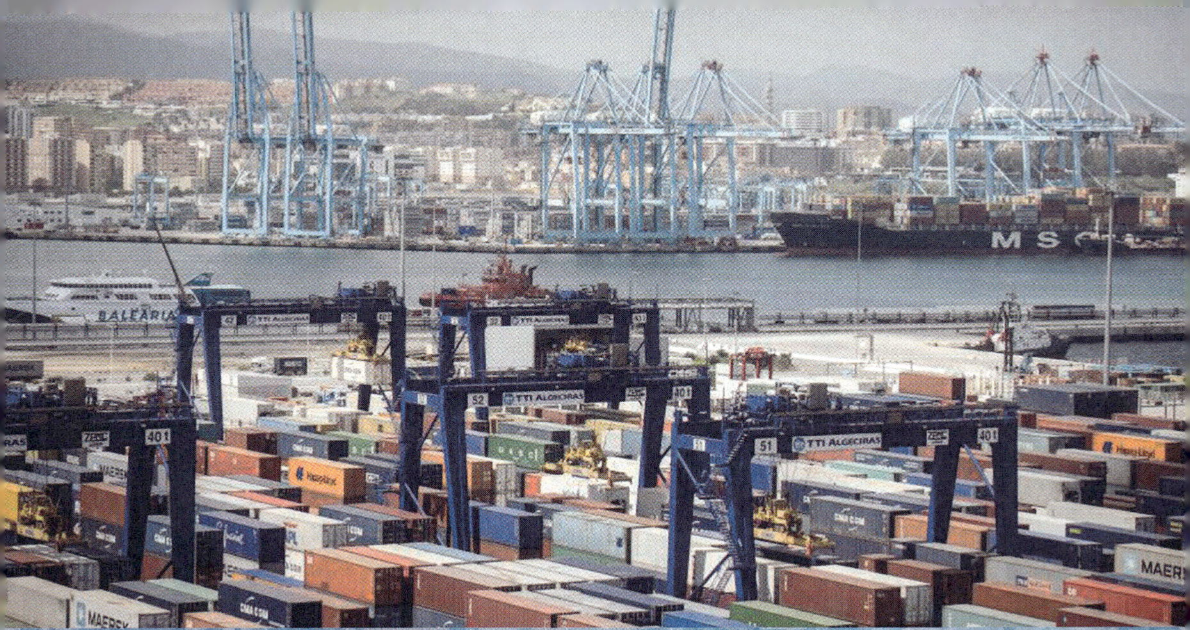

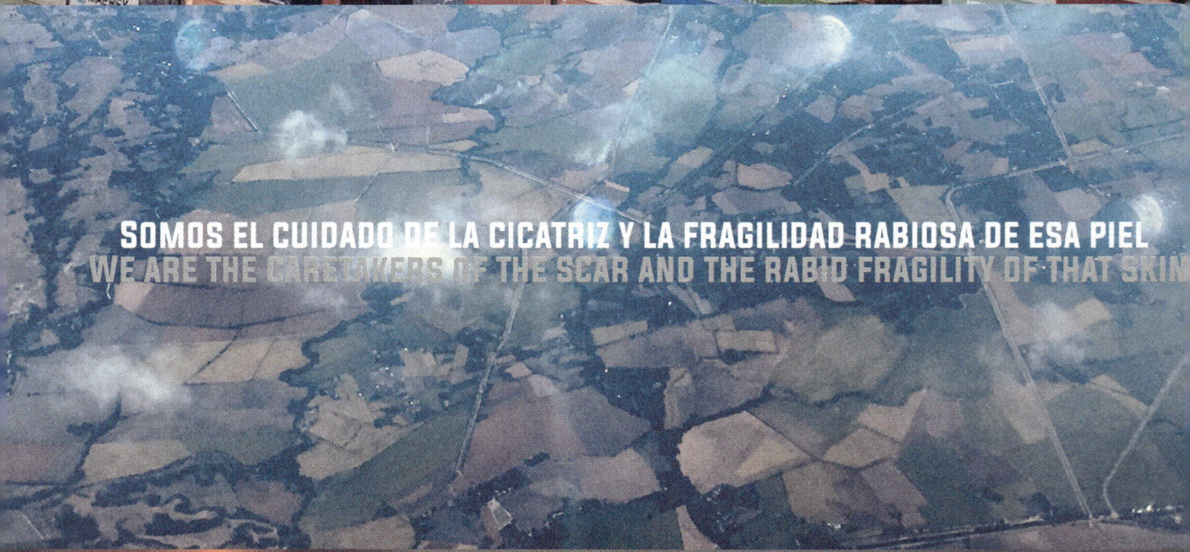

SOMOS EL CUIDADO DE LA CICATRIZ Y LA FRAGILIDAD RABIOSA DE ESA PIEL

WE ARE THE CARETAKERS OF THE SCAR AND THE RABID FRAGILITY OF THAT SKIN

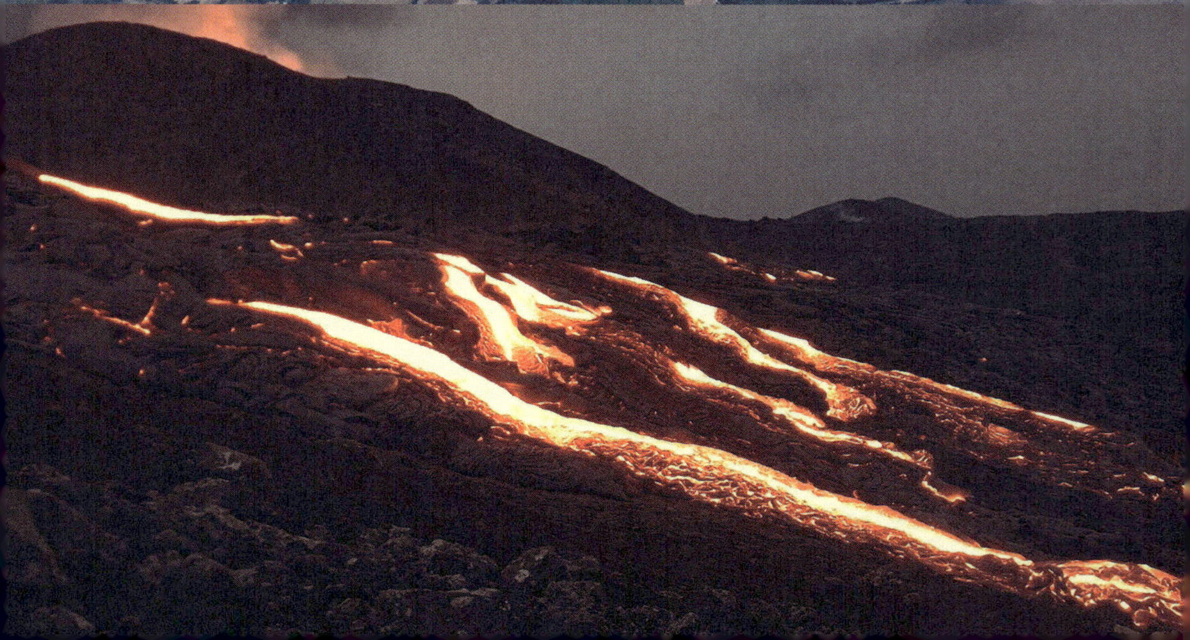

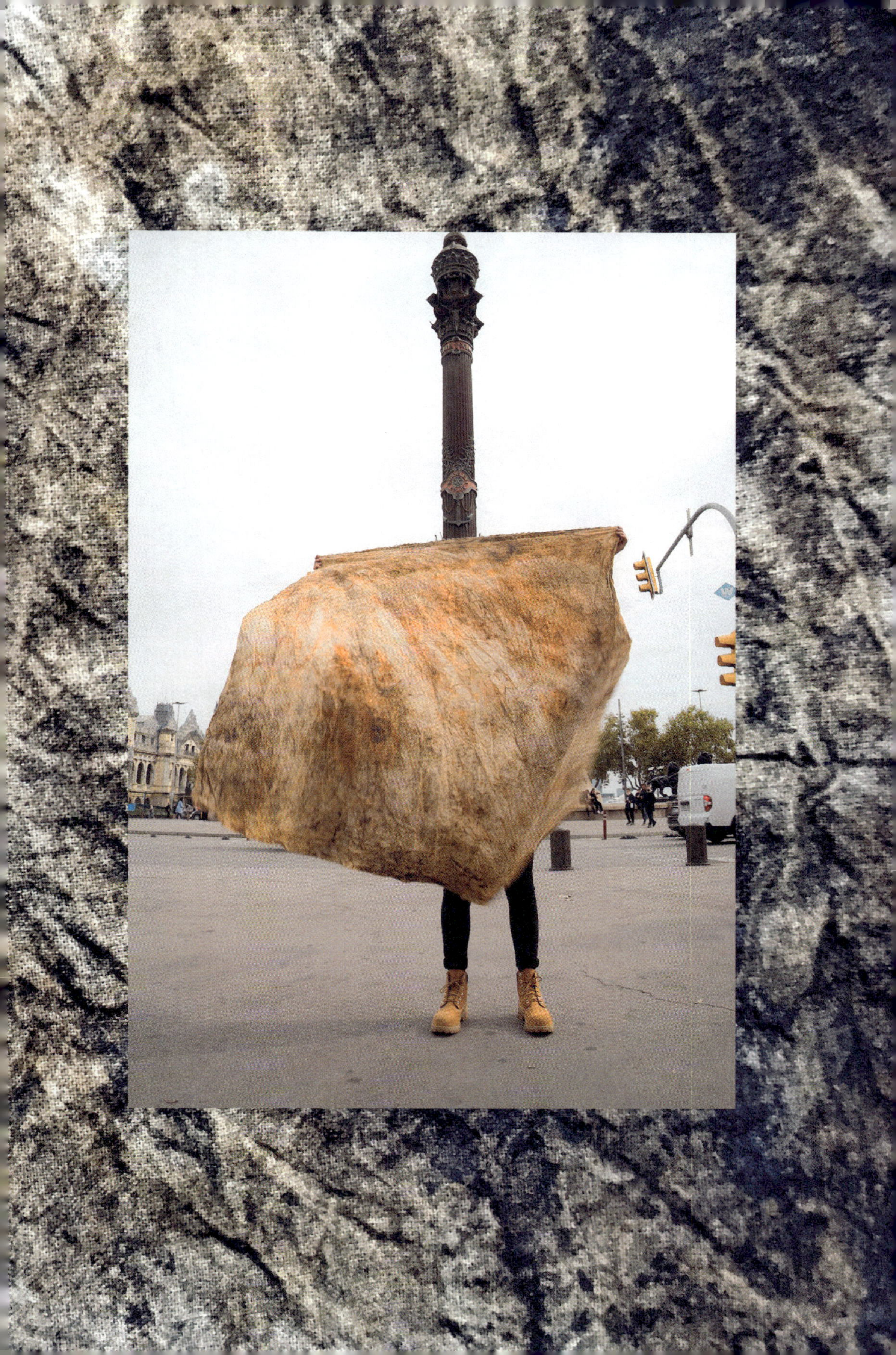

Decolonize, Democratize, Deelitize:

Notes on the Museo Nacional de Arte, La Paz, Plurinational State of Bolivia

—Max Jorge Hinderer Cruz

Between March 2019 and June 2020, I had the opportunity to direct the Museo Nacional de Arte (MNA) in the city of La Paz in the Plurinational State of Bolivia. Decolonization was a key issue from the moment I was invited to take the job up to the moment I was dismissed. You could say that my proposal to decolonize the museum was both the reason I was hired and the reason I was fired. But let's take it one step at a time, since my arrival and departure each took place against a specific political backdrop that was inseparable from what I was proposing to do at the MNA between 2019 and 2020.

What does it mean to decolonize a museum? What it doesn't mean: burning down the museum, or destroying its colonial architecture and artworks. It doesn't mean making anything disappear. On the contrary, it means making things appear, rendering visible structures and relationships previously made invisible. In a way, decolonizing means changing how we see the museum, how we see the works in the museum, and how we display works in the museum. Decolonizing the museum means intervening in its logic, questioning things we take for granted. At the same time, a process of decolonization must necessarily take into account its specific local context, figure out exactly what type of museum it is. For example, decolonizing the Musée du quai Branly in Paris involves starting from an entirely different set of premises than the one we would use to decolonize the Museo Nacional de Arte in La Paz. The process of decolonization cannot make the same mistake as colonization itself: supplanting local customs and presences in order to impose a new, universalizing principle. The following notes are an overview of some of the criteria we developed over my year and a half as director, which aimed at decolonizing the MNA and made apparent that no decolonization can happen without democratization and deelitization, of both the museum and the dominant notions as to what constitutes art.

Decolonize

There has been much talk of decolonization in recent times, and not just in Bolivia. For the past ten years, I have regularly been invited to talk about decolonizing the arts at universities and institutions of the so-called international art world. However, contrary to expectations, in the Bolivian context I have found a fair amount of upfront resistance to engaging in any debate about a possible decolonization of the arts. In February 2019, for example, in a press conference where I was introduced as the new director of the MNA, even before I had officially taken on the post, a member of the audience reproached me for talking about decolonization, alleging that my goal was nothing less that to destroy the colonial artworks in the museum's collection. My response is very simple: decolonizing art does not mean destroying art from the colonial period or from the viceroyalty; it does not mean burning them or making them disappear. On the contrary: destroying, weeding out, toppling, and burning cultural artifacts has—historically speaking—been the way of the colonizer.

And yet, depending on who you ask, five hundred years ago, as an act of legitimate self-defense, it might have been seen as a good idea to kill off all the white people and burn everything they had brought with them, since it would have saved the Indigenous Peoples of our lands five centuries of oppression, genocide, cultural extinction, raids, rape, extractive mining, and irreparable environmental destruction.

But in the early twenty-first century, it is a different story. The most likely beneficiaries of destroying colonial artwork would be the very reactionary forces who uphold colonial legacy against any form of decolonization, be it in art, general culture, or politics. As far as our heritage is concerned, the most powerful decolonizing effort in the realm of art is, in fact, to preserve the art of the colonial period, to study and understand it, so as to learn from it what colonialism was really about. What I mean is: to decolonize art, we must first of all carry out an exhaustive study of colonial art. We need to understand how colonial art worked and what its purpose was, here, in our part of the world, as well as in comparable contexts elsewhere.

I hold great respect for the hugely important research going on in the field—built on a foundation developed by the unequaled, pioneering work of Teresa Gisbert—but nevertheless Bolivian art history is still a long way off from consolidating itself as a fully fledged discipline, and even further off from establishing itself as a critical discipline that can be read on par with, but also in comparison to, Eurocentric art histories. We urgently need to rethink these narratives, whose main objective is the depiction and glorification of the cultural expressions of the colonial period. To press ahead with the project of creating our own art history, as an academic and a critical discipline, we must overcome the descriptive phase, that initial step of inventorying our heritage, and instead focus on putting our capacity for critical analysis to work. We must ask questions to understand how colonial art worked, what its purpose was, and who it benefited. And we must construct arguments so that we can explain why, in seeking to decolonize art, our primary responsibility is to care for it, make it accessible, make it known.

Paradoxically, colonial paintings are as fascinating as they are horrifying—theirs is an appalling beauty. Their allure is matched only by the repulsion of the system they depict. Colonial paintings are at once works of singular beauty and documents of a regime structured by the utmost violence, a regime that left a profound mark on our history, the wounds and negative consequences of which continue to afflict us today.

This very beauty of colonial paintings is evidence of the arrogance of the colonial project. But in a trial, it isn't the paintings we would summon as defendants: in the process of decolonizing art, the artworks are rather our witnesses and, therefore, our most important allies. In this trial, a gallery of colonial artworks is a room full of witnesses who have grown weary of being called on to testify.

Decolonizing art is not a simple matter of getting rid of a museum's colonial artworks. Taking them off the walls is merely a prerequisite for dusting them off and conserving them, for opening the doors and windows to let some fresh air into the old galleries, enough oxygen to finally get down to the real work of decolonization, which consists of rehanging the works, but putting them in their proper place.

Democratize

Culture is a fundamentally political technology. History's most effective projects of political usurpation have always been carried out on at least two planes: a project of military intervention and domination, and a project of colonizing the "hearts and souls," of governing the ideological, of conquering people's emotions.

When the Spanish reached the Americas, they destroyed the local temples and *huacas*, and in their place built churches where they trained the Indigenous Peoples to experience fear, guilt, and a sense of inferiority. In Germany, the Nazis stoked hate and racism, evoked resentment, and instigated civil violence and a disdain for Jewish people, those with disabilities, and homosexuals, among others, and with this discourse set fire to the Reichstag, the central symbol of the young, democratic Weimar Republic.

Revolutions seeking equality have also been adept at valuing the role of emotions, feelings, and perceptions. Europe's bourgeois revolutions of the late eighteenth and early nineteenth centuries had an ethical and cultural project behind them, including the desire to free people's aesthetic judgment, to emancipate the aesthetic experience. This idealistic proposal sought nothing less than the equality of all, both before the law and in the face of beauty. For the German bourgeoisie of the period, the very concept of *Kultur* was revolutionary, despite the fact that it continued to be fundamentally racist and sexist. At the outset, the Russian Revolution also included plans for a cultural revolution that envisioned a complete change in the habits and design of everyday life, that sought a revolutionary art and even sexual emancipation and gender equality.

It is from this last context that we in Bolivia inherited our concept of cultural revolution. And the comparison is a fair one: over the last twenty years, with the movements opposed to the neoliberal governments, we have been experiencing a process of cultural democratization previously unheard of in this country. Palaces haven't been burned down, but people's souls have caught fire. The people have shaken ideological pillars—in particular racism and sexism—which, for five hundred years, have propped up the false sense of superiority of the few over the many. It is in this sense that we can speak of revolution: a shift, a change of course, a change in how things are going. But you can't pull off a cultural revolution by putting on a play or buying a ticket to the movies. It is tough, long, and drawn-out work that—yes—requires its own form of commitment and militancy. And there is still a lot of ground to be gained. The self-determination of women's desires and bodies and respect for the dignity of nature, for example, are two points that must be emphasized in this process.

The great merits of the process of decolonizing culture have included the recognition of the dignity and value of Indigenous Peoples' contributions and the reassessment of women's role in the foundational narratives of contemporary Bolivia. But the process of democratizing culture is not solely carried out within the cultural sphere and its narratives. It also involves a negotiation as to what can be said, how to say it, and who has the right to talk about what culture should be. Because doing culture is nothing more and nothing less than doing politics with other means.

To democratize culture, then, is necessarily to renegotiate what "culture" itself could actually mean: to question the culture of the colonial period and of the former Bolivian Republic, to stop taking it for granted as something natural and understood, as a universal, unifying, and homogenizing cultural experience and belonging. Within the logic of colonialism, and even within the logic of the former Republic of Bolivia, culture is something that one simply "possesses" or "doesn't." Following this same analogy, with the bourgeois glorification of the principle of private property, "to have culture" defines one's position within a social hierarchy. It is, first and foremost, a marker of class. From the point of view of cultural democratization, then, renegotiating what is naturalized as a cultural norm also means fighting for a redistribution among those who do and do not own a share of this "property."

It is because of this shift, this redistributing of property rights, that the "owners" of Bolivian culture today—that is, the representatives and heirs of colonial and republican culture—are so afraid. Paradoxically, to maintain the legitimacy of their inheritance, they need to obscure their own historical condition and, likewise, the political mechanisms they have employed: colonialism and the hyperexploitation of the Indigenous workforce, feudalism, structural racism, and the innate patriarchy of colonialism, which forged the very conditions that enabled this culture to take shape.

Interestingly, these are the same people who have of late spoken out in favor of "democratic culture" while at the same time engaging in two types of implicit omission: first, confusing their privilege with freedom (the liberal approach), and, second, confusing their privilege with rights (i.e., conservatives, chauvinists, and the petite bourgeoisie).

In the face of silence and omission, it is not enough to say that one is nonracist: one must be antiracist. It is not enough to say that racism exists: one must truly understand in what forms it exists, both explicitly and implicitly, and where and how race is implemented as a social and political technology. Silence, omission, and confusing one's own privilege are all structural and fundamental parts of both racism and sexism.

To be successful in our context, any attempt at democratizing culture must therefore include a keen awareness of who its enemies are: they are the ones who talk about democratic culture without questioning their own historical conditions or actively fighting for the full eradication of racism and sexism. These other calls for democracy will never be anything but a sham.

Deelitize

A national art museum—for what and for whom? In Bolivia, in order to democratize, we first have to deelitize culture and the arts. If the heritage preserved in the museum belongs to all Bolivians, what the museum owes the public is, at the very least, to question why entering the museum feels natural for some but not for others. It should ask itself why some people identify with the cultural artifacts housed in the museum while others do not—and all the more so if we are talking about the colonial paintings that were part of the MNA's so-called permanent exhibition.

As its very name indicates, the Museo Nacional de Arte is a national museum. On the one hand, then, it is a public museum that answers to a system of public institutions and also to public oversight. In Bolivia this means, in particular, that the museum is susceptible to political shifts. But, on the other hand, despite the November 2019 coup d'état, constitutionally we have remained a plurinational state. So, starting with the country's official name—the Plurinational State of Bolivia—we can already see a certain contradiction between a *national* museum and a *plurinational* state, which in the case of Bolivia—per its Constitution—encompasses "thirty-six originary, indigenous, peasant and afro-diasporic nations."

While I was director of the museum, this led us to question the very nature of what the museum of a nation might be. Along these lines, the first question I asked when I took up the post was: How is it possible for a plurinational state to have a national museum? The restructuring of the museum that we tried to carry out, then, revolved around an expansion of its objectives, based on three fundamental guidelines: firstly, "opening up" the museum, meaning reaching out to new audiences, opening up new spaces, and getting out word on the museum's activities among both local and international audiences; secondly, rethinking narratives, shifting from a representational approach (the art of the nation) to an analytical one (who does the exhibited art represent?), and transforming the museum from a *repository* of exhibitions to a *producer* of exhibitions, research, and knowledge; and, finally, implementing an education- and research-centered department emphasizing the importance of community outreach to diverse audiences, as well as arts education for kids, teens, and specialist audiences, thereby transforming the museum not only into the country's foremost exhibition center but also into a public education institution.

All of this led us to think of a deelitized museum. To get there, we had to imagine a museum outside the museum, to go out and look for it elsewhere, beyond its usual location. Of course, for our exhibition and education proposals, we used the artifacts contained in the museum; but as to what the museum would be—for what and for whom—we decided to look elsewhere, outside the museum. We also looked outside the museum to answer the question "What is art?" We weren't satisfied with the answers already contained in the museum. The MNA has a collection of over nine thousand cultural artifacts, from colonial and republican to twentieth-century and contemporary, of which roughly two-thirds date from the twentieth century to the present.

Founded in 1964, the MNA has lived through a variety of administrations, including those of President Evo Morales and his Movement Toward Socialism (Movimiento al Socialismo), a policy priority of which was decolonization, and, in 2009, the implementing of a new Political Constitution of the State, which declared Bolivia a plurinational state. There were many changes in political, social, and economic structures, as well as in certain social hierarchies. For example, a new Indigenous economic and political elite emerged that had never before been taken into consideration as a political factor. And this new elite entailed, for the first time in five hundred years of history, the integration and active participation of sectors of the Indigenous population in matters of governance, in terms of both representation and decision-making.

The decolonization plan was very broad and highly publicized. However, it was a process that, in the art world, went nowhere. In fourteen years under the Morales administration, we did not see the same changes that we saw taking place in other sectors of social and political life. The MNA remained a "national" museum, in the sense of representing a cultural elite that had been in place since the colonial period but that had little to do with the new plurinational Bolivia. According to the 2001 National Census of Population and Housing, 62 percent of inhabitants—nearly two-thirds of the population—consider themselves to be Indigenous. The MNA, in representing a nation according to the ideology of the former Republic of Bolivia, represents a white cultural elite that is in fact a tiny minority within the Bolivian population. And it represents a nation that is heir to the colonial forces and the colonial elite. They remain, in fact, practically the same families. In Bolivia, the white cultural elite and "traditional" republican families constitute very small and exclusive circles. The fact that these groups are the same ones who have been in charge of the Museo Nacional de Arte for generations—since its founding—is at odds with the reality that Bolivia has the largest Indigenous population of any country in South America. And, as a plurinational state, it is certainly at odds with the lived reality of the country that Indigenous populations were never taken into account as audiences, much less as the protagonists or authors of even a single exhibition, and never given opportunity to express their opinions on what is or isn't art.

To decolonize the museum, we needed to change this concept, and to expand what "national" means for this museum, we had to go out and look beyond the museum, outside the restricted circles of the traditional elite. We had to look for people who had never set foot in the museum and who belonged to the nations that make up the majority of the Bolivian population. A deelitized museum—a museum beyond the museum—allows the world outside its walls to affect the world inside its walls. So, returning to our question as to what and who the Museo Nacional de Arte is for, we had to ask ourselves who the museum and its collections did and did not represent within the Plurinational State of Bolivia.

This is why our proposal marked a shift in the museum's guidelines and profile. The first thing we needed to do was open up the institution, which meant creating new spaces and reaching out to new audiences. We wanted people who had never even thought of going to the museum to now come in, feel welcome, and understand that the MNA's collection belongs to everyone, and that it is a collection that should raise questions. We wanted them to know that the policies governing the museum should be questioned, as should the parameters and aims with which the museum's collections were created. So, for example, we organized free guided tours in the Aymara language. La Paz is located in an Aymara-speaking region, and although every day scores of Aymara speakers walk past the museum's doors, many had never set foot inside the institution or thought that they might be welcome there. This includes people who work right near the museum and whose children go to school next door. What the tours in Aymara did was open up the museum to a community that had never visited it before. One of the most important results was a process of reflection and dialogue with the visitors and with the tour guide, the Aymara historian Isaac Callizaya, as to the translatability of the very term "art," designed by a modernist, Western culture and as such lacking an exact equivalent in the Aymara *cosmovision* (worldview). How can we talk about art if we don't have the word "art" to work with, or if we can't agree on its meaning? What can this teach us about Eurocentric understandings of art?

> Our second task was to rethink narratives. For us, it was crucial to understand the museum as more than just a space of representation. We didn't want to represent the artistic expressions of a genocidal regime like that of the colonial period, nor the art of a regime of inequality like that of the Republic of Bolivia, which also barred Indigenous participation. So, apart from opening up the institution, we also needed to rethink the museum's narratives and museology. We wanted to effect a shift from a logic of representation to a logic of analysis, by asking the very questions I mentioned at the outset: Why this art and not another? What purpose and what people did it serve? What was its function in the past and what is or could its function be today? Who found colonial art beautiful and who did not? These are the questions we focused on as we transitioned from the logic of representing the cultural expressions of a genocidal regime to a logic of analysis within the context of the Plurinational State of Bolivia. We cut down the number of exhibitions per year to give ourselves more time: more time to produce them, to ask ourselves what innovative museological approaches we wanted to use to hang the paintings, to do research and generate knowledge, to prepare a catalogue on par with our project of innovation, to develop educational and outreach materials, and to plan out the exhibitions as comprehensive projects.

For example, in the 2020 annual exhibition of works from the permanent collection, "Dios y la Máquina. Serialidad y singularidad en la pintura colonial andina" (God and the machine: The serial and the singular in colonial painting from the Andes), which included roughly seventy colonial paintings from the sixteenth to the eighteenth centuries, distributed across both floors of the Casona Diez de Medina building, we decided to display the paintings suspended in space, instead of the traditional approach of hanging them on the walls. We wanted to see the paintings from our collection in a new light, to literally see them from new perspectives. Displaying them in the middle of the space, with their verso sides visible, entailed a shift in the narrative: we are convinced that there is something about the backsides of these paintings that is crucial to understanding them.

When we look at a painting straight on, we often forget that it has an invisible or hidden side, an invisibility that—and this is our hypothesis—is part and parcel of the way we are used to seeing paintings in museums. We see paintings from just one side, without considering that the other side might be hiding countless histories and pieces of information that could add to or even alter the meaning of what we see on the front side.

But meaning isn't everything. The point is to understand a painting not only as a more or less masterful figurative illusion, a more or less beautiful surface. Each painting is also an object, and objects are complex. They consist of paint and a support, of layers of material, work, and history; they are body, texture, and time.

The third important point in redeveloping the museum's profile was integrating a research and education department. We wanted to understand art across the multiple historical and political shifts that have structured and restructured our society from the sixteenth century up to the present. We argued that it was impossible to move forward with a museum in a context like that of Bolivian culture without promoting public education and learning about history and about the context around us. The backbone of our research and education efforts was the Decolonial Studies Program in the Arts (Programa de Estudios Descoloniales en Arte; PED), which encompassed various modules. For example, the "PED-diálogos" was a weekly discussion series around the question "What is art?" The first session addressed this question from Afro-Bolivian and Afro-Latin perspectives. The next discussion looked at art from the perspective of El Alto, considered the youngest metropolis in the Americas. The city has approximately one million inhabitants, more than 80 percent of whom are Indigenous migrants from the Altiplano highlands and the Bolivian Andes. El Alto is a very unique metropolis, in that it

> only became a community and city less than fifty years ago. It is a city that, moreover, found its own political and civic identity in 2003, with the notorious Gas War, when the Sánchez de Lozada administration ordered the murder of more than eighty people in multiple massacres that took place during protests in the city.

We also held a session on art from the perspectives of the Quechua and Aymara cosmovision, during which we of course discussed the experience of the guided tours in Aymara with historian Isaac Callizaya. The question as to the translatability of the term "art," and of the MNA's conception of art, is at the origin of the "PED-diálogos." Alongside Quechua Aymara artist, weaver, and researcher Elvira Espejo Ayca—who has been a friend and collaborator of mine for more than ten years—as well as a mutual friend of ours, the writer, educator, and curator Pablo Lafuente, we discussed a very simple question: If our understanding of the word "art" is that of European, Western, colonialist, and imperial cultures, how can we find translations in the languages and cosmovisions of our First Nations that can have a place of their own in an art museum? And, more than this, how can we render intelligible the value added to the term when translating it back into Spanish from these Indigenous languages? How can we back-translate in such a way that these other meanings enhance our own understanding of art, instead of being taken as substitutes or competitors? This is an exercise not only of translation but also one of respecting and ennobling "the Other" and an act of self-deprogramming. In Bolivia, the ideology that separated "art" (attributed to whites and mestizos) from "craft" (attributed to Indigenous people generally) remains alive and well, and it is those privileged by colonialism and who have benefited from racist violence who shout the loudest when we propose that art be understood from other perspectives, when we propose decolonizing, democratizing, and deelitizing our notions of art and our notions of the museum. What decolonizing the museum actually means is setting ourselves a fundamental ethical objective: that the main purpose of art be to strengthen the unconditional equality of all and every person's nonnegotiable right to live in difference. Alongside this principle, we proposed a permeable museum that would exist both inside and outside its own walls, and whose doors would be open to everyone.

Postscript on the Current Political Situation in Bolivia

I was appointed director of the Museo Nacional de Arte by the Administrative Council of the Cultural Foundation of the Central Bank of Bolivia (Fundación Cultural del Banco Central de Bolivia; FCBCB), which governs the MNA and other important cultural institutions in the Plurinational State of Bolivia. The members of this council, who are designated by the Central Bank and the Ministry of Cultures and Tourism, were completely replaced between February and April 2020. The FCBCB president under Evo Morales, Sergio Prudencio, was replaced by Guillermo Mariaca. On June 1, the directors of all the museums, centers, and archives governed by the FCBCB were asked to "make available" their positions, so they could be either confirmed or dismissed. On June 23, I was informed by email that I would not be confirmed in my post and that my last day at the museum would be June 30.

Mariaca justified the move to the press by stating that it was "only natural" for a change in the presidency to bring with it a change in the directors of these institutions. However, not all directors were forced to resign. The only ones affected were those of us who had worked toward inclusive policies, toward strengthening cultural diversity and oral history, or toward problematizing the colonial past, racism, and sexism. The decision, therefore, was not "only natural." It was blatantly political.

The other civil service employees affected by this situation were Máximo Pacheco, a historian and writer from Chuquisaca, until then the director of the National Archive and Library (Archivo y Biblioteca Nacionales de Bolivia) in Sucre, and Elvira Espejo Ayca, the aforementioned artist and recipient of the 2020 Goethe Medal, who was dismissed from her post as director of the National Museum of Ethnography and Folklore (Museo Nacional de Etnografía y Folklore) in La Paz.

It is important to understand that the problem we are up against is a structural one. Jeanine Áñez, appointed as interim president in November 2019 for the sole purpose of calling general elections within ninety days, did not hesitate to undertake structural interventions in the state apparatus, even after elections had finally been confirmed for September 6, 2020. In June of that year, the Ministries of Communication, Sports, and Cultures and Tourism had all been eliminated, and, along with the latter, also the Vice Ministries of Decolonization and Diversity as well as the Directorate of Depatriarchalization. In other words, we witnessed not just the violent demotion of culture's status within state politics but also the elimination of the key apparatuses by which the state might ensure the equality of all Bolivians.

Strengthening equality through difference is one of the unique powers of culture. But when Áñez unexpectedly seized power, after the police staged a nationwide insurrection and the top brass of the Armed Forces "recommended" that Morales step down, Áñez entered the Palace of Government with her collaborators clutching a Bible and saying that she was going to extirpate Pachamama, to kick her out of the Palace and replace her with "the Word of God." Meanwhile, Áñez's followers staged public burnings of the Wiphala, the Andean flag that, along with plurinational statehood, came to represent the Indigenous populations of Bolivia and other parts of the Americas.

It was grotesque, and what's worse, it continued: on July 1, 2020, the police cleared the National Museum of Archaeology (Museo Nacional de Arqueología) in La Paz, which belonged to the Ministry of Cultures, forcibly removing the staff and leaving the institution's priceless archaeological artifacts completely unattended. The Áñez administration's open disdain for both ancestral cultures and contemporary cultures committed to social inclusion and the institutions that help ensure it is a clear reflection of the discourse of hatred against Indigenous populations that Áñez deployed in order to take power.

Culture is a fundamental tool in education against hate, racism, and sexism. The Áñez government's drastic increase in defense spending and, at the same time, brutal cuts to culture leave no room for doubt as to the intrinsic relationship between these decisions. It is no coincidence that Espejo, one of the most renowned Indigenous figures in Bolivia, was among those sacked from their positions; it was an attempt to eliminate her from the public sphere. It was, I insist, a structural operation.

Before being asked to take on the directorship of the MNA, I was living in Brazil. There, I witnessed how, after the coup d'état against Dilma Rousseff in 2016, the interim president Michel Temer, in one of his first acts as president, eliminated the Ministry of Culture and, throughout the rest of his brief term, brought about a backslide of historic proportions in the field of Indigenous rights. The result, shortly after, was the presidency of Jair Bolsonaro, an overt racist who incites civil violence and organizes protests in favor of closing the National Congress. The process we experienced in Bolivia had many points in common with what we witnessed happen in Brazil.

What this interruption of the democratic order and its open hostility toward culture has shown us is that our institutions and their infrastructures are fragile. We can only hope, now that democracy in Bolivia has been restored through the general elections of October 18, 2020, which led to the reinstating of the Ministry of Cultures (now the Ministry of Cultures, Decolonization and Depatriarchalization), that some of the previous efforts can now be taken back up by the country's arts and culture institutions, and thereby strengthen the ethical and social mandate afforded them by the Plurinational State of Bolivia. The 2020 elections marked the beginning of a new cycle, and with it, the possibility of returning to the tough road that is the decolonization, democratization, and deelitization of the arts and culture in our country.

This is a translation of "Descolonizar, democratizar, deselitizar," published in *Transplurinacional. Perspectivas desde el arte sobre un territorio en mutación*, ed. Santiago García Navarro and Douglas Rodrigo Rada (Santa Cruz de la Sierra, Bolivia: Kiosko, 2021), 116–33. Translated from Spanish by Nicholas Callaway.

Dan Perjovschi

Drawings (2020–21)

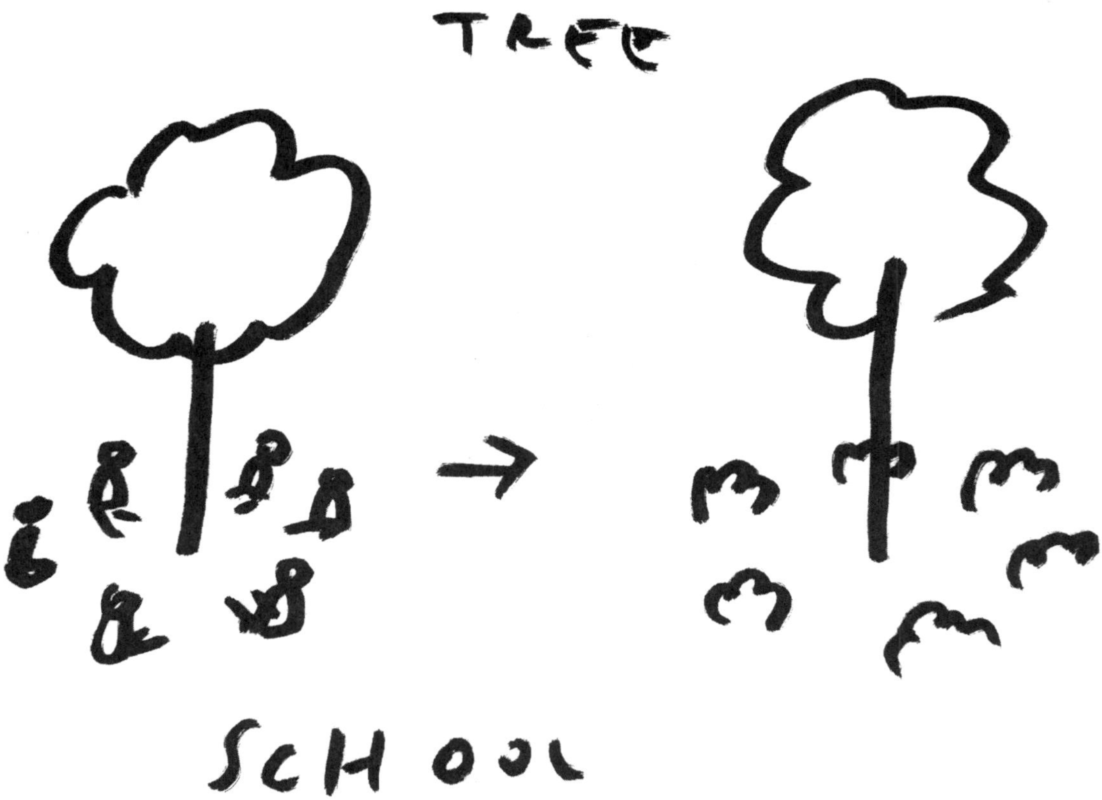
TREE
SCHOOL

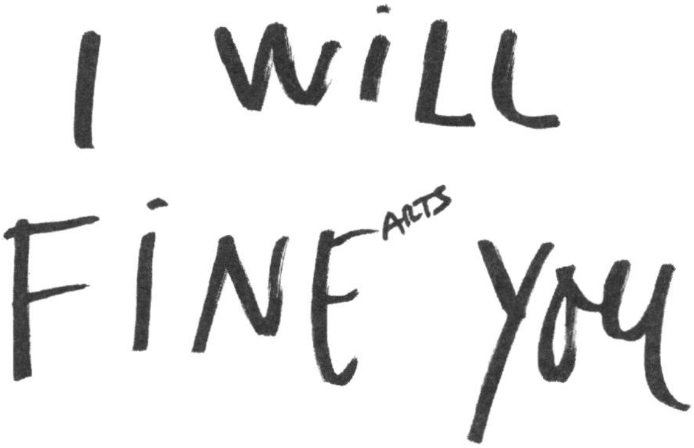
I WILL
FINE ARTS YOU

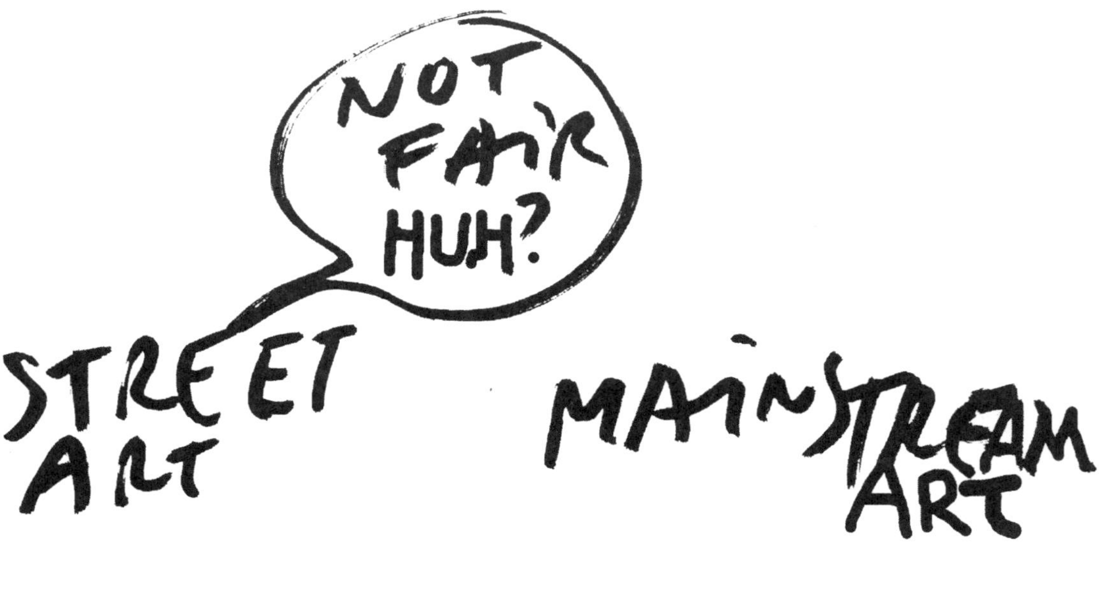
NOT FAIR HUH?
STREET ART
MAINSTREAM ART

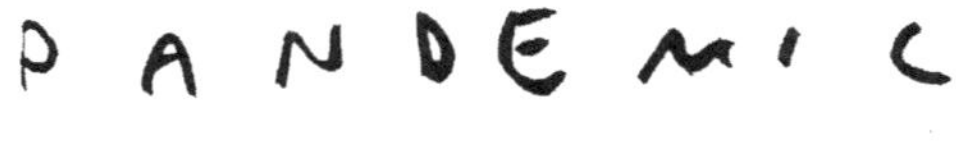
PANDEMIC

JO BURI

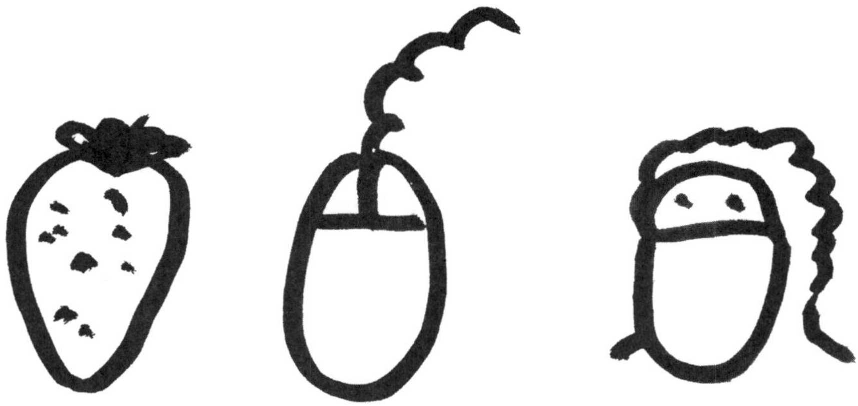

WESTERN OPPORTUNITIES
FOR EASTERNERS

Local Maximum: On Popular Technical Pedagogy

—Pirate Care

In 2019, we initiated a research process called Pirate Care.[1] Its content was inspired by the many initiatives of disobedient organizing of care that we saw emerging amid the global "crisis of care,"[2] engendered by decades of austerity and centuries of extractivism. We wanted to learn from these care practices and to invite others to learn with us. Methodologically and technologically, Pirate Care was inspired by the phenomenon of #Syllabi, developed by several social movements in the mid-2010s as a tool of radical pedagogy (e.g., #StandingRockSyllabus, #FergusonSyllabus),[3] as well as by the shadow libraries that have emerged to provide digital access to books where public libraries have not been allowed to. The resulting Pirate Care Syllabus[4] is the fruit of a collective writing effort of over twenty activists, artists, and researchers to whom we are profoundly indebted.

For the writing of our syllabus, the programmer among us (Marcell Mars) developed an experimental publishing platform, striving to embed in the technology the political values we are committed to in our intellectual practice: to foster as much autonomy, collective intelligibility, and independence from capitalist forces as practicable.[5] Sandpoints remains under continuous development and is now used by a number of collectives according to their own needs, including the Machine Listening curriculum[6] and *Dotawo: A Journal of Nubian Studies*.[7] The nonprogrammers among us have been putting together an accompanying workflow to facilitate the sharing of skills and a pedagogical process that complicates the received notions and roles in the production of critical knowledge.

In the following text, we attempt to orient ourselves as we embark on a new adventure of trying to link political pedagogy with technological literacy. We start from a set of intuitions: that technical pedagogies are indispensable to political autonomy; that the plebs, the proletarians, and the poor have historically devised ways to pass on technical knowledge; that the collective capacity to understand technological systems was lost with the fragmentation of the labor movement; that digital environments have perpetuated that collective deskilling; that today we are lacking a nonexpert mass technical pedagogy and critical usership to be able to deal with the impact of digital environments on our social world; and that technologies can be designed to foster such critical usership and a relative autonomy for users. These assertions remain at the level of intuition, though, and therefore, borrowing philosopher Isabelle Stengers's words, we invite the reader to "hesitate together" with us through these pages.

Technical Training between Pacification and Revolution

Before we can look at the concept and processes of technical "deskilling," which is a central concern of our work, we must first look at how such a vast bundle of insight and know-how that we call "technical knowledge" was historically exercised and passed on among the plebs—the working (and unworking) poor. Spending time in the archives reveals that, just as there is no such thing as a neutral technology, there is no such thing as a neutral technical pedagogy.

> Many cultures have developed regimes of apprenticeship; however, if one focuses on recent history, what clearly emerges are certain patterns concerning the political contexts in which technical training was first conceived and administered on a mass scale.

Three characteristics mark the development of vocational training programs since its "foundations [...] were laid most of all in the 19th century,"[8] revealing this branch of education as a terrain of power struggle over the governance of industrialization. Firstly, these programs were "developed most of all in national state contexts and [were] publicly or state-regulated."[9] The tensions between the emancipatory promise of education and the subjugation of waged labor were keenly modeled as part of nationalist and colonial development projects. Secondly, this unfolded "precisely at the time of the appearance of photography and mass communication by way of posters, leaflets etc."[10] As such, the development of vocational training paralleled that of the emergence of new identities and subjectivities within the working classes, most significantly the growing gap in self-perception between skilled and unskilled workers, which was a major obstacle for union organizers and socialist or communist party members. And, finally, these programs were developed mostly in social-democratic and Christian contexts, building up an offer that often stood in ideological opposition to the independent efforts of working-class organizations to provide a worthy and partisan education to their members.[11]

A review of the broader tradition of "independent working-class education"[12] reveals that, while proletarian culture was seen as a means not of social mobility but of political emancipation, the status of technical training was ambivalent. Many radical teachers were keen to politicize workers, and while the pure theory was recognized as insufficient, and there was general consensus around the need for political learning to be rooted in the practices and everyday struggles of the workers, a recurrent tension arose between the educational offerings of the education organizers and the desires of the pupils, who often were more interested in acquiring practical rather than analytical skills. Even though counter-institutions—such as peoples' houses, labor colleges, and popular universities—were striving to develop a distinctive pedagogy that opposed the hierarchical models and supposed neutrality of knowledge predominant in the bourgeois educational establishment,[13] it was hard for teachers committed to an anticapitalist stance to develop different methods, especially where technical knowledges were concerned.[14] The limitations of independent working-class education in nineteenth- and early twentieth-century Europe were exacerbated by the conditions of hardship and deprivation in which workers lived. Full-time courses were a luxury few could afford. There was also a perennial lack of spaces to meet and of "appropriate reading matter which could foster an anti-capitalist stance," forcing participants to instead "be active producers of an alternative literature and teaching resources."[15]

After World War II, the world's political and economic systems were newly reconfigured, and this impacted the status of popular technical pedagogy once again. In parts of the world where socialist governments were in power, the technical know-how of workers gained a positive ideological status and was largely supported via official institutions. In regions of the world engaged in anticolonial struggles, militant intellectuals began a process of sieving through notions and techniques received through the colonial apparatus to begin disentangling knowledges that could be reappropriated for achieving liberation from those knowledges that were technoscientific manifestations of colonial rule. Perhaps the most influential figure in this latter process was Amílcar Cabral, the leader of the anticolonial movement in Guinea-Bissau and Cabo Verde. Trained as an agricultural engineer in Lisbon, Cabral placed pedagogical activities at the center of liberation struggles, founding a variety of schools and insisting on "providing agricultural training for the farmers and militants, both before and during the liberation struggle."[16] As contemporary artist and filmmaker Filipa César notes, "Cabral understood agronomy not merely as a discipline combining geology, soil science, agriculture, biology and economics but as a means to gain materialist knowledge about peoples' lived conditions under colonialism."[17]

Echoes of these two radically different pedagogical efforts in the socialist and decolonizing parts of the world shaped the ways in which social movements and workers' organizations articulated their desires in capitalist Europe, too. In the 1960s and 1970s, students demanded (and partially obtained) reforms in the public education sector, while workers' organizations (including feminist organizations, expanding the very category of those who counted as "workers") asserted the need for autonomous technical learning. To cite one example paradigmatic of the struggles of this historical phase, in 1973 Italian trade unions managed to secure an unprecedented mechanism for the right to study as part of their renewed national collective agreement on employment. Named "the 150 hours," this new institution guaranteed employees a maximum number of hours of paid leave to be used for learning.

According to the Free Women University of Milan, which organized courses that fell under this program, the 150 hours were

> *a cultural experiment run by the vanguards of the trade unions themselves. They took over decision-making about objectives and methods of study, negotiated formal recognition of the curriculum with the state, and trained the teachers. The pupils were the avant-garde workers who had led the struggles of 1968 with students, and the teachers were those same students who flocked to these schools en masse. It was a serious attempt to reappropriate and change culture, its outcomes, its use, its meaning, on the part of the lower classes.*[18]

Alongside the many courses that helped workers complete their primary education, several experimental initiatives developed novel pedagogical approaches and subject areas, including pioneering courses in workers' health and safety. Here, technical and scientific know-how was intertwined with autobiographical and creative methods, since the intention was to impart useful skills for everyday life. For example, the teaching of arithmetic and accounting would start with learning how to correctly read one's payslips, then move on to graphs and percentages, and finally look at piecework and taxation mechanisms.

Popular Technical Deskilling

The political history of popular technical pedagogies is paralleled by a history of evolution and devolution of *technical usership*, which we define as the skillful application of tools others make, in the course of the industrial capitalist development and technological restructuring of the social world. To understand the crisis of popular technical pedagogy, it is useful to look at how the relations between users and technologies developed. For our purposes, this development can be roughly divided into three contexts: first, the relation between workers and their tools of production; second, the relation between participants in a public sphere and the technological apparatus that allows them to communicate; and, third, the relation between people and everyday smart objects that make up their domestic and leisure worlds.

Tools of Production

The ascendancy of industrial capitalism, employing an army of labor to attend to increasingly complex machinery, created a mass base of workers who could use their collective knowledge and material resources to organize, set demands, and achieve rights. The growing concentration and skills of industrial workers thus created the prerequisites necessary to exercise *power from below*, which the political scientist Francis Fox Piven proposes to see as a disruptive collective capacity grounded in interdependence.[19] The interdependence of labor processes on the shopfloor created the conditions to produce collective intelligibility of the factory, which in turn allowed organized workers to ameliorate the drudgery of work, game production quotas, and disrupt production processes to the greatest effect.

However, in the latter part of the twentieth century, the downskilling and automation of labor, accompanied by the creation of global production chains, led to a fragmentation and disaggregation of the working class and the collective intelligibility of the factory, which is now a diffused and fluid entity.[20]

Today's workers in the digital economy log on to networked systems that allocate, coordinate, and dictate their labor across a translocal geography in ways that are neither easily legible nor contestable. Furthermore, platform capitalists, from Uber to Amazon, actively suppress worker organizing, resulting in what has been described as a regime of digital neofeudalism.[21] Indicative is the case of Smart, a Belgian freelance workers' co-operative that, in 2016, started a campaign on behalf of couriers to challenge Deliveroo's algorithmic rule. Eventually, Deliveroo agreed to transfer its data to Smart's information systems, allowing couriers to gain labor protections and guaranteed shifts. This led to 90 percent of Deliveroo couriers shifting their work processes to go through Smart. However, because Deliveroo thus became liable for the basic protections of its couriers, it decided to terminate its contract with Smart at the end of 2017.

There are other notable attempts on the part of workers to regain some control over the digital tools of production by experimenting with autonomous, worker-led platforms. Such "platform co-operativism" efforts have been proliferating: examples include Fairbnb.coop, for short-term apartment letting; Fairmondo, for ethical goods and services; and a number of local ride-sharing projects. However, the capacity of these cooperatives to scale up and become economically viable has been limited. It couldn't be otherwise, as they face the competition of digital monopolies that have troves of money to burn, using their excessive valuations to cover the cost of expansion and operating losses (for instance, Uber has lost US$25.5 billion over the last five years).

Digital Media

The opacity of the technological systems that govern production is mirrored in the opacity of digital communication environments that extract value not only from people in formal contractual arrangements but also from societal relationships at large. Digital media strive to make interfaces as simple as possible for their users. Yet, these simplified interaction patterns occlude the complexity of computing infrastructures and the intricacy of the social behaviors they generate. Data-driven engagement algorithms have pushed social networks and online media to fragment the information they communicate into clickbait snippets to keep readers clicking and scrolling. That time of engagement is the most valuable asset in the contemporary attention economy—and one that is producing a number of mental health issues. At the same time, this fragmentation and the information overload it creates are increasingly contributing to a disinterest in attentive reading and understanding of context—in other words, a condition of aliteracy, which seems to be growing in inverse proportion to the degree of attention our increasingly complex and technologically mediated reality calls for.

> These processes have contributed to the creation of a "disinformation machine" whose virally proliferating content is created more for its affective load than its informational content. The production of affect is not a negative thing; however, clickbait aimed at stirring outrage serves to disable an intelligibility of systemic injustices that could open up avenues for a variety of what Baruch Spinoza would call "sad passions" to transform into effective forms of collective action. The growing scrutiny, including from government regulators, of the effects fake news has had on political processes and during the COVID-19 pandemic has forced Facebook, Twitter, and YouTube to introduce fact-checking of the ad content they support. However, to first uncover how user data is captured to drive surveillance and viral content, we needed whistleblowers such as Edward Snowden, Timnit Gebru, and Frances Haugen. Their actions have had a sobering effect, but it hasn't contributed much to increasing online platforms' accountability to their users nor empowering users in general.

Smart Things

Finally, as digitization permeates everyday tools and objects as they increasingly incorporate bits of software to become "smart" and automated, the experience of users with the very "stuff" that makes up our everyday activities is also changing. Behind a rhetoric of consumer empowerment, the so-called "internet of things" is impacting material cultures by further reducing the autonomy of use. Much more than in the past, companies are in a position to dictate what the "correct" uses of a given object are, by reducing the scope for retooling, misusing, or repurposing their products. They accomplish this by limiting the property rights attached to objects, especially in relation to sharing and collective usage, as well as through predetermining products' life cycles through planned obsolescence and proprietary software, which together make independent repair impossible.

The three above-described macro-tendencies of deskilling are by no means intended to present an exhaustive picture of the issues with the present technological infrastructure. Rather, we use them to attempt to draw out what we have identified as the three principal zones of contact between technologies and diffused forms of technical usership in contemporary societies—three zones that we can therefore identify as being potential fronts of political struggle. In each case, the introduction of ubiquitous digital technology coincides with a loss of autonomy that takes on the contours of an experience of deskilling. The advent of what media scholars have been calling the "post-digital condition"[22] has coincided with a recoiling of social contexts in which one person's technical knowledge is able to make a significant impact on their own well-being, their chosen forms of life, or the life of their communities.

To Zoom or Not to Zoom

The prominence of digital technologies in shaping the politics of everyday life has, since the start of the COVID-19 pandemic in early 2020, come into full relief. The last two years have ushered in a widespread awareness of the materiality of our relations as mediated through the digital,[23] an awareness that previously was shared only by practitioners and scholars with an interest in computation. The shift of digital tools from cutting-edge, optional gadgets to intrusive, unrefusable essentials affects many domains, from home deliveries to access to care, yet there is something distinctive to the way the recent migration online has impacted the practices of knowledge production in critical circles and autonomous scenes. An iconic example of this unease can be found in the admission we have heard many times: "We know Zoom is problematic, but we ended up using it because there is no other service with a connection stable enough."

In all their banality, such statements shed light on the material conditions of critical knowledge production. And we couldn't agree more: once the need for such video-conferencing technologies surged beyond any expectation, Zoom was by far the most stable tool. The problem with the lack of viable alternatives, in our view, is not a problem of ethical consumption. The problem with the monopoly of Zoom is that it became the institution that mediated and profited from all our exchanges. As we have written elsewhere,[24] whoever owns the means of production within an institution de facto runs that institution. The unavoidable reliance on Zoom makes us realize not only that critical thought is being pushed out of academia and cultural organizations but also that its mode of existence online is prey to a similar fragility of conditions. While the discourses of institutional critique, inclusion and diversity, and, more recently, decolonization and decarbonization have proliferated, the digital sphere enmeshes our relations in an infrastructure of seemingly immaterial yet very concrete conditions of toxicity, oppression, and exploitation. But the route toward establishing convincing, sustainable, and at-scale modes of technopolitical resistance is blurred, its genealogies intricate to excavate.

Critical interventions in technical usership that were widespread among the "progressives" of twenty years ago seem to have dwindled in size and relevance. To name but a few: the creation of GNU Linux and free software tools; the production of independent news through networks such as Indymedia; having one's email or blog hosted on servers maintained by hacktivist collectives; the development of Wikipedia and various other wikis; the sharing of pirated movies, music, and software; using anonymizing browsers such as Tor; and the construction of alternative social networks (such as n-1 in Spain). All this appears to be conspicuously missing today.

The relations between a politicized hacker movement and the countercultural scenes that used to intersect seem to have cooled down, too. Among other factors, the intersectional focus of many of the recent struggles has proven difficult to harmonize with the demographics of hacker circles, known to be rather homogeneous in their racial and gender composition. More recently, a novel infrastructure of fablabs (small-scale "fabrication laboratories") and maker spaces has opened up a potential space for grassroots, inclusive, and conscious approaches to technology. However, maker scenes cultivate an entrepreneurial positioning that curtails more radical critical uses of technological tools whenever they do not meet funders' preferences or do not guarantee a margin of profit.

We should also mention the highly motivated activist movement that aims to expose the racist and sexist biases embedded in algorithms. This movement has been gaining traction at a moment when algorithms are becoming ubiquitous: from the allocation of credit scores to the selection of employees, from determining parole for incarcerated people to tracking citizens' movements without authorization. Some actors in these nascent struggles are Data for Black Lives and Big Brother Watch. Yet these initiatives do not so much articulate a mass politics of usership as fight at the level of radicalizing experts in the field, such as programmers, mathematicians, researchers, and lawyers.

While the present standing of technopolitics within social movements is opaque, we feel it's useful to explore some of the ways in which political activists and radical pedagogies have confronted the problem of technical knowledges in the past. Such historical perspectives must inform our quest to find meaningful forms of intervention in the present.

Local Maximum: A Critical Usership Perspective

The brief historical overview undertaken by this text allows us to appreciate how technical training was a core element of the political division of labor, its unequal valorization, and the attempts at creating greater autonomy from the dictates of factory work and capitalist relations. However, the capacity of nonexpert masses to collectively understand and learn how complex technological environments structure both the world of work and the world of everyday life was greatly lost to deskilling and fragmentation. That process was only exacerbated by the fact that technological systems are embedded in and have been designed to support illegible corporate structures, which operate across regulatory arrangements and territories to avoid accountability, taxation, and contestation.

Yet, technological environments can be reorganized to be legible and to empower by transferring to users varying degrees of autonomy.

In the sphere of labor organizing, platform cooperatives—though experimental and small—have demonstrated that the technological systems developed by big tech can be replicated and readapted to increase the autonomy, working knowledge, and welfare of workers and users. In the sphere of knowledge production, arguably the most successful of such attempts remains Wikipedia. Built on the simple syntax of the MediaWiki software and an evolving set of community rules, this technological environment places a low barrier on the acquisition of skills and enables nonexpert users to achieve a *relative maximum of autonomy within the system*. It is not an absolute autonomy, however, but one that operates within the conditions created by the developers of MediaWiki, a system designed to empower users to build increasingly complex entanglements of technology and community structures. In the sphere of data aggregation, a notable effort at creating a relative "digital sovereignty" is the DECODE project, which brings together hacktivists and the municipalities of Barcelona and Amsterdam to create tools that put "individuals in control of whether they keep their personal data private or share it for the public good."[25] Thus we can see that encounters between technologists and constituencies can create more convivial tools that allow increasing degrees of skill and autonomy.

Similarly, with our own Sandpoints platform, we have been developing a tool for collective writing, learning, and experimental publishing. Access to infrastructure, access to learning materials, and formats of access are political matters. Sandpoints thus supports offline editing in situations of limited internet access (e.g., war zones, prisons) and where vulnerable groups need their content to never be accessible online. It allows readers to easily copy onto a USB drive a single folder that contains the whole website, alongside a PDF library of all included references, and to read it offline in a browser or move it to another server. Furthermore, in situations that call for paper, Sandpoints automatically exports the publication into a well-paginated PDF that is ready for on-demand print.

With Sandpoints, users decide how far they want to engage the technological environment: whether they want to only contribute text and let more tech-savvy collaborators do the rest, or whether they want to level up and become editors, responsible for the collective process of writing. Or they can decide to become administrators, responsible for entering texts into the system and structuring the publication. Barriers to entering all these roles are low, and acquiring basic technical skills in Markdown, Git, and our custom tools goes a long way in building collective technical capacities for critical pedagogy.

> Over the last twenty years, activists have often demanded that the free software community follow the latest technological trends; that is to say, they would adopt a tool only if it replicated the usership models of corporate tools. Rejection of tools as too complicated—as most noncorporate tools are perceived to be—is endemic. Ironically, though, users have been learning new skills all along; they just haven't seemed to notice because these skills were acquired through the use of corporate tools.

Technical pedagogy is a way to intervene in this complicity: we need to get to know the tools we use better. This is what we are trying to achieve in the micro-environment of Sandpoints. It provides an environment similar enough to Wordpress that it feels familiar, but at the same time it tries to teach the reflexive use of technology in collective practices. If organizing is urgent, then we do not need to care about how we do it—we can use Facebook or whatever tool works best for our cause. But there remains this vital question (and this is something we'd like to invite readers to think about): What does organizing require of the technological surround in the long run? And, furthermore, what degree of autonomy does a particular technology allow us to practice? Our mission does not revolve around anticorporate sentiments where we merely want to avoid big tech. Ours is not a contribution to the politics of consumption but rather to the politics of usership. With our tools, we as Pirate Care want to intervene in the division of labor that entangles us with our machines and our peers—and, in that context, we ultimately see it as our responsibility to maximize entanglements of technical pedagogies and collective organizing.

Should you wish to hesitate together with us, as Isabelle Stengers recommends, on this quest for developing autonomy-supporting technologies, pedagogies, and critical usership, please send your thoughts to info@pirate.care.

NOTES

1 For more information, see our website at https://pirate.care.

2 Nancy Fraser, *Fortunes of Feminism: From State-Managed Capitalism to Neoliberal Crisis* (London: Verso, 2013).

3 Valeria Graziano, Marcell Mars, and Tomislav Medak, "Learning from #Sylla-

bus," in *State Machines: Reflections and Actions at the Edge of Digital Citizenship, Finance, and Art*, ed. Yiannis Colakides, Mark Garrett, and Inte Gloerich (Amsterdam: Institute for Network Cultures, 2019), 115–28.

4 At the time of writing, the Pirate Care Syllabus comes with a full library of reference materials and covers thirteen topics, each broken down into sessions that can be adapted for various learning situations. See https://syllabus.pirate.care.

5 For more on the technopolitics of the Pirate Care project, see Valeria Graziano, Marcell Mars, and Tomislav Medak, "Care in a Techno-Capitalist World," *Ding: A Magazine about the Internet and Things*, December 15, 2021, https://dingdingding.org/issue-3/care-in-a-techno-capitalist-world/.

6 See Machine Listening's website at https://machinelistening.exposed/curriculum/.

7 *Dowato* is available at https://pages.sandpoints.org/dotawo/journal/.

8 Esther Berner and Philipp Gonon, "Introduction to a History of Vocational Education and Training in Europe: Cases, Concepts and Challenges," in *History of Vocational Education and Training in Europe*, ed. Esther Berner and Philipp Gonon (Bern: Peter Lang, 2016), 11.

9 Berner and Gonon, "Cases, Concepts and Challenges," 14.

10 Berner and Gonon, "Cases, Concepts and Challenges," 17.

11 Rachel Sharp, Mervyn Hartwig, and Jan O'Leary, "Independent Working Class Education: A Repressed Historical Alternative," *Discourse: Studies in the Cultural Politics of Education* 10, no. 1 (October 1, 1989): 1–26.

12 Sharp, Hartwig, and O'Leary, "Independent Working Class Education."

13 Sharp, Hartwig, and O'Leary, "Independent Working Class Education," 22.

14 Jean-Louis Guerena and Alejandro Tiana Ferrer, eds., *Formas y Espacios de la Educacion Popular en la Europa Mediterranea*. Siglos XIX y XX (Madrid: Casa de Velasquez, 2016).

15 Sharp, Hartwig, and O'Leary, "Independent Working Class Education," 20.

16 "Conversation with Amilcar Cabral: From Agronomist to Liberator," *Health of Mother Earth Foundation* (blog), August 18, 2020, https://homef.org/2020/08/18/conversation-with-amilcar-cabral-from-agronomist-to-liberator/.

17 Filipa César, "Meteorisations: Reading Amílcar Cabral's Agronomy of Liberation," *Third Text* 32, nos. 2–3 (May 2018): 254–72, https://doi.org/10.1080/09528822.2018.1492073.

18 Paola Melchiori, "Le 150 ore, un esperimento di vita e di cultura," 1973, *Libera Università delle Donne*, http://www.universitadelledonne.it/le_150_ore.htm. Our translation.

19 Frances Fox Piven, "Can Power from Below Change the World?," *American Sociological Review* 73, no. 1 (2008): 1–14.

20 Mario Tronti, "Factory and Society," in *Workers and Capital* (London: Verso Books, 2019).

21 Jodi Dean, "Neofeudalism: The End of Capitalism?," *Los Angeles Review of Books*, 2019, https://lareviewofbooks.org/article/neofeudalism-the-end-of-capitalism/.

22 Florian Cramer, "What Is 'Post-Digital'?," in *Postdigital Aesthetics: Art, Computation and Design*, ed. David M. Berry and Michael Dieter (London: Palgrave Macmillan UK, 2015), 12–26.

23 Yuk Hui, "Towards a Relational Materialism," *Digital Culture & Society* 1, no. 1 (2015): 131–48.

24 Marcell Mars and Tomislav Medak, "Against Innovation: Compromised Institutional Agency and Acts of Custodianship," *Ephemera: Theory and Politics in Organisation* 19, no. 2 (May 2019): 345–68.

25 DECODE home page, n.d., https://decodeproject.eu/.

Teuta Gatolin
Of the Earth
(2021)

Of the Earth is a book of poetry made by remixing the text of James Hutton's 1788 geological study of sedimentary rocks and deep time, titled *Theory of the Earth*. The artist book *Of the Earth* is interested in relations between language and historical narratives about nature up to current perceptions of ecology, and the need to build new narratives and practices of cohabiting with a planet whose ecosphere has been injured. The work consists of a remixed book in English and one in Croatian, translated by the artist.

I

observable
composition, dissolution, disillusion,
and restoration *upon the Globe:*

.

Where so many living creatures are
Where so many living creatures are

we are not to look for nature in a quiescent state;

matter itself is in motion,

and the scenes of life are a continued series

of c h a n g e s and

e v e n t s.

we are not to estimate the powers of nature by the measure of our own.

III

various purposes of this world are
accomplished

by the operation of varieties:

obtained, blessed,

(un)possessed,

like the beneficial artificial light and
culinary fire.

V

we,
circulations of organized bodies
within the earth's rotation.

"we"
a habitable word?
a habitable world?

we—

irregular bodies.

(*my irregular body raised above the level of the ocean*
by the virtue of the land
sustained in this world because
surrounding it is the body of the atmosphere.)

a mass, a mess.
a distress.

a n i r r e g u l a r b o d y
a h a b i t a b l e world

a h a b i t a b l e word

to animals
to the water of the ocean

for arthropods
and anthropos.

The Origin of Story

A theory which is founded on a new principle is needed.

a theory which has to make its way into the public mind

by overturning the opinions commonly told by

philosophising men,

the men of authority

who disregard

the earth,

as prophets of profit.

A theory which is founded on a new principle

is needed

is knitted

is nettle.

Earth thinks.

rivers carry the materials of our stories,

and histories.

History is dislocated.

all the strata of the earth,

all the data of the earth,

have had their origin at the bottom of the story,

by the collection of sand, gravel, shells, coralline, and crustaceous bodies, and of

earths and clays variously mixed, separated, and accumulated as

nature

recoiling from the abyss.

our fertile plains are formed from the ruins of the mountains
our fertile plans are formed from the ruins of the mountains
our fertile plans are formed on the ruins.

this is

a collection of earthly matter

of compression
of compassion

kind kin,

they make a warmth which is very durable.

we shall be led to admire the wisdom of nature, providing for the continuation of this living world, and employing those very means by which

this beautiful structure of an inhabited earth seems to be necessarily going into destruction

or

we yet might be the spiders molting.

Dan Perjovschi

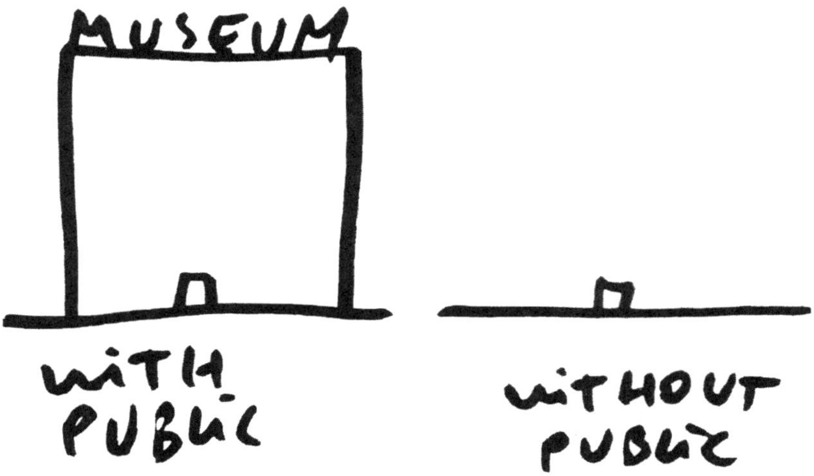

Drawings (2020–21)

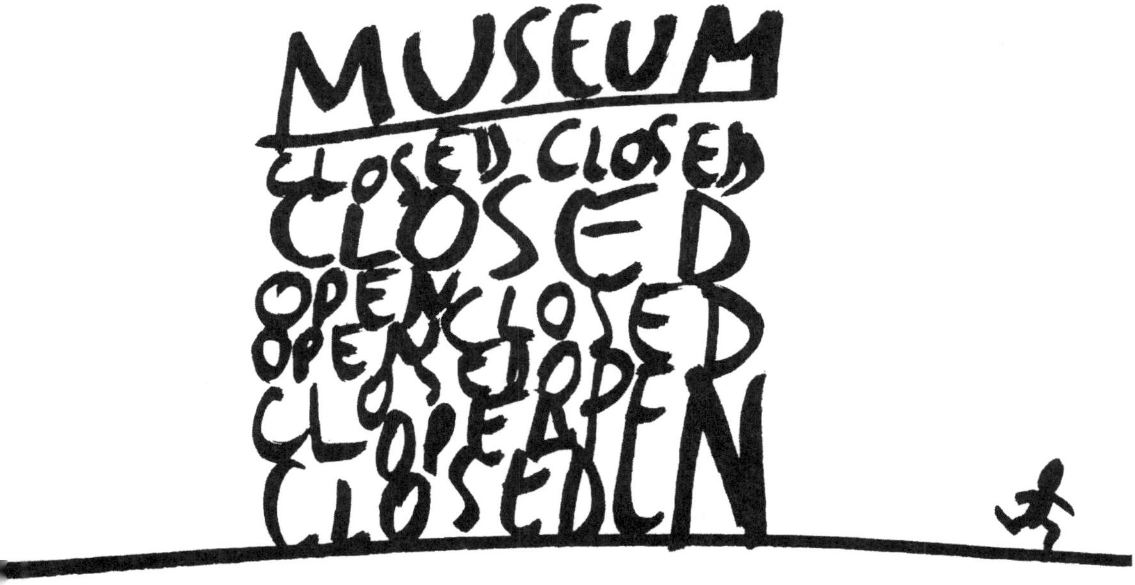
MUSEUM
CLOSED CLOSED
CLOSED

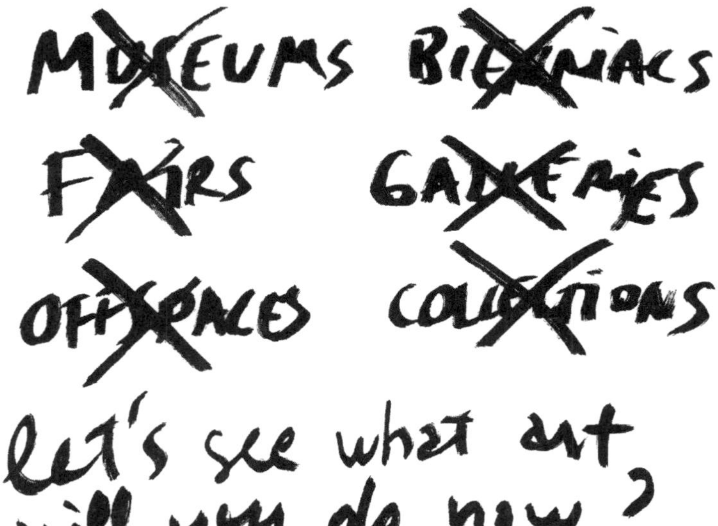
let's see what art
will you do now?

CON TEMPORARY ART
CLOSED

MUSEUM USE

AFTER
EDUCATION
RECENT STAFF
AND
"NONESSENTIAL
WORKERS"
CUTS

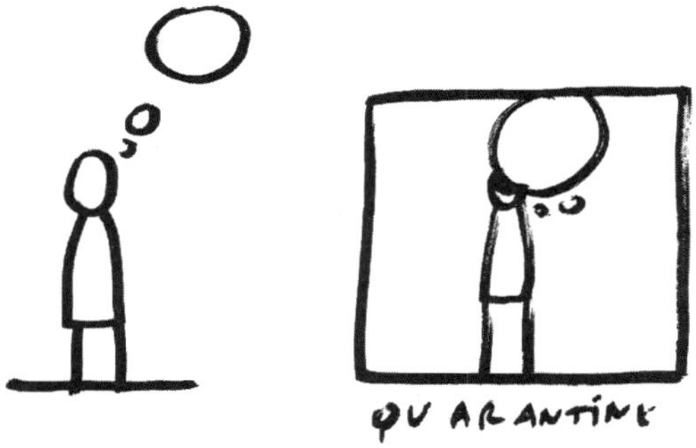
QUARANTINE

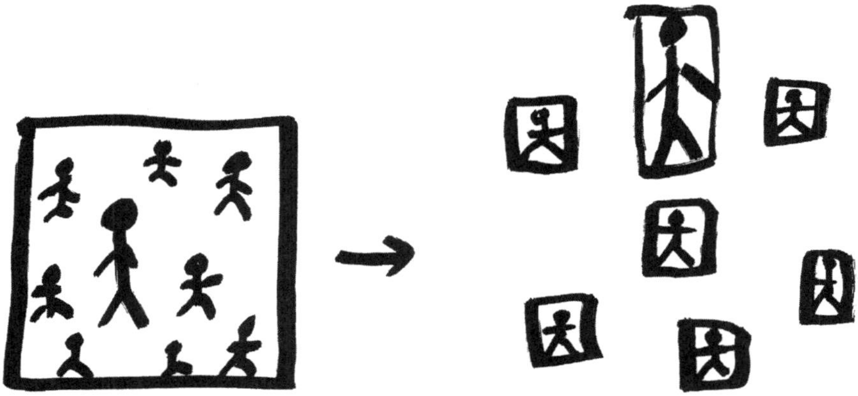

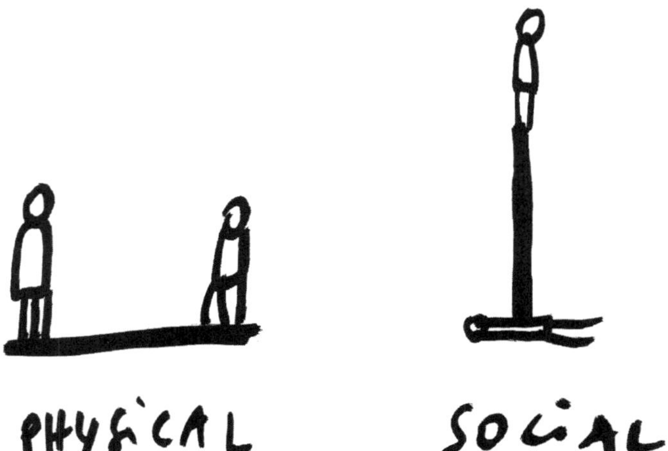
PHYSICAL
SOCIAL

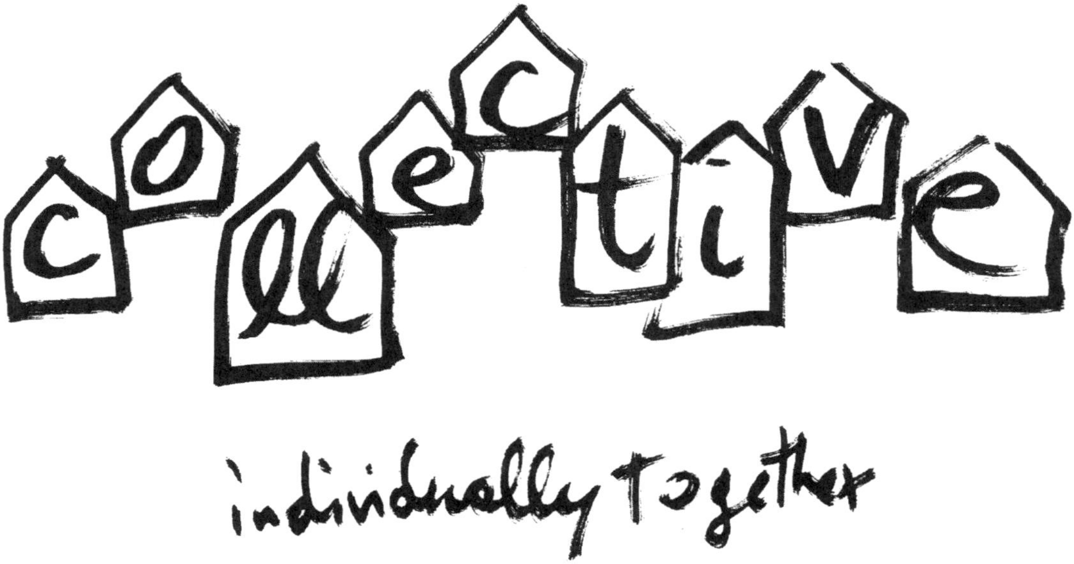
collective
individually together

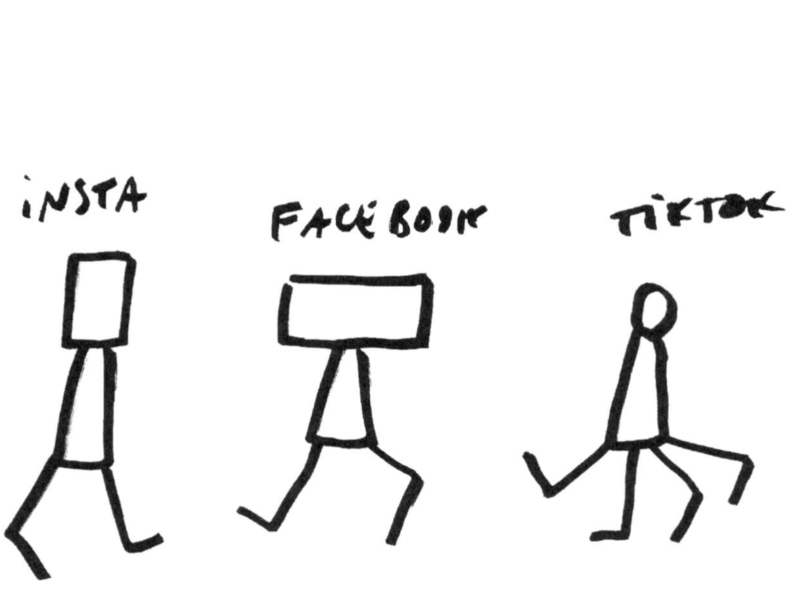
INSTA
FACEBOOK
TIKTOK

CAConrad

Shards (2021)

our
little
places
within
are not
dungeons
remember
remember
astronomers point
satellites into space
the military points
them down at us
the inverse relationship
between love we offer
and what we give
this on and
off button
is another
opportunity
to believe
there are
only two
choices
this too
must end

what was
the point
of today
nothing
more than
microscopic
creatures on
my eyelids
reaching for
sunlight with me
how hard is your
historical memory
as in gay
bashing 101
same day you
learn hieroglyph
means *sacred carving*
elegy is not a form
it is a state of being the
poet must write from
a faggot takes a beating
from another holy book
and the band said
this is my four leaf clover
what did they say
this is my four leaf clover

to
desire
the world
as it is
not as
it was
falling
feather
attaches
to new life
for a moment
when the hammer
approached we thought
is that thing coming this way
we are the fractal
drop to hear
our own
harmonics
in the muffled
underground
hum of seeds

Healing as a Transformative Praxis

—Valentina Desideri & Denise Ferreira da Silva (The Sensing Salon)

in conversation with Emily Pethick

As part of their Sensing Salon, art theorists Valentina Desideri and Denise Ferreira da Silva apply various forms of healing in their search for alternative knowledges and to deepen our understandings of the world.

EMILY PETHICK: **I've been fortunate enough to meet you both at the Sensing Salon. I thought it would be nice to hear about how you started collaborating as well as about your individual practices.**

VALENTINA DESIDERI: Denise and I met in 2011 in Naples at a conference on Frantz Fanon. At the time, I was starting to develop fake therapy and political therapy. I had started approaching healing as a practice from an artistic perspective. I heard Denise talk and heard about her double life as an astrologer, tarot reader, and herbal healer, and we began our exchange from there.

DENISE FERREIRA DA SILVA: I think that was in May of 2011. I was coming to the end of my first year of teaching at the Queen Mary University of London. It was a crucial moment in my career because, after a few months in London and teaching at Queen Mary, I thought that maybe I should do something else—I shouldn't be only an academic. In the ten years before, I had focused on political theory and critical legal studies, and I had been writing primarily on police brutality and racial violence. Anyway, at that restaurant in Naples, Valentina was telling me about her practice and I remember saying, "We should do something together." That became the poethical readings.

EP: **Can you talk about the different practices that you're working with in the Sensing Salon?**

DFS: I've been studying astrology since I was a teenager. Every time you look at a chart, there is so much to consider. I have read my own chart many times and still it's not exhausted. That is also how we do the poethical readings in general. We are not looking for causal relations, like if you have your sun in Gemini it will make you a certain way. Instead, our readings open up sense and meanings, rather than close or resolve signification.

VD: We look for possibilities; it's not about determination. A reading is a possibility to *image* what we're talking about—whatever question, situation, or problem that instigated or initiated the reading—in a different way. So when we look at how planets are aspecting the sun in the astrological chart of a person or an event, we look for possible descriptions of it—a different image.

EP: When you talk about the "image," how does that differ when you're working with a body practice, like reiki, for example?

VD: It comes in different ways, so sometimes it comes as text, as language, and sometimes it comes as sensations, and other times it comes as images. For the poethical readings, we adapted reiki treatment in a way where we use the treatment as a reading. For each chakra, we have a question. So it is a treatment, but we also ask things like: What grounds the question? How does it relate? What does it manifest? So for each chakra we take whatever sensation we feel, or whatever image arises, as being an answer or in relation to what we're asking.

DFS: This can come up in very interesting ways, because sometimes the answers are cryptic and you have no idea. Sometimes it's pure poetry. All seven questions come together as poetry where the meanings are not fathomable, and sometimes they are descriptive and more informative, too. Now, when we speak of the image, we have in mind a meaning different from the usual idea of representation. How do I talk about something that exists but is not and (many times) cannot be named because it is not identified or identifiable? The term "representation" usually presupposes some kind of mental apprehension that provides the immediate meaning of whatever is under consideration. The image, in our view, is already mediated. It is a reading, a composition made by the tool—astrology, tarot, reiki, whatever the case may be. When reading such compositions, we add yet another composition; so each reading is a recomposition.

VD: It is also a form of composing, recomposing, and decomposing the question that we perform together. The image emerges in the moment we share the reading.

EP: I think I see that in the tarot cards. The readings that I've done have started with a question, but they are also about something bigger—cycles or processes. They are often about transformation. In the cards you see the end of the cycle and another horizon. What do you read in the cards as a system?

DFS: There is a composition—a spread is a composition. One tarot spread we use more frequently is the Celtic cross. This composition might be complex, but it is a very traditional way of describing things. There is an inner cross: the first two cards. And there is an outer cross, with two lines: the vertical line (conscious and unconscious aspects playing out in the inner cross) and the horizontal line (past and future aspects of the inner cross). In addition, we identify different possible compositions within those two given composition. Something else we highlight when talking about how we read the tarot is that it's intrinsically collaborative. That's true for the other practices too, because when you learn how to use them—when you're initiated and you practice—you are always learning from somebody who has learned from somebody.

EP: What I noticed from the readings is that it becomes a way to think in a nonbinary or nonlinear way—to think *across*, in a very lateral, connective way. It creates a way to turn something. Quite often the crisis is about being stuck, and tarot somehow enables you to turn your thinking. You come out with another perspective.

DFS: Yes, and weird things can happen. We had somebody come in with a question about religious spaces at the airport. We had no idea what the question was about, and we didn't ask because we never do. But as we talked about it, we suddenly understood each other. Nobody knew anything about the other—the person didn't know how to read the cards, we didn't know of their situation—and that conversation brought something out. I was amazed.

VD: The question was actually about a relationship that wasn't going well. But the cards recomposed the situation in such a way that it illuminated what the initial question was about. Through how the Celtic cross operates and how we look at the different aspects of the composition, it became clear.

EP: The concept of entanglement is something that comes up a lot in relation to this practice. Why is it important?

DFS: I think astrology and tarot—as I have come to understand as we have practiced more and more over the years—presume that everything that you know exists in what I call deep implicancy (that is, entangled or confused with, inseparable from one another).

What is actual is implicated, but it's also implicated with what is potential and virtual, what might and will never become actual, right? "Actual" in the sense of being real in space-time, solid, or visible. That assumption allows for a connection between combinations of planets at a certain moment, for instance, and the infinite implications on a person's life. Of course, we think that this is about animism or similar premodern or nonmodern ways of thinking. Francis Bacon, one of the four fathers of the scientific method, was very much concerned with magic and developed his observation of nature precisely as a way of moving away from magic while keeping the basic elements. Magic is concerned with efficacy, with cause and effect, with how certain things or combinations of things may bring about a certain effect. In modern thought, similar elements are used, but there is a preoccupation with isolating the specific aspect (which Bacon calls its "form" or "essence") of a thing that brings about a particular effect, and what is privileged is knowing a particular thing's efficacy: that which distinguishes it from other things. Formally, it also has to make sense, and the formalization or abstraction also creates separation. Our reading is different, because we read under the presumption of *intricacy*, not efficacy. While the usual modern scientific or interpretive mode of approaching gives meaning, it only works because it presumes separability in the description of relations, of cause and effect, and also in the identification of what is related through those abstract forms. So, without considering the subject, we consider the world as it is organized from the perspective of the subject, in terms of efficacy and implication.

EP: Could you speak a little bit about "sensing" as a practice, considering the intuitive aspect of how you're working?

VD: When we did the first Sensing Salon, I think at that point we were still calling it the Healing Salon, because it was about healing tools and the healing arts. Yet we had a problem with the word "healing" and all the connotations it carries. At some point in our conversation, Denise and I realized that what we engage in is actually "sensing." Through the complexification of the issue and its de/re/composition through the elements and the different tools, you end up making different sense of what is happening to you. Not at just a cognitive or intellectual level, about which you can say,

"Oh, well, it wasn't like this—it was actually like that. And I have the correct description now." Rather, it's a movement of sensing, a moving through something and sensing your way through, so that you have a different experience. The word "sensing," then, brought those two elements, those two layers, or those two aspects of sensing and sense-making, together. Because sometimes what happens is not sense-making—sometimes you don't make any sense, and yet you feel differently. It's about the way we think of the situation and the way we experience it, and that these are not separated.

EP: So, in a way, the outcome doesn't need to make sense.

VD: Yes—that's how the practice extended naturally into the study group. We thought to ourselves: What if we were to use those tools to ask the kinds of questions we would ask in a classroom, or in a meeting, or in a moment where we want to think about something? What other sense becomes possible? I remember in one Sensing Salon, we asked about climate change, and we wanted to know what happens if we think about it through heat. How does our understanding of it change?

DFS: And that was another weird one, because we did a reiki reading for that question with around forty people. Everybody was treated. Because, as we're doing the reading, we're also treating. That had an effect, which was to bring out the emotions—how everyone was feeling about climate change. It all came out very strongly. But it was necessary.

VD: I think it's amazing in relation to study, because when you think about climate change, it's difficult to feel anything. It's very hard to make the connection and to feel the catastrophic dimensions of it, without which maybe it's impossible to think about any way out. That was very instructive.

EP: Now that you've been working on this for ten years, how do you feel about where you've gotten to today, and where else do you want to take it?

VD: The practice has changed over time. We started with an interest in political questions and how to image their complexity through our tools. Then we realized that what was also happening was the sociality, the coming together that readings bring about. Reading in this collaborative way creates a certain way of being together, and relationship are established. We have seen these relationships grow into a kind of tissue that holds many. The act of transmitting the tools also became important, as it enabled more people to read and to read together with us, to make study groups, so that we can really rest on our entangled existence.

DFS: One of the things that the COVID-19 pandemic is doing—what crises always do—is that the usual ways of living and doing things, going about resolving situations, do not count anymore. Because of this, I think people are actually paying more attention to the readings. Individuals, groups, and institutions have increasingly asked us for private readings, which we started to do, since our specific approach—especially to the more traditional tools, such as tarot, astrology, and reiki—seems to directly and effectively address the current challenges.

VD: Finally, we also made a website where we document the various editions of the Sensing Salon (with short descriptions and photos) as well as texts and recordings we have produced over the years.

DFS: We also have a new project that was born of a suggestion from the artist Jason Dodge to make something with the poems of the late American Japanese poet Ai Ogawa. He sent us the poems and we knew: "OK, yes, we'll do this."

VD: We immediately did a tarot reading to see what this new project would be, and in the reading we found out that it is a new deck: it's a whole tarot deck we need to make. So we are doing poethical readings for each poem paired with a tarot card, in order to know how to read that card in this new system. So a new reading tool is in the making!

Originally published as a translation into Dutch in *Metropolis M*, no. 6, December 2020/January 2021. The text has been edited for republication.

“Even without gene editing we are already mutants, capable, for instance, of carrying out our daily lives while aware that catastrophic events are occurring all around us, including the destruction of our ecological environment and the slow death of many people now living on our streets, whom we daily pass by without much of a thought or an emotion. What threatens us are not only that the machines are taking over, but also that we are becoming like machines. Thus we do not need any more robot-like individuals produced by a new breeding industry, this time located in medical labs.”

—Silvia Federici, *Beyond the Periphery of the Skin: Rethinking, Remaking, and Reclaiming the Body in Contemporary Capitalism*

Eva Ďurovec *Iolaus' Atlas of Hydra's Heads* (2021)

News, messages, numbers, and warnings, forming the overall picture of the day, which disappears in the latest catastrophic report, are captured and frozen as some evidence on the growing body that was once mine. His bodily development, his newly acquired abilities, but also the description of the day filled next to patient but exhausting care work, bump up against records from the surrounding world and capture the space where the child's body is located. The metallic silver text on the red lining rhythmically changes direction: once horizontal, then vertical, it lies and then stands, failing to copy modern architecture and its right angles. An urgency, exacerbated not only by the birth of a descendant but, above all, by the exceptional situation of a deepening crisis as a result of a pandemic that has exposed devastating dysfunctions in many spheres of society and in the face of which the most vulnerable are paying most dearly.

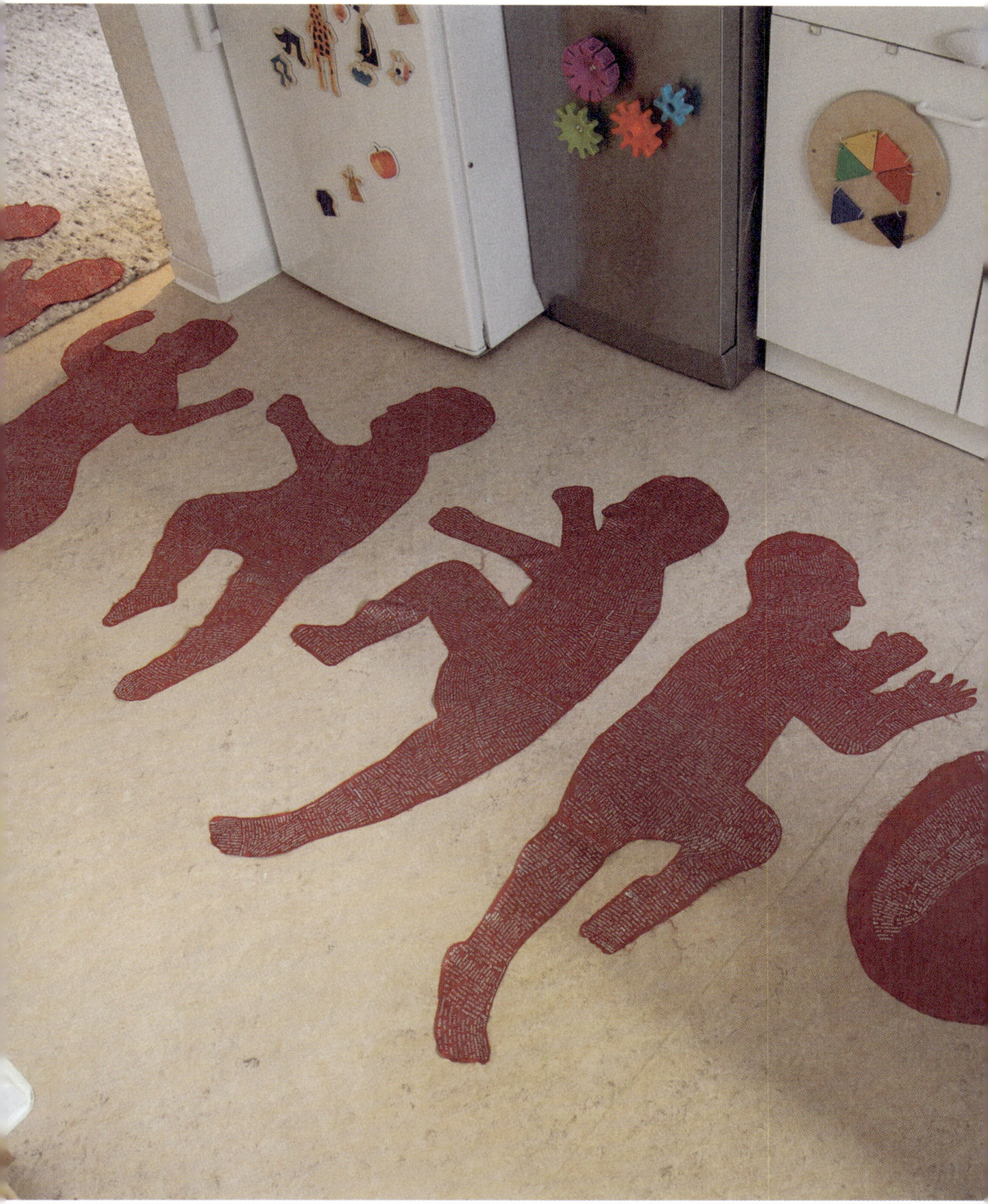

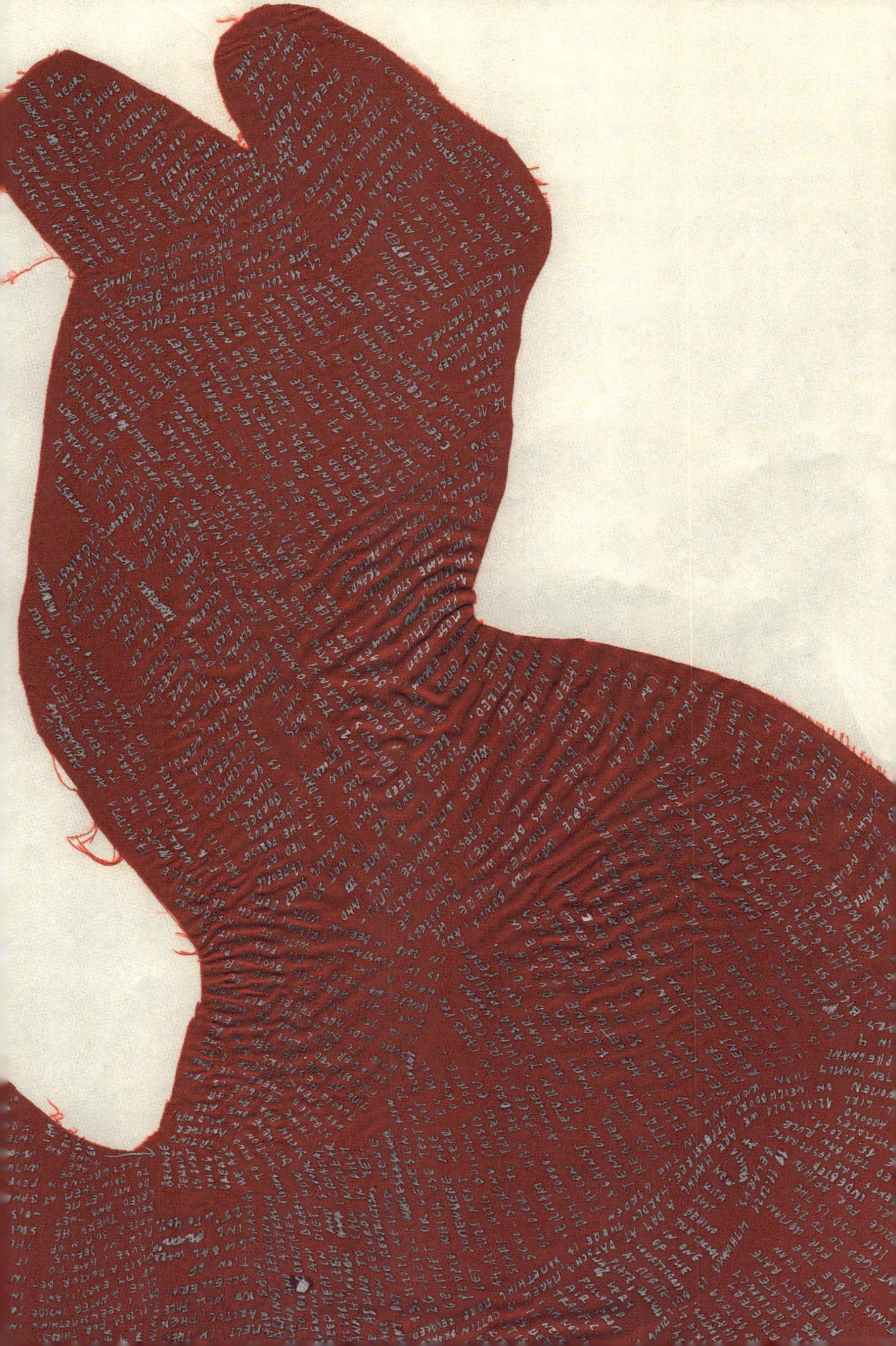

25.9.2020 WE ARE IN FAMILY CAFE TO FIND PLACE WHERE JERGUS COULD PLAY AND I COULD WORK. IT DOESN'T WORK AND HE STILL CANNOT MANAGE TO PLAY LONGER THAN 1 MINUTE THE SPACE IS ALSO MADE FOR OLDER KIDS. IN ANOTHER COWORKING SPACE OFFERS DAY CARE FOR 11-15 EUR AND DESK FOR 4 HOURS FOR 9 EUR. IT WOULD BE THEN 24 EUR FOR 4 HOURS
WE MET DAVID IN SWEDEN
SINCE 70s FARMERS IN INDIA ARE UNDER PRESSURE OR CAN'T REPAY LOANS. SINCE 1995 286 438 INDIAN FARMERS COMMITED SUICIDE.

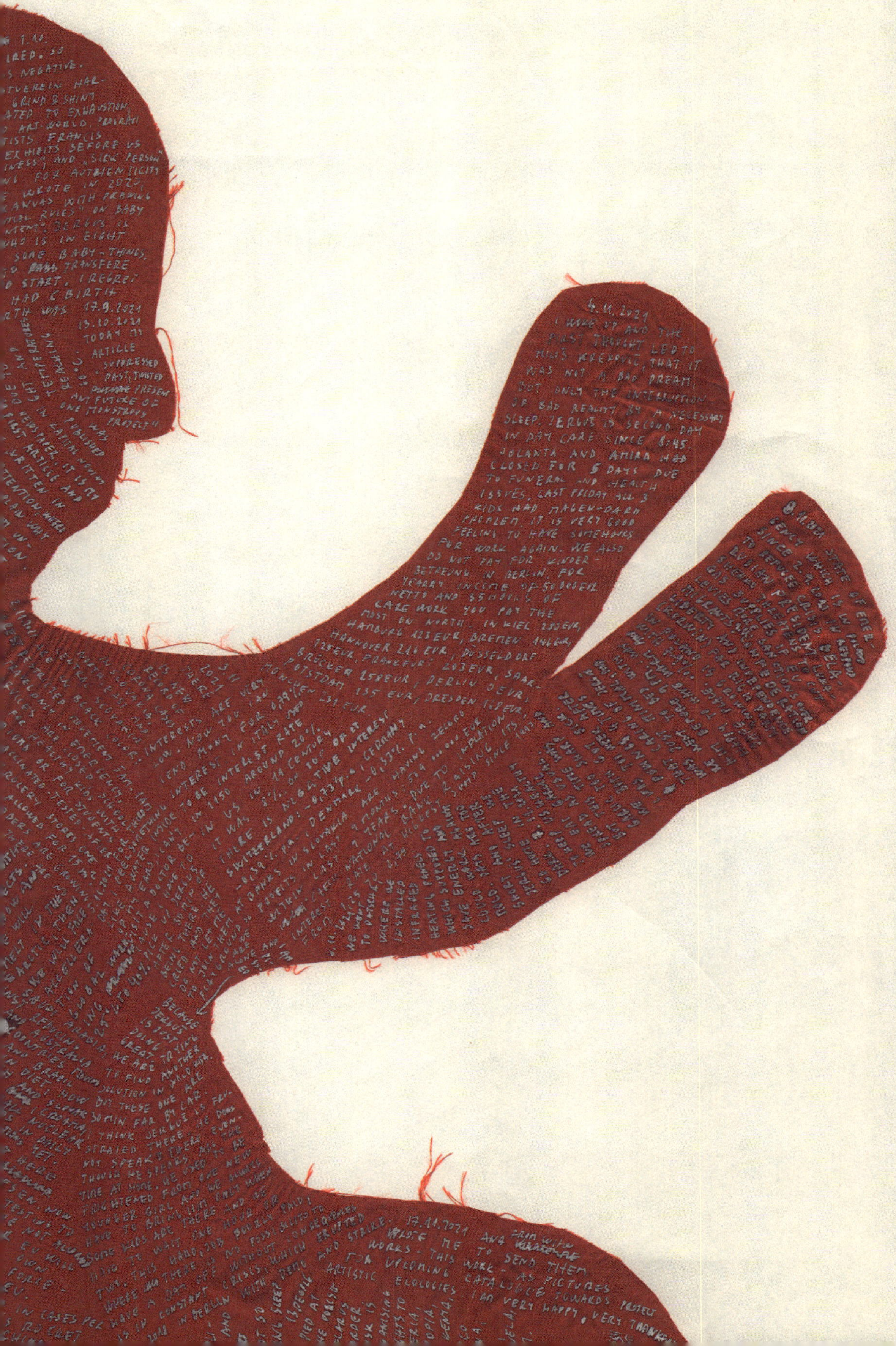
4.11.2021
I WOKE UP AND THE FIRST THOUGHT LED TO THAT IT WAS NOT A BAD DREAM BUT ONLY THE INTERRUPTION OF BAD REALITY BY A NECESSARY SLEEP. JERGUS IS SECOND DAY IN DAY CARE SINCE 8:45. JOLANTA AND AMIRA HAD CLOSED FOR 5 DAYS DUE TO FUNERAL AND HEALTH ISSUES. LAST FRIDAY ALL 3 KIDS HAD MAGEN-DARM PROBLEM. IT IS VERY GOOD FEELING TO HAVE SOME HOURS FOR WORK AGAIN. WE ALSO DO NOT PAY FOR KINDER-BETREUNG IN BERLIN. FOR YEARLY INCOME OF 50 000 EUR NETTO AND 55 HOURS OF CARE WORK YOU PAY THE MOST ON NORTH. IN KIEL 280 EUR, HAMBURG 123 EUR, BREMEN 146 EUR, HANNOVER 216 EUR, DÜSSELDORF 125 EUR, FRANKFURT 203 EUR, SAARBRÜCKEN 159 EUR, POTSDAM 135 EUR, BERLIN 0 EUR, MÜNCHEN 231 EUR, DRESDEN 168 EUR.
17.11.2021 ANA FROM WHW WROTE ME TO SEND THEM WORKS. THIS WORK AS PICTURES FOR UPCOMING CATALOGUE TOWARDS PROTECTIVE ARTISTIC ECOLOGIES. I AM VERY HAPPY, VERY THANKFUL

One Is Always a Plural: Moving Together over Distance

—Yael Davids

in collaboration with
Hannah Dawn Henderson & Lotte Lara Schröder

The following is an abridged, edited transcript of the workshop "One Is Always a Plural: Moving Together over Distance," part of the series *Artistic Ecologies, New Compasses and Tools*, organized by the collaborative initiative *Education from Below*.

Contributing participants and co-organizers were Ana Dević, Curator, What, How & for Whom / WHW • Virág Szentkirályi, Residency and Programme Coordinator, Rijksakademie van beeldende kunsten, Amsterdam • Nataša Ilić, Curator, WHW • Sabina Sabolović, Curator, WHW • Pablo Martínez, (then) Head of Programming, MACBA – Museu d'Art Contemporani de Barcelona • Ivet Ćurlin, Curator, WHW • Emily Pethick, Director, Rijksakademie.

ANA DEVIĆ: Over the past five years, Yael Davids has trained in the Feldenkrais Method, which she uses as a research device for comprehending the structure of bodies, institutions, and artworks. She collaborated on an exhibition with the Van Abbemuseum in Eindhoven, titled "A Daily Practice" (2020), for which she invited the exhibition team to each select an artwork from the museum's collection based on its significance to the exhibition's context and concept. From these selections, Yael then developed and led Feldenkrais lessons so that the audience could experience the artworks through somatic engagement. Similarly, as part of developing an exhibition at the Migros Museum of Contemporary Art in Zurich that opened in the spring of 2021, Yael worked with the museum's staff and provided weekly Feldenkrais lessons over Zoom. That exhibition, titled "One Is Always a Plural," was likewise designed as a learning schema in itself.

Drawing on the methodologies used at the Van Abbemuseum and Migros Museum, Yael has invited members of the *Education from Below* team to choose an artwork that symbolizes our respective experiences of the pandemic's circumstances—our fears and hopes, as well as other emotions buried in our bodies—and this will act as the framework for tonight's Zoom session. The co-organizers will first say a few words about why they chose these particular artworks. After that, Yael will briefly introduce the Feldenkrais Method, which will then segue us into the workshop. You are all invited to actively take part; please make sure your camera is on and you're in a well-lit space.

The Works

Trying (1998) by Liza May Post
SELECTED BY Virág Szentkirályi

VIRÁG SZENTKIRÁLYI: I chose this piece, I guess, not only because there is a certain symbolic meaning in it—regarding the pandemic as the elephant, and how everybody has tried and is still trying to tackle this problem, endlessly. I also had a more personal reason: I realized that I identify with the woman and her endless efforts. I like how Liza May Post examines attitudes, movements, and actions, placing them into this dreamlike scene.

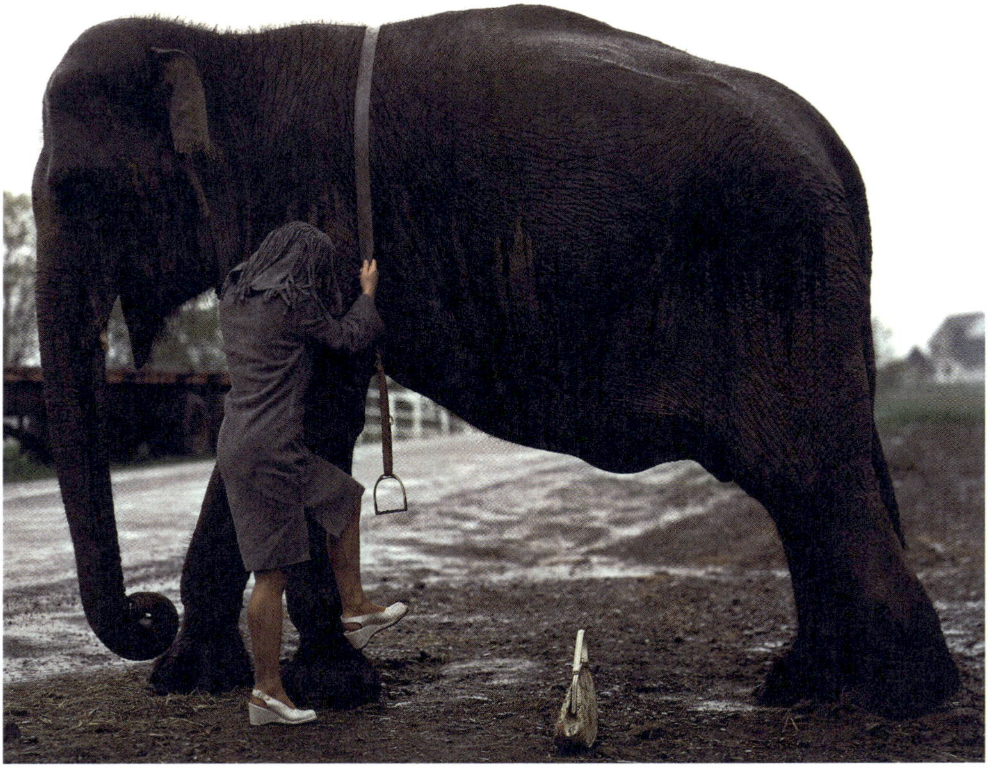

Courtesy the artist

YAEL DAVIDS: What is prominent is the lack of ground support. Firstly, due to the way she is dressed—the high heels—but also you feel that she cannot use the ground effectively while climbing, and she has this precarious way of addressing her own relation to the ground.

DIVORCED (1981–82) by Sanja Iveković
SELECTED BY Nataša Ilić

ANA DEVIĆ (*reading on behalf of* **NATAŠA ILIĆ**): "I suggest that Sanja Iveković's drawing *DIVORCED* is all about body parts disintegrating, and hopefully about reintegrating. The title in Croatian is closer to 'dismembered' than 'divorced,' but it means both. Iveković chose to translate it as 'divorced.' Obviously, it's a woman's body, and this tension between dismembered and divorced I hoped could be a good starting point. I really like the drawing—it's full of floating limbs that need some anchoring."

YD: I think it's a great name. Of course, what I see is fragmented and it again comes in relation to the idea of wholeness. Here it is clear that every detail is always in relation to another, just as we all are. The whole is greater than the sum of the parts—once the details return together, it's not only the image of a person or a woman, but much more.

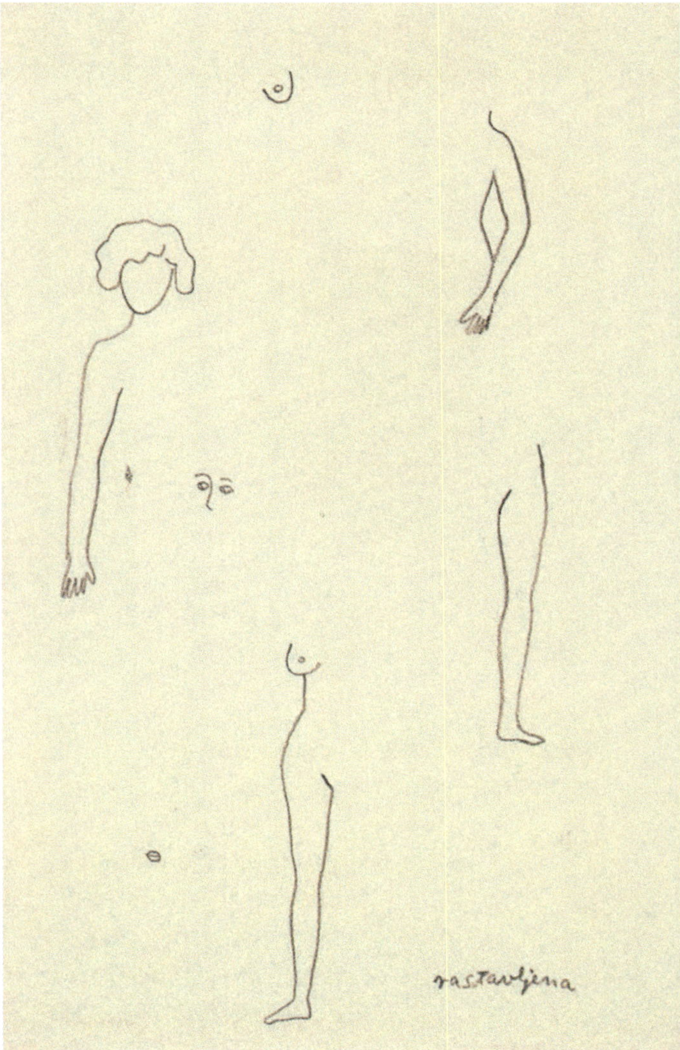

Courtesy the artist

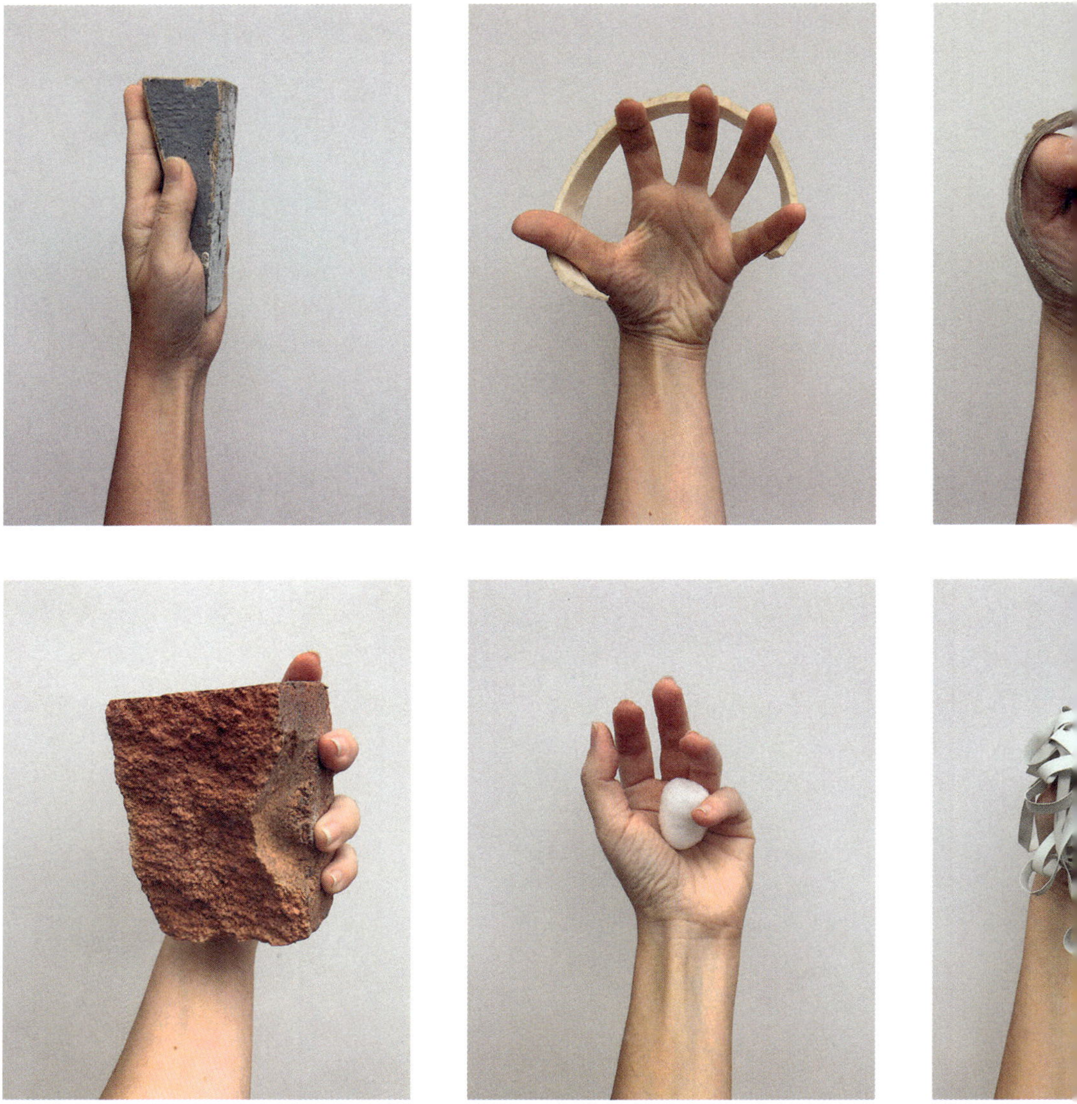

Courtesy the artist

Monuments (2018) by Vlatka Horvat
SELECTED BY Sabina Sabolović

SABINA SABOLOVIĆ: I found it beautiful how, in a way, with scattered materials and with this simple gesture of holding them in a fist, the artist completely changes our reading of the materials. For me, the present circumstances feel like a moment in which all the big narratives are dissolving—tracing something that we cannot so easily comprehend, yet it's also something valuable and dear.

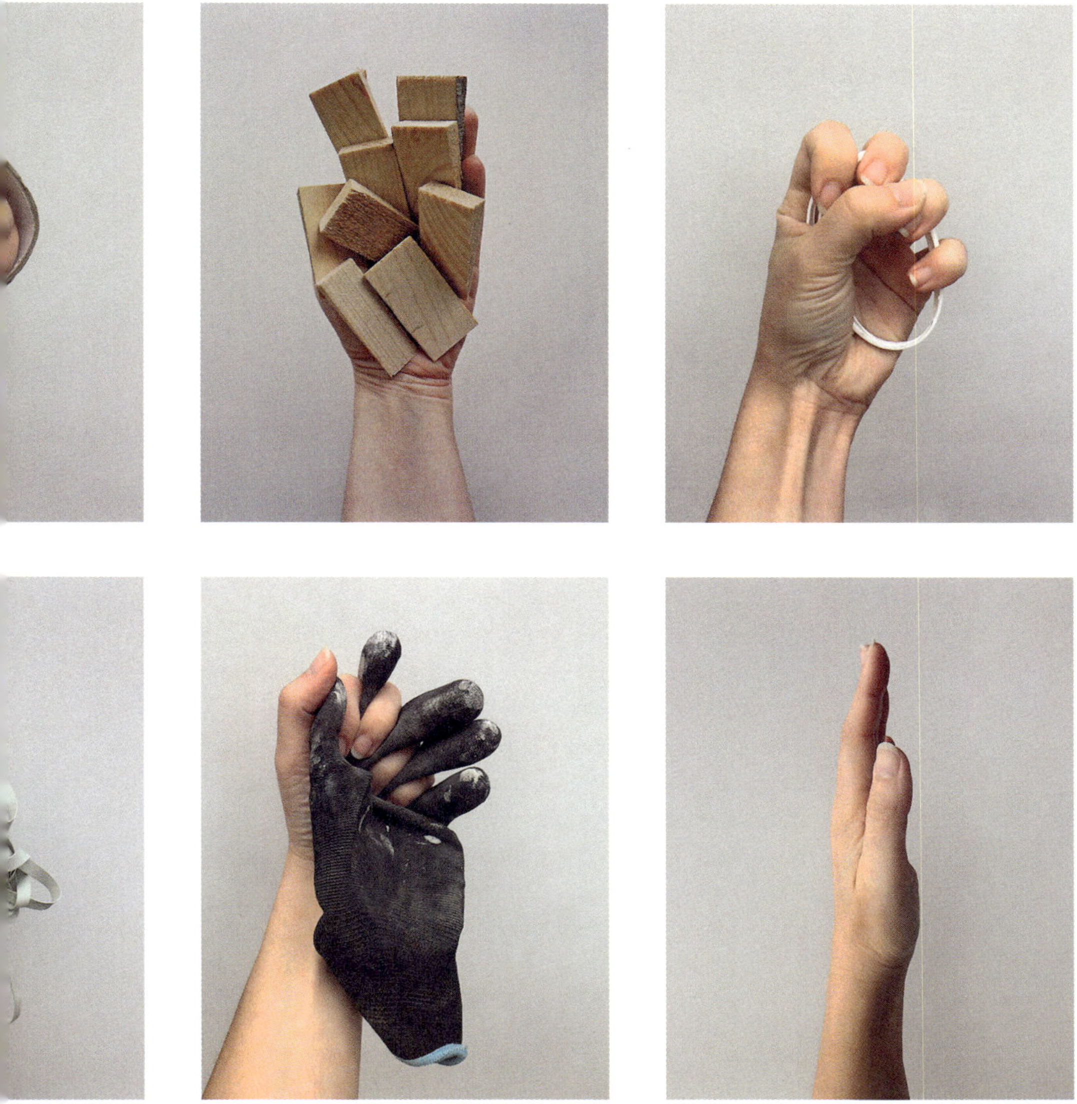

YD: In Feldenkrais, we understand the body as a whole, and our primary motivation is the functional integration of what we practice in the lesson into our daily life. There's an aesthetic of learning, but it's not an aesthetic in the sense of being a visibly beautiful movement. The movement always comes from functionality. In this work, there is a strong narrative of dominance and functionality between the objects and the artist's hands. One hand is holding the camera and the other hand is performing the act. The right hand is always taking the photo. My question is: Which is her dominant hand? Is it the one who performs or is it the one who shoots?

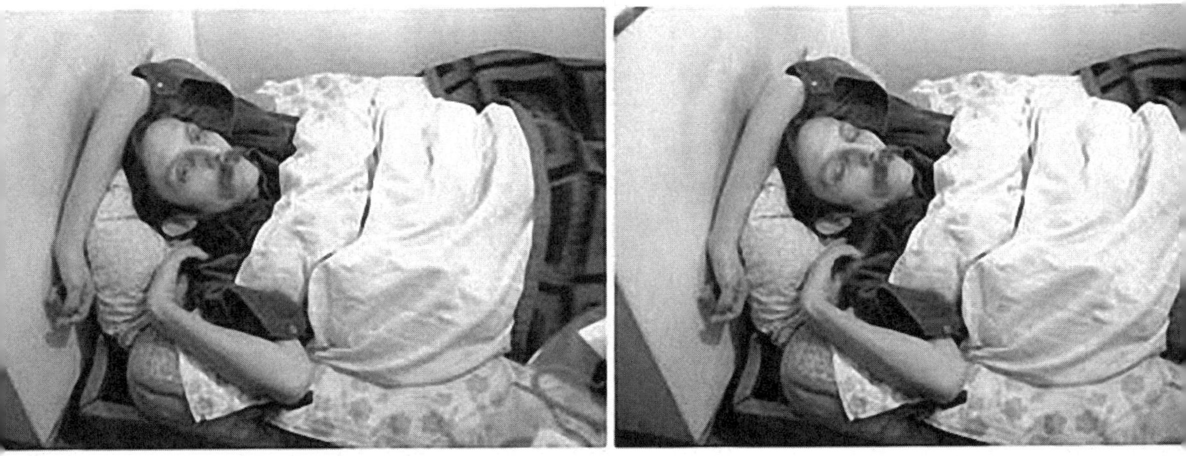

Artist at Work (1977) by Mladen Stilinović
SELECTED BY Ana Dević

ANA DEVIĆ: I chose this iconic work because of its theme of laziness—because it was also a bit of a lazy choice from me. In relation to the pandemic, for me it's about the pressure to be hyperproductive. One of the interpretations of the work is that it protests against this obsession with production and also comments on the immaterial labor of artistic work. That it's a kind of work that never stops, even when one is sleeping or pretending to sleep.

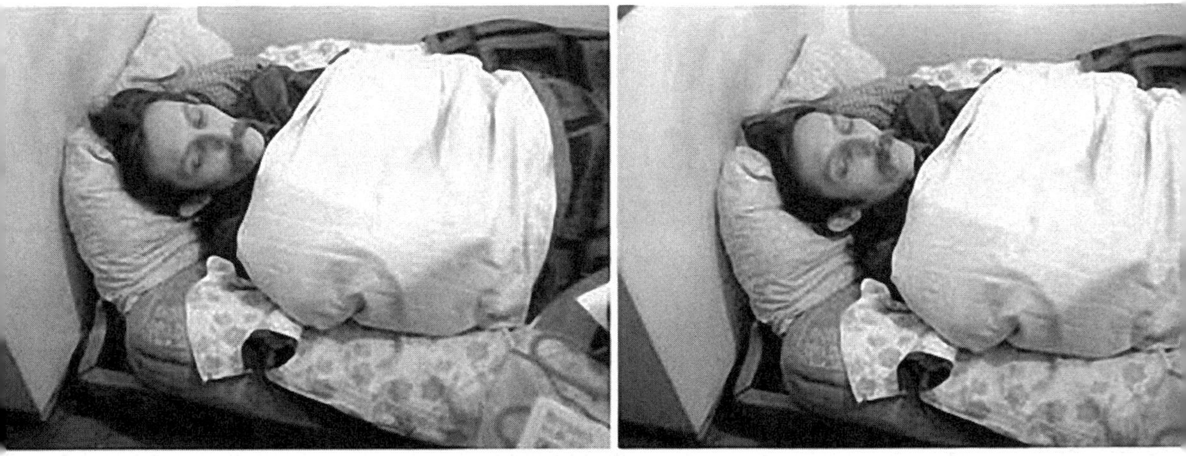

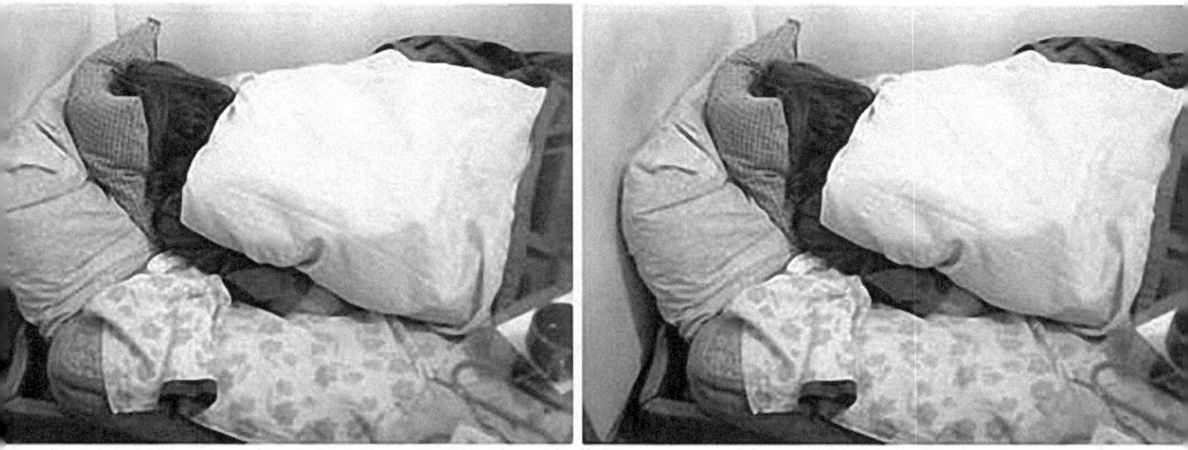

YD: In Feldenkrais lessons, we always pause throughout, albeit not because the work is so complicated or so difficult. Moshé Feldenkrais was interested in neurology, and he understood that the learning process happens during rest. We need pauses, because that's when the brain makes connections. I also notice this in regard to my daughter—I've often had tutors remark that she has problems with concentration, with daydreaming. But daydreaming also has a role—it's when children make connections. So, that which we call "laziness" is actually one of the most important moments for the brain.

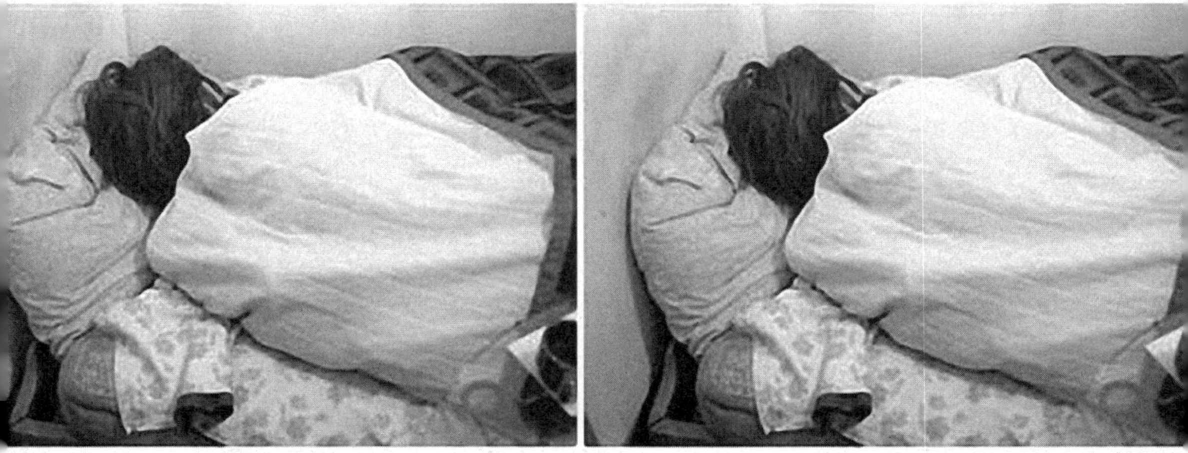

Courtesy the artist's estate and Branka Stipancic

***Woman-Tree (Documentation of the Performance Carried Out in November 1973 in Sant Llorenç del Munt, Spain)* (1973) by Fina Miralles**
SELECTED BY Pablo Martínez

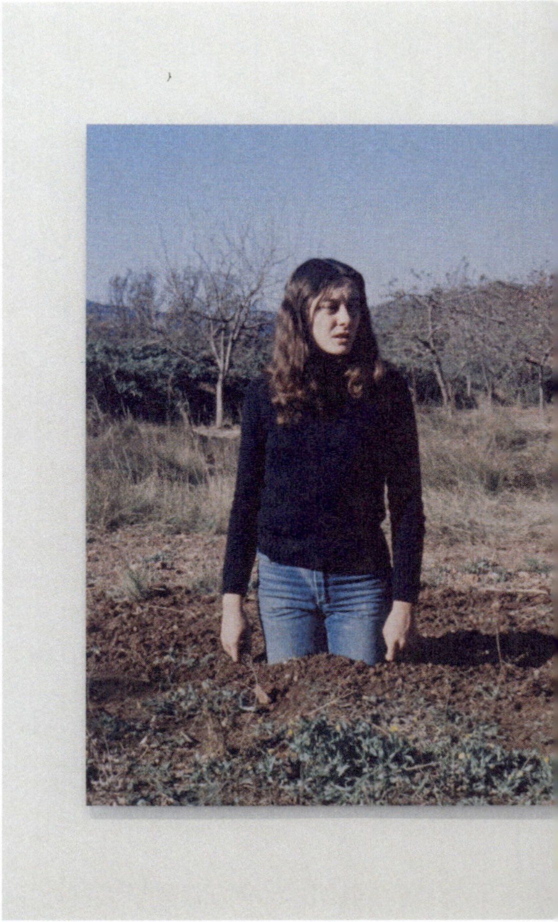

PABLO MARTÍNEZ: We currently have an exhibition of Fina Miralles on at the MACBA, and I am connected to her work these days. In relation to the lockdown, the work seems to reflect the paradoxes that we are living in. How we are stuck, how we are confined and in lockdown, but at the same time more connected to our context, our land, our territory. We can also read other aspects into this image, as it was made under dictatorship—we can think about the role of women at this time, and also the relation to environmental destruction within Spain due to the development of tourism and the new industrialization of the country during this period.

YD: The first thing that came to mind is, again, the lack of mobility and the lack of using the ground. I mean, using the ground in a different way. And I was interested in the idea, in this case, of the advantage of lacking mobility. One can assimilate into nature and observe more—like becoming a tree. What we interpret as movement, as human beings, is usually omnidirectional—front, back, sideways, bending down, and stretching up. Trees are also very active, but their movement orientation is different—it is downward and upward. Trees have a mechanism called gravitropism: the tree's cells detect gravity, and that is how it directs its

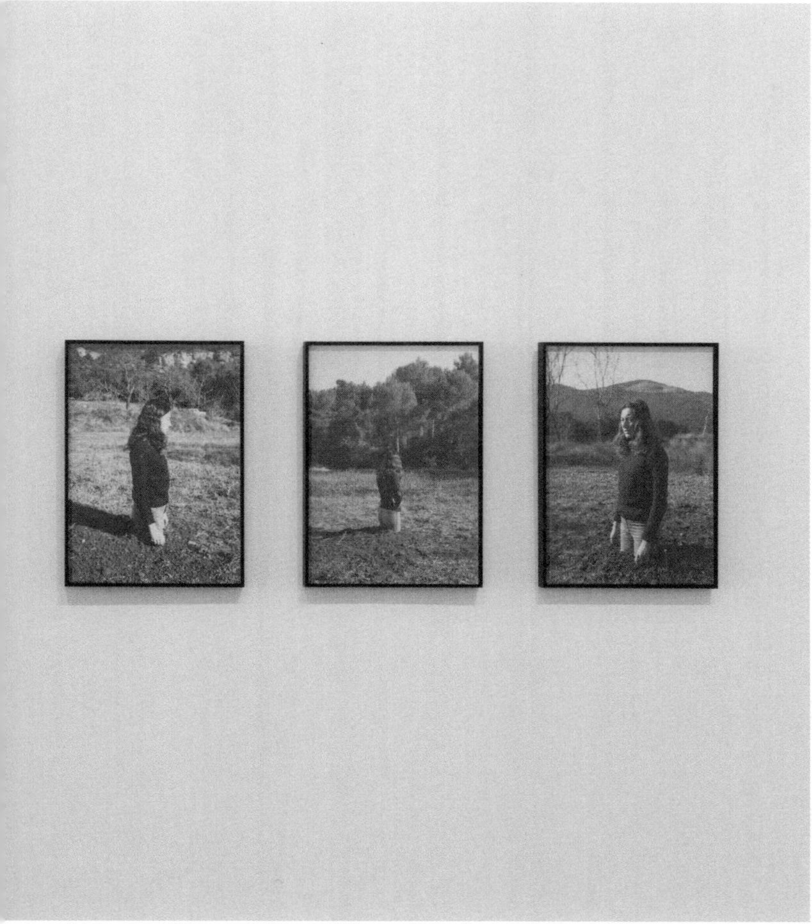

Courtesy the artist and MACBA, Barcelona • PHOTO: Roberto Ruiz

roots. In the other direction, trees possess a hormone called auxin, which detects light. The tree will always grow toward the light in order to generate energy. So, there are always these two forces in a tree: one going down and one going up. You will notice in the lesson that we use it a lot—that you need the ground in order to stand.

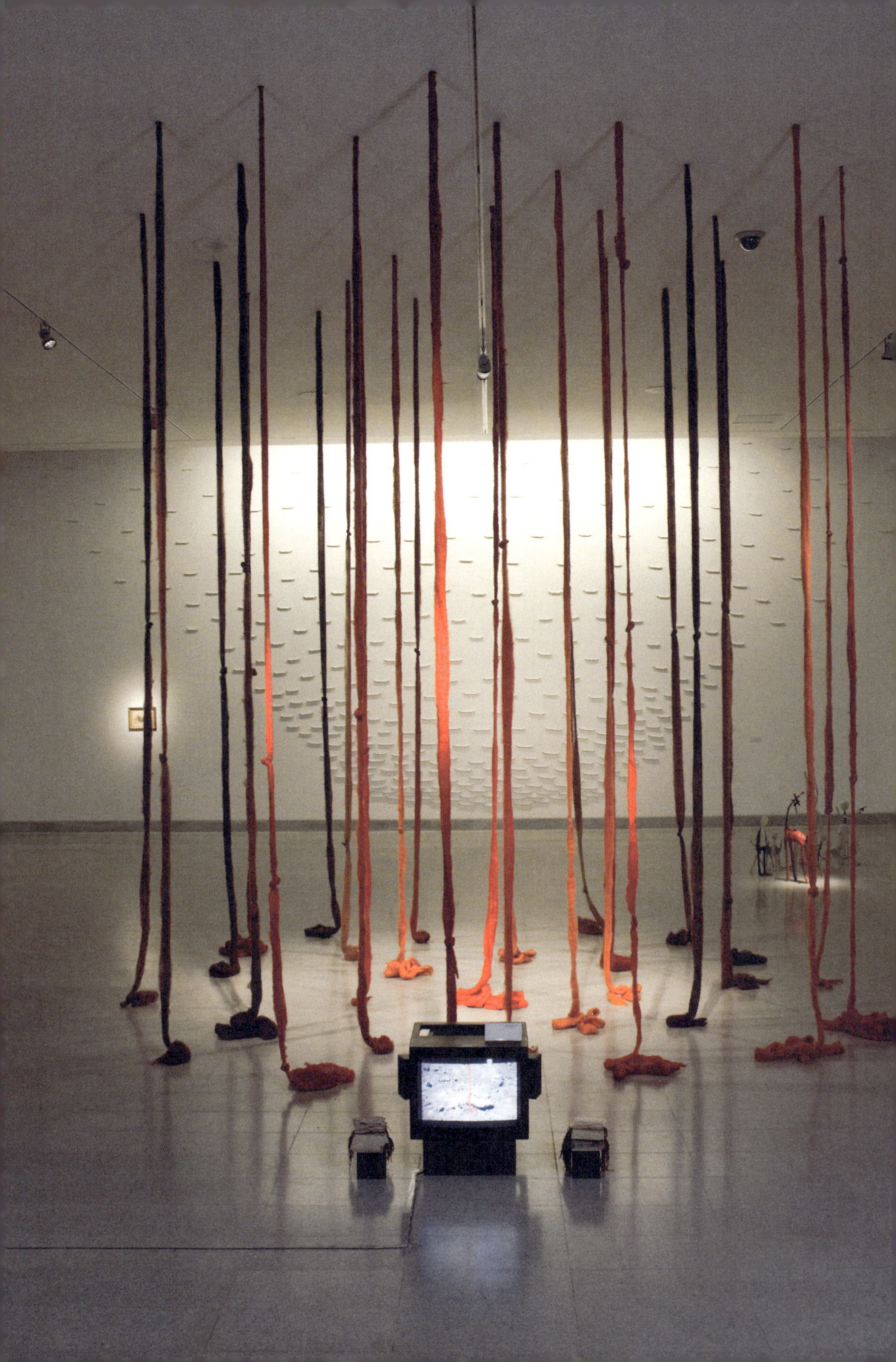

Menstrual Quipu, The Blood of the Glaciers (2006) by Cecilia Vicuña
SELECTED BY Ivet Ćurlin

IVET ĆURLIN: Cecilia Vicuña made this work when the socialist Michelle Bachelet, Chile's first female president, was elected in 2006. She installed these twenty-eight threads, colored with menstrual blood, at the bottom of Cerro El Plomo, a mountain in the Andes. The quipu is a mode of communication used by the Indigenous people of the Andes. It is a system of writing history, of archiving, and it was forbidden by colonial forces for years. So, this return to the quipu and to the feminine principle is very much a resurrection of Indigenous knowledge.

The installation stood at the bottom of the mountain for a while and then, later on, when Vicuña exhibited it inside a gallery, she included a letter to Bachelet in which she asks the president to override the authorization of gold mining in the Andes, which is actually destroying them. It's a piece asking for consideration for the environment, for protecting the environment. I also chose it because it starts from something very female, intimate, and secret. Something that is associated with vulnerability and something that women are supposed to hide, and then the work transforms it into something beautiful and public—like a public statement. I think in these times of pandemic, we are much more aware of how our bodies are actually interacting and being influenced, but also influencing the world around us.

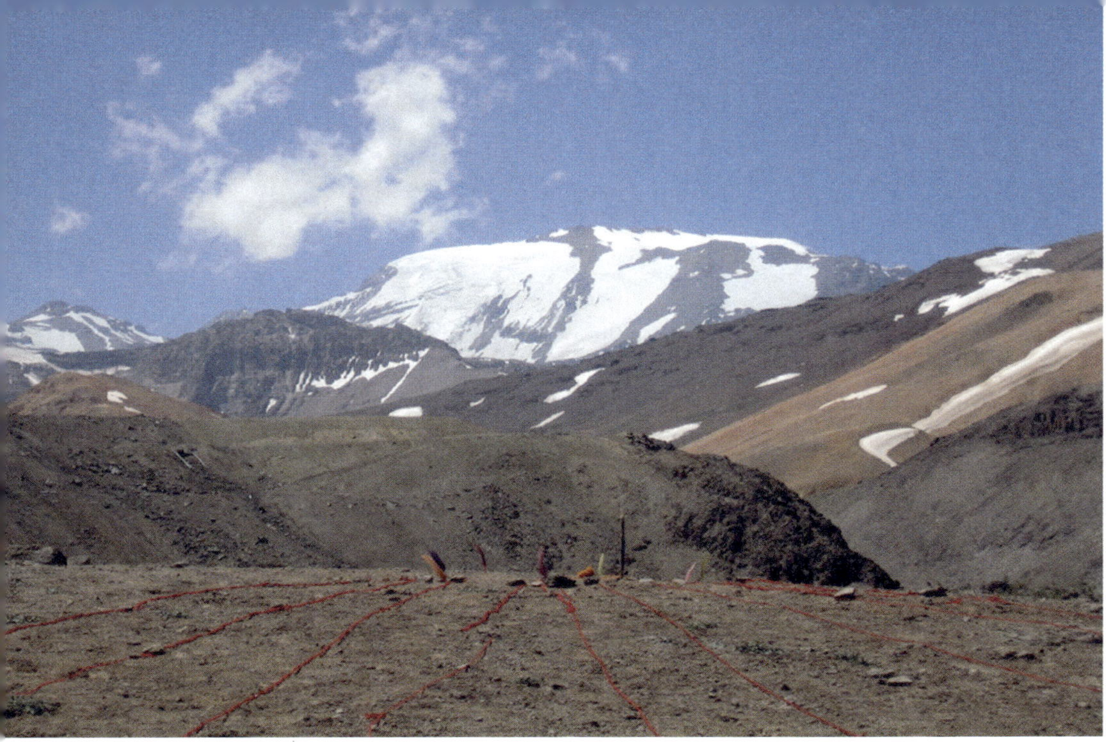

Cecilia Vicuña, *Menstrual Quipu, The Blood of the Glaciers*, 2006
Courtesy the artist and Lehmann Maupin, New York, Hong Kong, Seoul, and London • PHOTO: James O'Hern

YD: I would like to read something in relation to this work from Moshé Feldenkrais. This is a free translation from a lecture he gave in 1964 at the School of Psychological Sciences in Tel Aviv:

> *The dichotomy between the body and spirit is unacceptable to the mind. There exists a unity between the two that, at its foundation, relates to either energy or matter. There is a complete unity on the basis of matter. As we know, matter is energy. So, ultimately everything emerges from matter. Without matter activity, without muscular activity, there are no thoughts, no anxieties, no feelings.*

There is a relation between anxiety and gravitational pull. How could we ever conceive matter as being separate from the spirit? How is it that we are told about all kinds of phenomena, thinking, emotions, without being occupied with bodily, psychological, and neurological systems? How can we think there is no relation between the human and the cosmos? Between one's world and the force of gravity is the rotation of the earth's axis. Consider this: for women, every twenty-eight or so rotations of the earth produces menstruation. How does it come to be? Menstruation depends on a certain number of days, the number of rotations.

> *There is a strong relation between the cosmos, astronomy, the body and its nervous system. All this impacts the body, the environment, the public, culture. All this involves the neurological system.*

Creature-Maquette (320) (1964) by Lygia Clark
SELECTED BY Emily Pethick

EMILY PETHICK: I was looking at this work in terms of movement—these spines and opening movements. Thinking about the current situation and its effects on us, I think this is a nice object to think with, in terms of movements that try to break these inside/outside binaries—and to think through a form, a movement, whereby you can let go. Working with the body and less with the mind. I think that's a way out from this lack of an "outside" that we are experiencing mentally at the moment. You're always in the situation (the pandemic), and this is a way to move out of it for a moment.

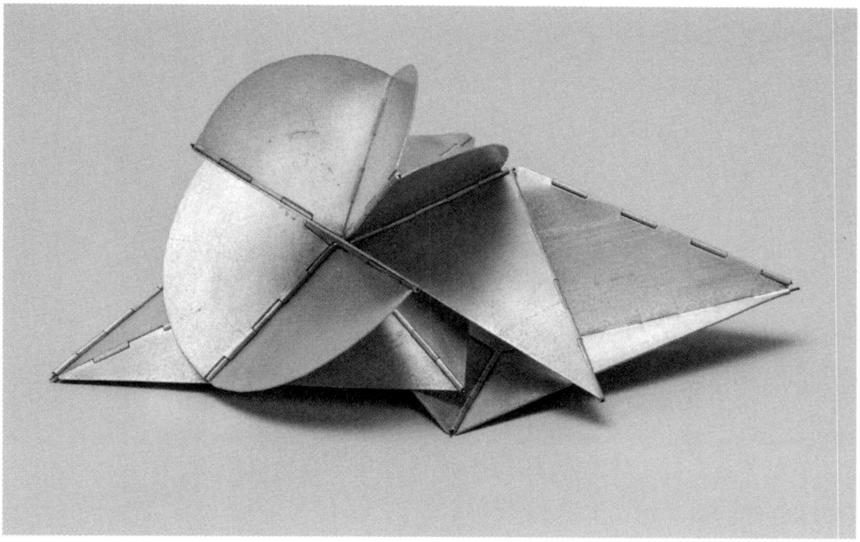

Courtesy O Mundo de Lygia Clark-Associação Cultural, Rio de Janeiro • PHOTO: Tate

YD: You immediately see the axis and the relation to the distant and the proximal. In Feldenkrais, we try to reach from the distal to the proximal, toward the center. That is what you can see here: you can unfold and enfold. We touch the edges in order to make movement through the axis. This work is from a series, and there's a very beautiful text the artist wrote about it in 1960:

> *The arrangement of the metal plates determines the position of* [*the sculpture*], *which at first glance seems unlimited. When I am asked how many moves* [*it*] *can make, I reply: "I don't know, you don't know, but it knows."* [...] [*It*] *is an organic entity that fully reveals itself within its inner time of expression.* [...] *There is no room for passivity in the relationship that is established between* [*the sculptures*] *and us, neither from them nor from us.*

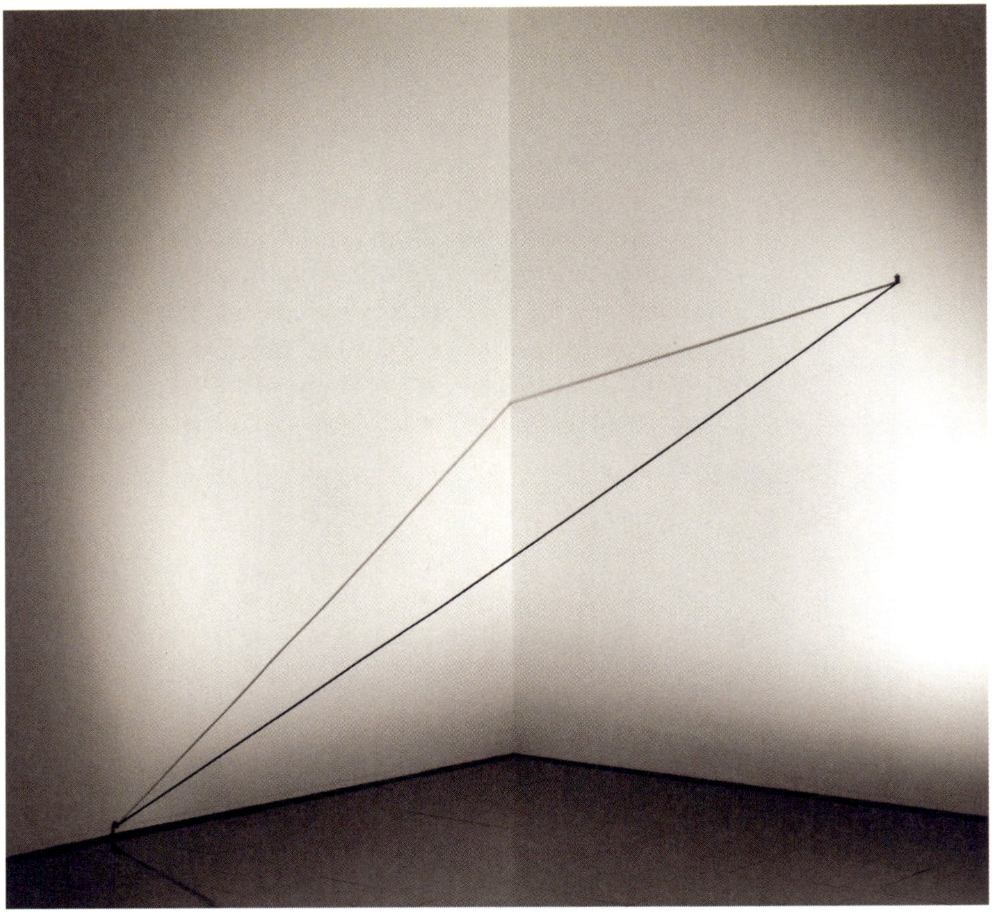

Courtesy the artist and MACBA, Barcelona • PHOTO: MACBA

***3 Points* (1970) by Àngels Ribé**
SELECTED BY Pablo Martínez

PM: I did not choose this piece because of the current situation. I was thinking more about the Feldenkrais Method, which I have never tried before. This is one of my favorite pieces in the MACBA's collection. It's so simple, so delicate. It's a minimal gesture within the existing architecture, but it's so powerful at the same time—it expresses tension while also expressing vulnerability and intimacy.

YD: It is beautiful how it explores the corner. For me, this work has much to do with direction. There is a very clear force between the three corners that hold these lines in exactly the right position. If it were too tight, it would break. If it were too long, there would not be a straight line.

The Skeleton and the Feldenkrais Method

YD: The skeleton is our support system. Each detailed part is very related to all the others. Any movement, even if it's small, includes the whole body. We're not interested in movement as such, but rather how we organize ourselves toward it. Often you have pain in the part that functions the best—this is the part that takes over the whole activity; it is hyperactive. So, we look at how to support this part with the other parts—how to invite the participation of other parts that are less active—and thus reduce the work from the most active part.

Here are some terms we will use [*indicating on a skeleton model*]: From the spine, we have the ribs. The spine extends to the skull. The ribs are connected to the sternum and to the clavicle. The clavicle is connected to the scapula, the shoulder blades. The shoulder blades are connected to the hand. So, for example, when we lift the hand, we are moving the shoulder blade, which moves our clavicle, which moves our sternum, which moves our ribs, which will approach our spine. The spine meets the pelvis, the hip joint, and thus the legs. If we think about reaching, for example, we reach through our whole body.

Now, in this specific lesson, we will look at the ribcage. This idea of a "cage" is embedded in many languages, but actually our ribs have a lot of mobility. You can feel it when you breathe. These connecting parts between the sternum and the ribs are called cartilage, soft sections that are movable, which is also the case between the discs of the spine. The more flexible parts of the ribs, the cartilage, mirror the position of cartilage sections of the spine. There is thus the potential for a parallel movement, too.

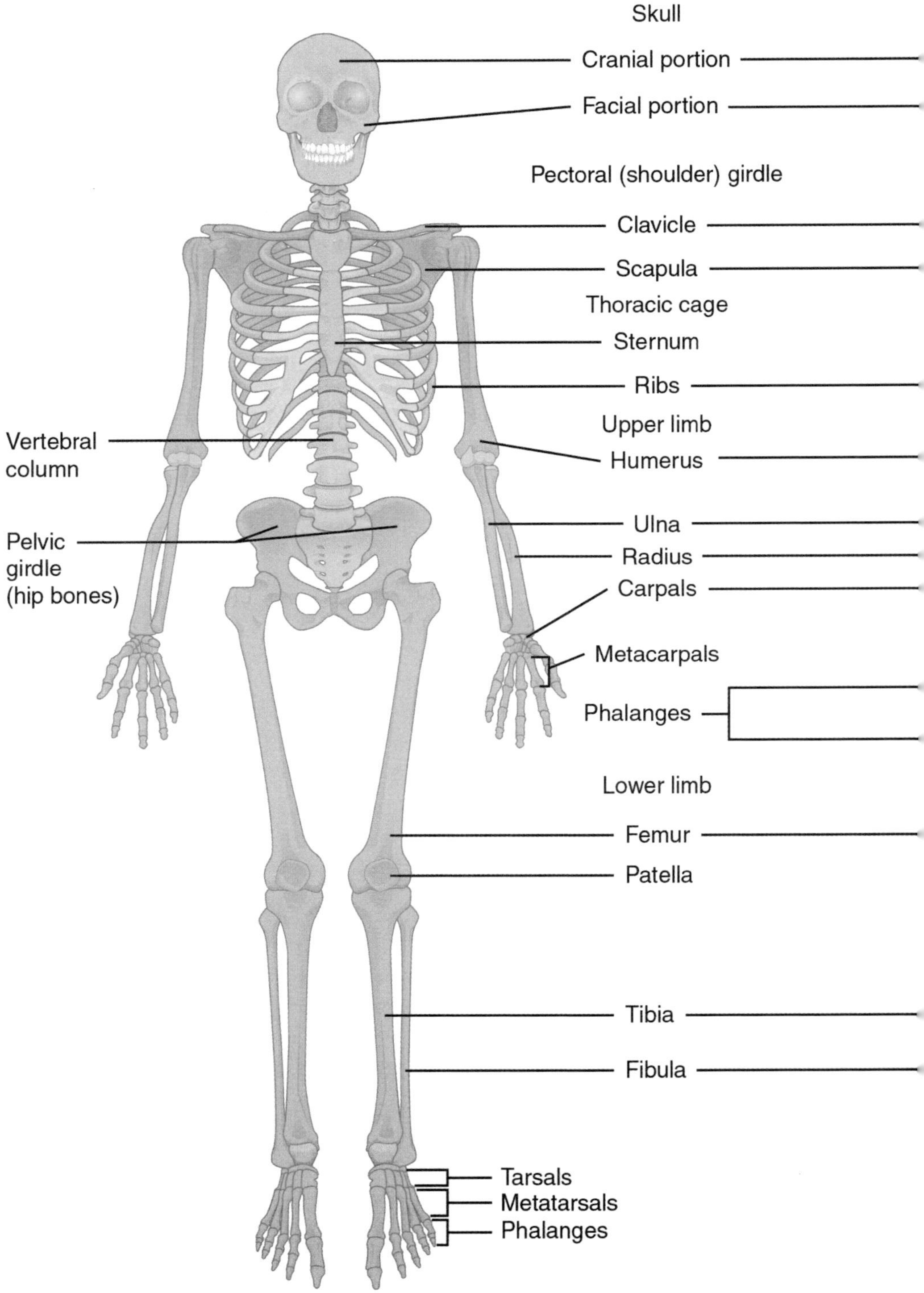

Anterior view

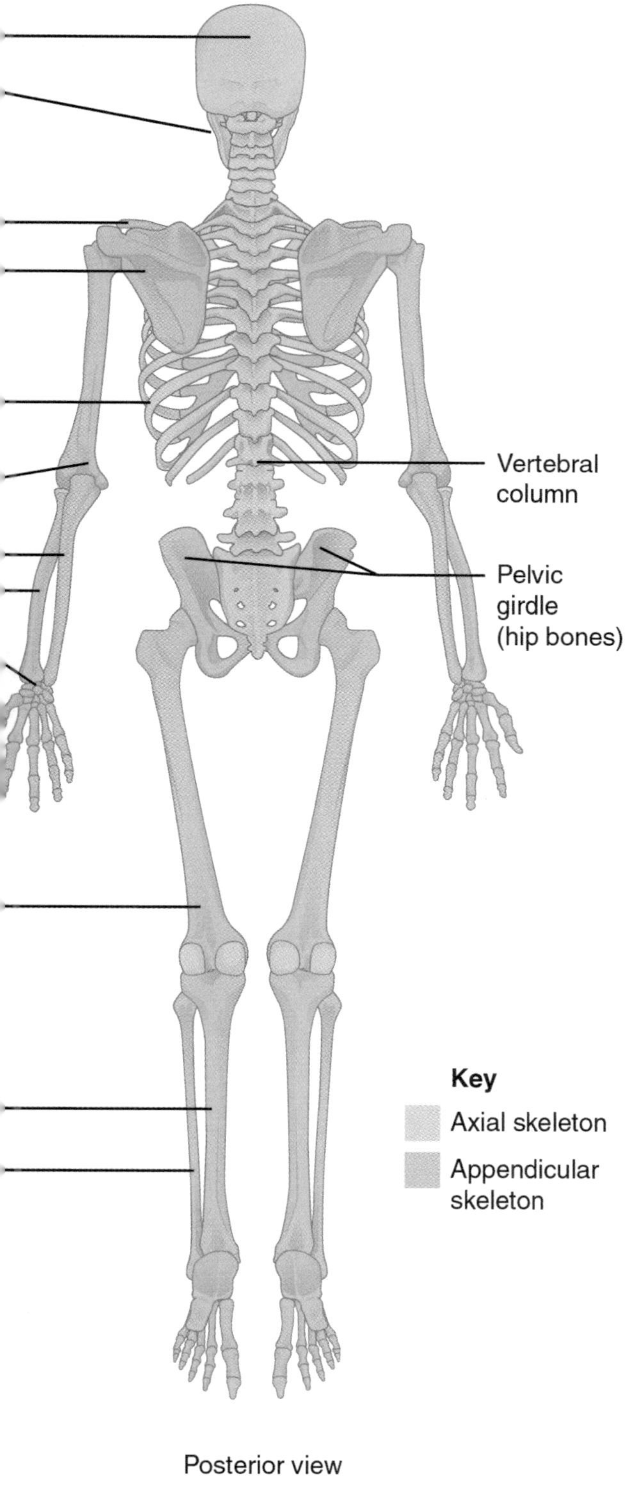

In Feldenkrais, we understand pain and excess effort as "noise," and in order to introduce optimal learning conditions, we would like to soften such noise. So, closing the eyes lessens the impact from outside. It is very important to use as little effort as possible. When we do things on a smaller scale, we often have much more of an overview of our bodily organization. If you feel any discomfort or pain, that is the place to stop. We have three options: reduce the scale of the movement to make it smaller, change the direction of the movement, or decrease the speed. When I use the word "look," it is always meant in terms of looking inward, imagining how you organize yourself. Being judged is not a nourishing experience, and it undermines the learning process. Therefore, I will not correct you. A movement that is right for you is the right movement. And how do you know? The right movement is a movement where you know what you are doing. That's the most important thing—*to know and be present in what you are doing.*

◄
Axial skeleton, illustration by OpenStax College (CC BY 3.0)

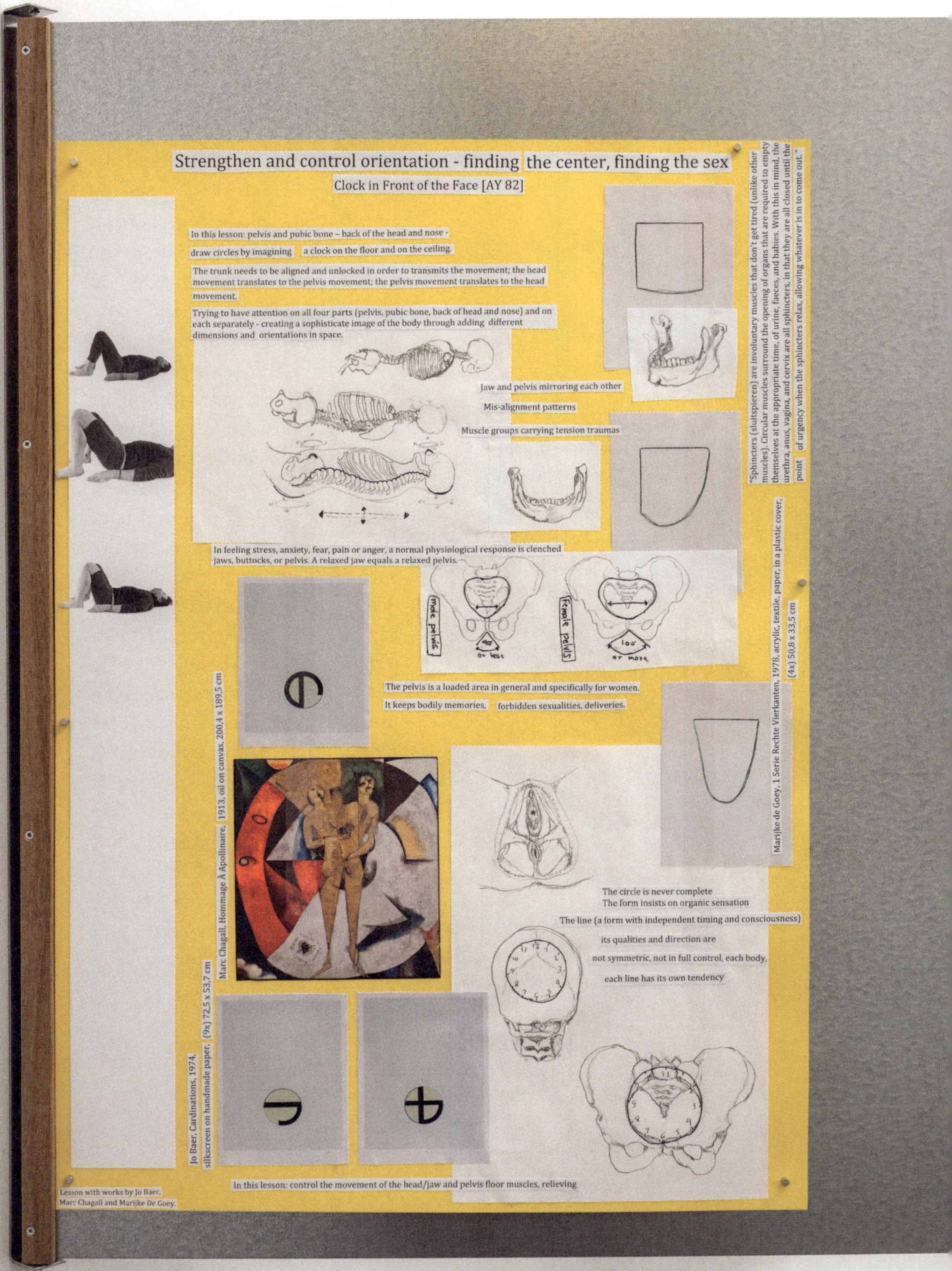
Strengthen and control orientation - finding the center, finding the sex
Clock in Front of the Face [AY 82]
In this lesson: pelvis and pubic bone – back of the head and nose - draw circles by imagining a clock on the floor and on the ceiling.
The trunk needs to be aligned and unlocked in order to transmits the movement; the head movement translates to the pelvis movement; the pelvis movement translates to the head movement.
Trying to have attention on all four parts (pelvis, pubic bone, back of head and nose) and on each separately - creating a sophisticate image of the body through adding different dimensions and orientations in space.
Jaw and pelvis mirroring each other
Mis-alignment patterns
Muscle groups carrying tension traumas
In feeling stress, anxiety, fear, pain or anger, a normal physiological response is clenched jaws, buttocks, or pelvis. A relaxed jaw equals a relaxed pelvis.
male pelvis
female pelvis
The pelvis is a loaded area in general and specifically for women.
It keeps bodily memories, forbidden sexualities, deliveries.
"Sphincters (sluitspieren) are involuntary muscles that don't get tired (unlike other muscles). Circular muscles surround the opening of organs that are required to empty themselves at the appropriate time, of urine, faeces, and babies. With this in mind, the urethra, anus, vagina, and cervix are all sphincters, in that they are all closed until the point of urgency when the sphincters relax, allowing whatever is in to come out."
Marijke de Goey, 1 Serie Rechte Vierkanten, 1978, acrylic, textile, paper, in a plastic cover, (4x) 50,8 x 33,5 cm
Marc Chagall, Hommage À Apollinaire, 1913, oil on canvas, 200,4 x 189,5 cm
Jo Baer, Cardinations, 1974, silkscreen on handmade paper, (9x) 72,5 x 53,7 cm
The circle is never complete
The form insists on organic sensation
The line (a form with independent timing and consciousness)
its qualities and direction are
not symmetric, not in full control, each body,
each line has its own tendency
In this lesson: control the movement of the head/jaw and pelvis floor muscles, relieving
Lesson with works by Jo Baer, Marc Chagall and Marijke De Goey.

The Lesson

Body scan. Lie on the floor. Close your eyes. Notice how you are lying.

We lie on the floor because this provides maximum support, and we use less of our strength to resist the pull of gravity. How do you know that you are breathing? See what it is that tells you that you are breathing. Accept the fact that you are alive. Look at what is changing in the ribs in relation to the floor.

Now notice how your right heel lies on the floor. Where is the place that it touches the floor?

The direction of your right toes, and your right ankle—does it have contact with the floor? Go to your right calf, your right knee, your right thigh, and the right side of your pelvis. Now try to imagine your right hip joint and make a line between the right heel and the right hip joint. Notice the quality of this line, and whether you can even call it a line. We are always looking for feedback from the floor. The more contact with the floor we have, the less mass we are holding.

Go to your left heel. Take a moment to compare it with your right heel: the location of the heel and the sense of weight.

Go to the back of your left ankle, your left calf, your left knee, your left thigh, and wherever you imagine your left hip joint to be. The hip joint we cannot see, so we are moving from where we perceive it to be. See where you perceive your right and left hip joints to be and make an imaginary line between the left heel and the left hip joint. Again, notice the quality of this line, and whether you can call it a line at all.

Imagine the sacrum—the base of your pelvis, above the tailbone—which is the lowest point of your spine, through the pelvis. Go along your spine.

◄
Feldenkrais lessons at Van Abbemuseum
PHOTO: Marcel de Buck

Try to follow the arch in your lower back. Try to sense the scale of this arch, its form. Where does the arch start and where do you touch the floor again? Can you locate the vertebrae that touch the floor back? Go along the spine, between your ribs, between your shoulder blades, your neck, and imagine where and how your head is situated. More on the right or the left, or toward

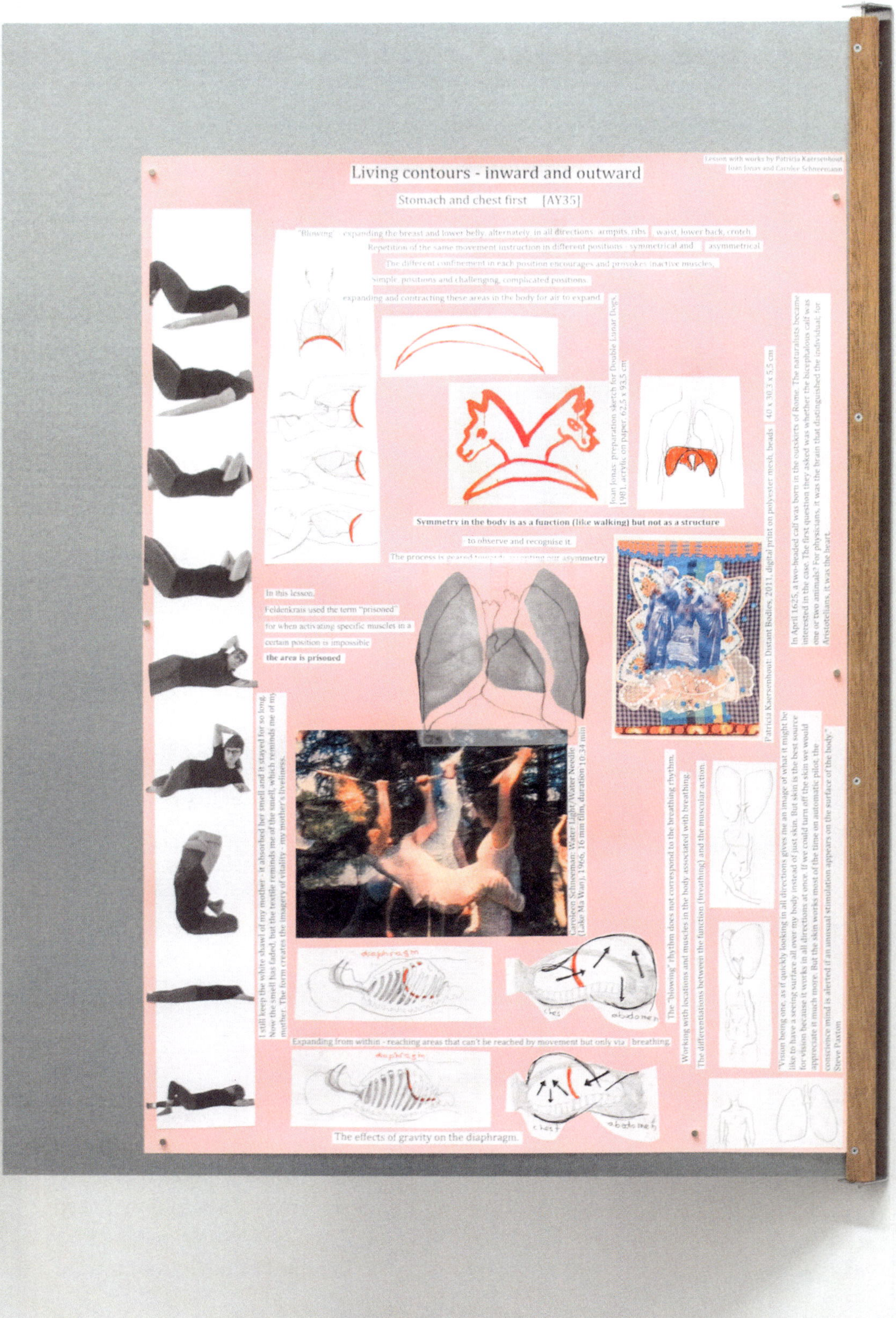
Living contours - inward and outward
Lesson with works by Patricia Kaersenhout, Joan Jonas and Carolee Schneemann
Stomach and chest first [AY35]
"Blowing" - expanding the breast and lower belly, alternately, in all directions: armpits, ribs, waist, lower back, crotch.
Repetition of the same movement instruction in different positions - symmetrical and asymmetrical.
The different confinement in each position encourages and provokes inactive muscles,
simple, positions and challenging, complicated positions.
expanding and contracting these areas in the body for air to expand.
Joan Jonas: preparation sketch for Double Lunar Dogs, 1981, acrylic on paper, 62.5 x 93.5 cm
Symmetry in the body is as a function (like walking) but not as a structure
to observe and recognise it.
The process is geared towards accepting our asymmetry
In this lesson,
Feldenkrais used the term "prisoned"
for when activating specific muscles in a
certain position is impossible
the area is prisoned
Patricia Kaersenhout: Distant Bodies, 2011, digital print on polyester mesh, beads 40 x 30.3 x 5.5 cm
In April 1625, a two-headed calf was born in the outskirts of Rome. The naturalists became interested in the case. The first question they asked was whether the bicephalous calf was one or two animals? For physicians, it was the brain that distinguished the individual; for Aristotelians, it was the heart.
I still keep the white shawl of my mother - it absorbed her smell and it stayed for so long. Now the smell has faded, but the textile reminds me of the smell, which reminds me of my mother. The form creates the imagery of vitality - my mother's liveliness.
Carolee Schneemann: Water Light/Water Needle (Lake Ma Wan), 1966, 16 mm film, duration 10:34 min
The "blowing" rhythm does not correspond to the breathing rhythm.
Working with locations and muscles in the body associated with breathing.
The differentiations between the function (breathing) and the muscular action.
"Vision being one, as if quickly looking in all directions gives me an image of what it might be like to have a seeing surface all over my body instead of just skin. But skin is the best source for vision because it works in all directions at once. If we could turn off the skin we would appreciate it much more. But the skin works most of the time on automatic pilot, the conscience mind is alerted if an unusual stimulation appears on the surface of the body."
Steve Paxton
diaphragm
chest
abdomen
Expanding from within - reaching areas that can't be reached by movement but only via breathing.
diaphragm
chest
abdomen
The effects of gravity on the diaphragm.

the back? Notice your shoulders, the right shoulder and the left shoulder. Do they have equal distance from the floor, or does one feel higher? And what is the distance from your ears—the distance from the right shoulder to your right ear, and from the left shoulder to your left ear?

Your hands—are they equally close to the body? And are they facing the same direction—toward the body or the ceiling or the floor?

As you lie there, take a moment to imagine the work of Lygia Clark. Try to see if you can imagine the different spines the work portrays, the different possibilities for folding in and out. Find a place where you can embody this work. And imagine the three strings of Àngels Ribé's work—the clarity of direction. See if there is any clarity for yourself, any clear lines in your body that you can trace. They can be short or long.

Bend your right knee upright. Very gently, imagine that you want to push the floor away from you.

What will move? When you push the floor away from you, the knee will go above the heel a bit and your right hip joint will lift from the floor. Try to feel through the structure that is pushing at the floor. In this movement, there is also a slight rotation in the spine. Try to trace this movement, known as ground reaction force—the way the ground gives you the force to initiate movement. Try to feel this force with the pushing and lifting, and then let it always return softly to the floor.

How far does a movement go through you? If you do not bring any straining or constraint, the movement might reach your head, your shoulder, reaching through all of you. See what stops the movement and whether you feel the places in the vertebrae and ribs that are taking part.

Take your left hand and put it upward and straight, still on the floor and alongside your head. Keep pushing at the floor with your right leg. Imagine that you want to elongate the hand through this pushing.

◄
Feldenkrais lessons at Van Abbemuseum
PHOTO: Marcel de Buck

See if by pushing the heel to the floor the movement reaches your left shoulder and—even if it is only by a millimeter—whether your left hand is elongating. Keep doing it.

Take your right hand and slide it, very gently, down in the direction of the heel—a very small movement—and then come back to the neutral position.

See how you are doing this, and whether this produces any movement in your ribs. Do you feel maybe that the right side of the ribs is getting a bit shorter? And, as the right side of the ribs gets shorter, maybe the left gets longer? What is happening in your shoulder? Your hand is connected to the shoulder. What does the shoulder take with it? Does it take the clavicle with it? What happens in the ribs? What happens with your head? You can move the head if you feel that there's an invitation for movement.

Let the head roll to the left, as if it wants to look at the hand.

Feel what amount of turning is asked for from the movement. Turn your palm to the floor, as if you want to touch the floor, like you really want to touch the floor. Notice when you do it—when you slide the hand down and the head is rolling—that something is happening in your sternum and in your ribs.

Feldenkrais was interested in organic learning, which means learning in the way that babies do—a learning led by curiosity and playfulness. So, imagine there is a toy there somewhere and you want to reach it. How can you change your organization to make your reach longer? When you take the hand down, the left shoulder also will go down and eventually it will affect the right shoulder as well. The right shoulder will probably shift a little bit upward.

Keep elongating the hand, but now keep the face parallel to the ceiling. Slide the back of your head, as if you want to bend your head toward the left side.

The left ear will come closer to the left shoulder. The right ear will move away from the right shoulder.

Let it go and rest a moment.

See if you feel any difference between the right and left shoulder blades and between the right and left sides of the ribs.

Bend only your left leg and now do the movement again. What is your natural way—will you rotate the head or bend the neck? Now, can you imagine combining both movements?

The pushing and reaching—try to see this play between what falls to the floor and what is lifted. They need each other. Nothing happens in your right leg. The right hip joint is falling to the floor. Allow the belly to go out. Each time, come slowly back. The smaller you do it, the more you can feel the unity of the parts. Try to see how you can organize your body so that all of you takes part in this movement.

Now bring your left foot a little bit closer to your hip joint—perhaps you can touch the ankle or heel?

Do the movements again. As you hold the left foot like this, take the pelvis down and up. Push the heel, lift the left hip joint, and then take it down slowly, very slowly.

Now, we will try the same movements on the other side.

[*The same movements are repeated on the opposite side*]

You remember we talked about the tree? Imagine how you need the ground so as to extend upward. You can feel how the movement and the force is coming from the ground, beginning in the feet. Try to see what invitation you receive from your ribs, from this part that we don't often move so much. Feldenkrais says people think they have a problem in the shoulder or the knee, but they in fact have a problem in the breast—because we do not move our breastbone, as it is busy with protection. The ribs protect valuable organs: the heart, the lungs. But it's also an emotional protection, this rigidity. It is not really necessary, actually. This stagnation is a process we all go through. But the more mobility we have, the better protection we have.

It's just interesting to think about weight as a force. There is somehow a negative connotation about weight. Weight is a force that acts on all objects—it acts on the Earth and Earth responds.

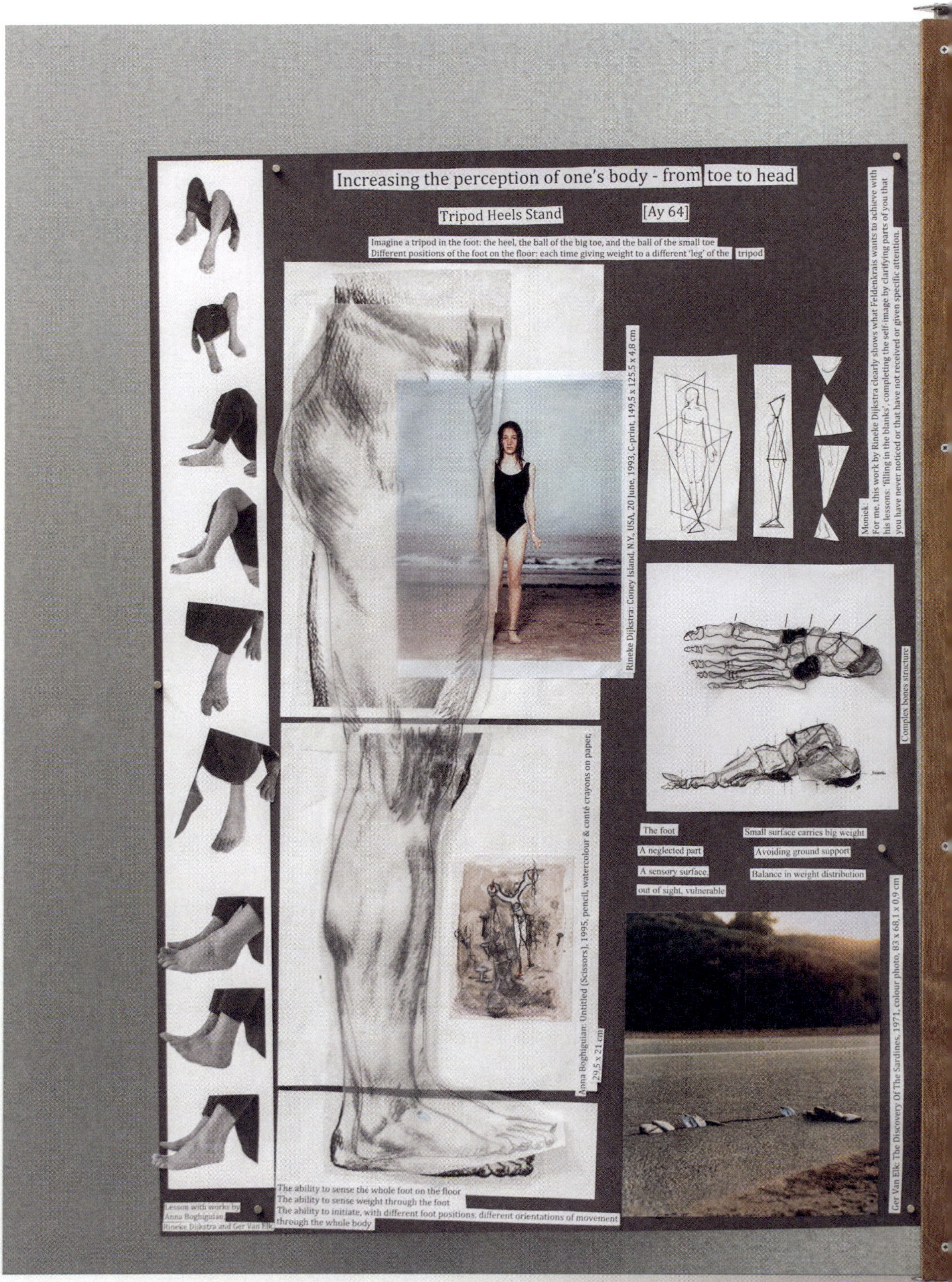
Increasing the perception of one's body - from toe to head
Tripod Heels Stand
[Ay 64]
Imagine a tripod in the foot: the heel, the ball of the big toe, and the ball of the small toe
Different positions of the foot on the floor: each time giving weight to a different 'leg' of the tripod
Rineke Dijkstra: Coney Island, N.Y., USA, 20 June, 1993, C-print, 149,5 x 125,5 x 4,8 cm
Moniek:
For me, this work by Rineke Dijkstra clearly shows what Feldenkrais wants to achieve with his lessons: 'filling in the blanks', completing the self-image by clarifying parts of you that you have never noticed or that have not received or given specific attention.
Complex bones structure
The foot
A neglected part
A sensory surface,
out of sight, vulnerable
Small surface carries big weight
Avoiding ground support
Balance in weight distribution
Anna Boghiguian: Untitled (Scissors), 1995, pencil, watercolour & conté crayons on paper, 29,5 x 21 cm
Ger Van Elk: The Discovery Of The Sardines, 1971, colour photo, 83 x 68,1 x 0,9 cm
Lesson with works by
Anna Boghiguian,
Rineke Dijkstra and Ger Van Elk
The ability to sense the whole foot on the floor
The ability to sense weight through the foot
The ability to initiate, with different foot positions, different orientations of movement through the whole body

So, the gravitational force of Earth pulls all objects down toward the center of the Earth, but then we have the ground reaction force, which comes from our weight—the force we direct back at the ground, which mobilizes a power in us. Often, when lying down, we bring along our habits from standing and sitting, which entail a lot of constraint. Try and see if you can allow yourself to drop and relax. The more availability we have in the skeleton, the less we use the muscles and the more the skeleton can come into function. If we work *with* the skeleton, we are much more efficient in our movement.

Bend both legs and both arms on the floor, but directed upward, and now try to elongate first the right hand and then the left hand.

You will notice that the head will probably move differently, if you are really able to be open to the differences and the asymmetry. You'll probably notice that you have a favorite side that is easier to organize. Do not move the knees. The knees stay facing the ceiling because we want to move the center, the torso—we want to invite movement there.

Interlace the fingers of the hands together, and put them on the floor, around ten centimeters from your head. In this arrangement, move your hands a little bit to the right and then a little bit to the left.

It's as if the respective elbow wants to come closer to the side of your ribs. The head stays still. The head does not move. Try to see if you feel this movement in the shoulder blades and imagine how they are sliding under your ribs.

Now let it go and rest. Notice how you are lying on the floor.

Put your hands on top of your eyes, and imagine them in their sockets, as if they are liquid. Imagine they are melting into the ground.

You might see some white points. See if you can find a dark spot and then concentrate on it, extending the darkness. A relaxed nervous system will have total darkness, but because we are never really relaxed, these kinds of white points reflect the work of the nervous system. We are trying now to introduce more darkness. Concentrate on one black point and make it larger and larger, so that the darkness spreads all over.

◄
Feldenkrais lessons
at Van Abbemuseum
PHOTO: Marcel de Buck

Lying like this, choose one work from the works we looked at. Choose one that you feel can stay with you for a while and notice where it is landing in your body.

And now, very gently, keeping your eyes closed, take your hands away from your eyes. Very slowly slide to your side. From the side, come gradually to sitting and then to standing. Stay standing for a moment.

Where do you lean on your feet, and where is the pelvis in relation to your feet? Is it above your feet, a little bit back? Where are your shoulders in relation to your pelvis and your head? Lift your right hand as if you want to reach something. Keep it up for a bit, and then try to elongate it.

Now let it go, and walk a little bit around the space.

YAEL DAVIDS'S ACKNOWLEDGMENTS

For their support and contribution, I would like to thank Ana Dević, who worked with me on developing the event, as well as Virág Szentkirályi, Sabina Sabolović, Nataša Ilić, Pablo Martínez, Ivet Ćurlin, and Emily Pethick for their participation. For their assistance, I would like to thank Lotte Lara Schröder and Hannah Dawn Henderson, as well as transcriber Jenny Wolka. Further, I would like to thank my longtime collaborators Nick Aikens and Frederique Bergholtz, as well as everyone who attended the evening via Zoom.

CAConrad

Shards (2021)

remember
our metal skin
when the planet
first caught fire
it was
years
before we
understood
the awful
thing we
held to our chest
whatever a poem can
send into the future
please send the
breath
we have
been trying
to catch
for as long
as you can
hold it
so glad
you came by
thank you
as always

swallowed
each other
until we
heard
each
other
think
queer pirates
I have loved
loosened my
wilderness
no
more
miscounting
butterflies in
our utopia
let's make
poems
that
can
rob
a bank

a storm of
handwriting
was this
poem's
first
shape
all that
matters
is which
decisions
today lead me
closer to you
do not fall
away one
two three
a paperboy
delivering his
father's obituary
a footnote to stumbling
in the dark as an artform
come sing
with me into
this dough
what song shall
we bake into
our supper

Dan Perjovschi

Drawings (2020–21)

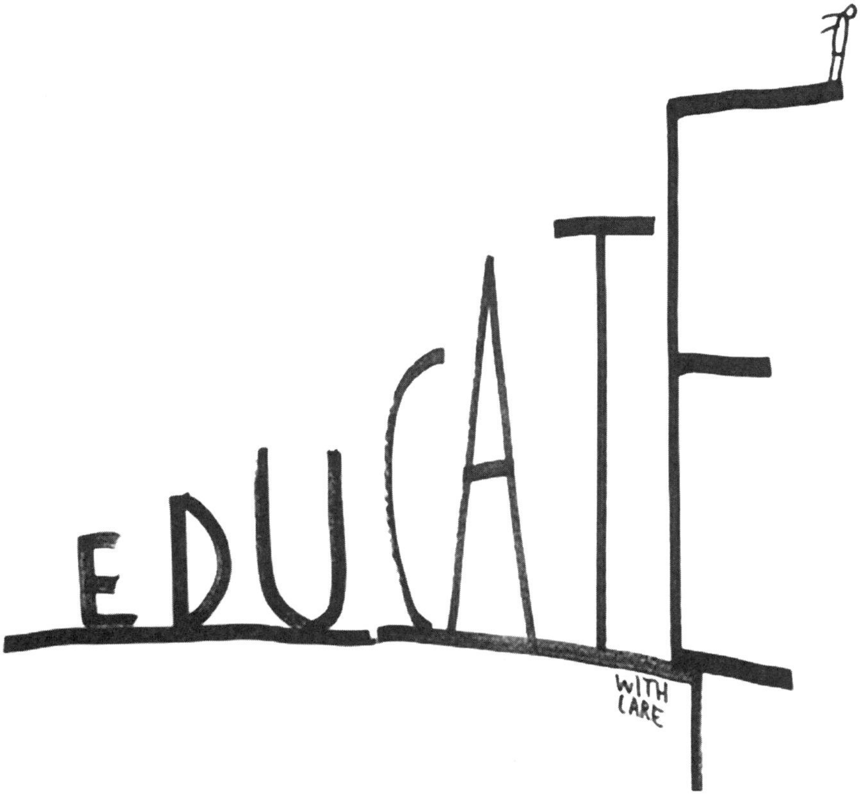
EDUCATE
WITH CARE

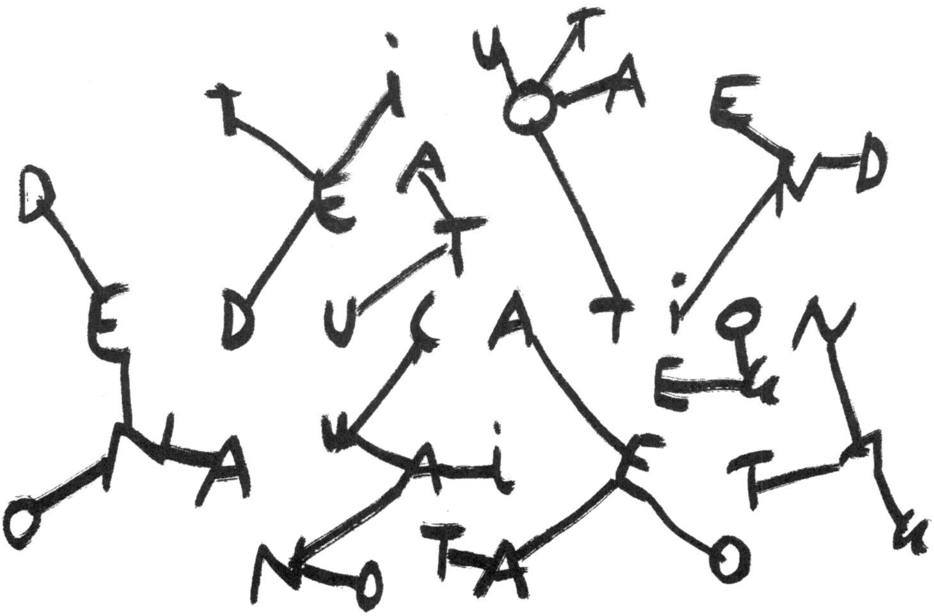
EDUCATION

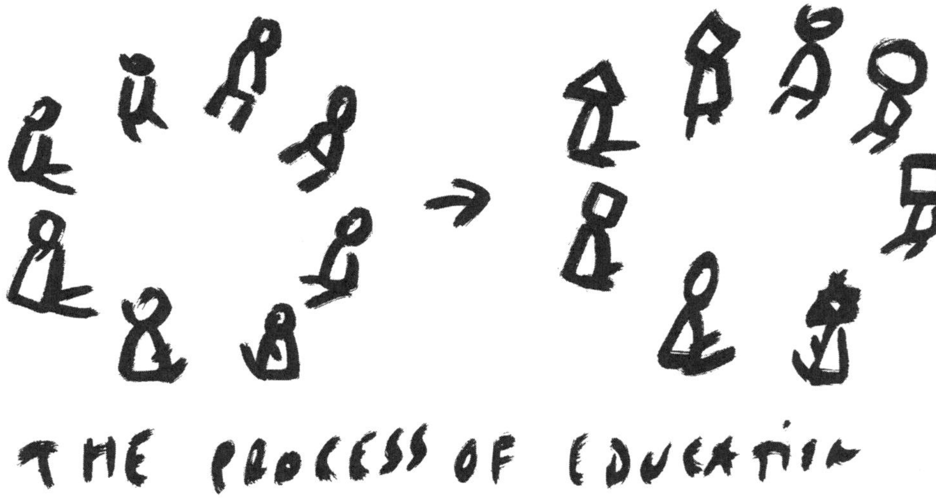
THE PROCESS OF EDUCATION

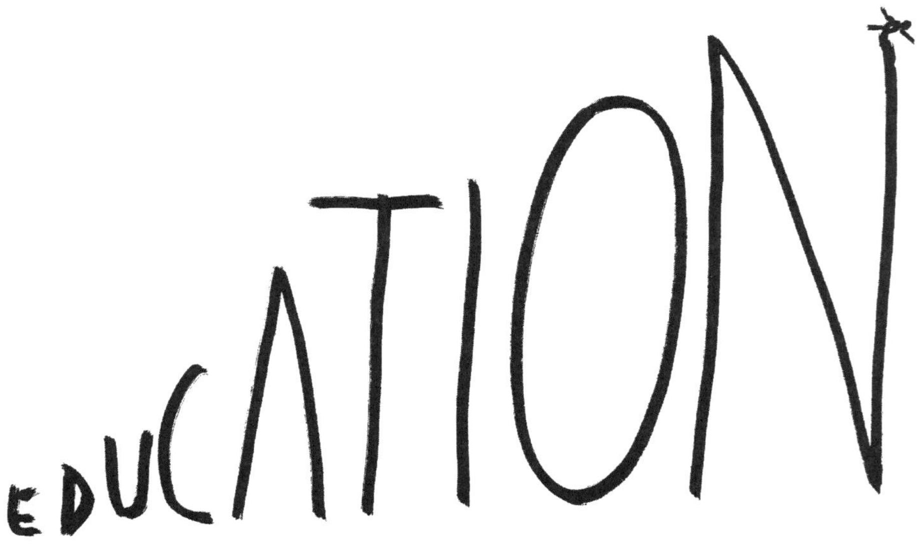
EDUCATION

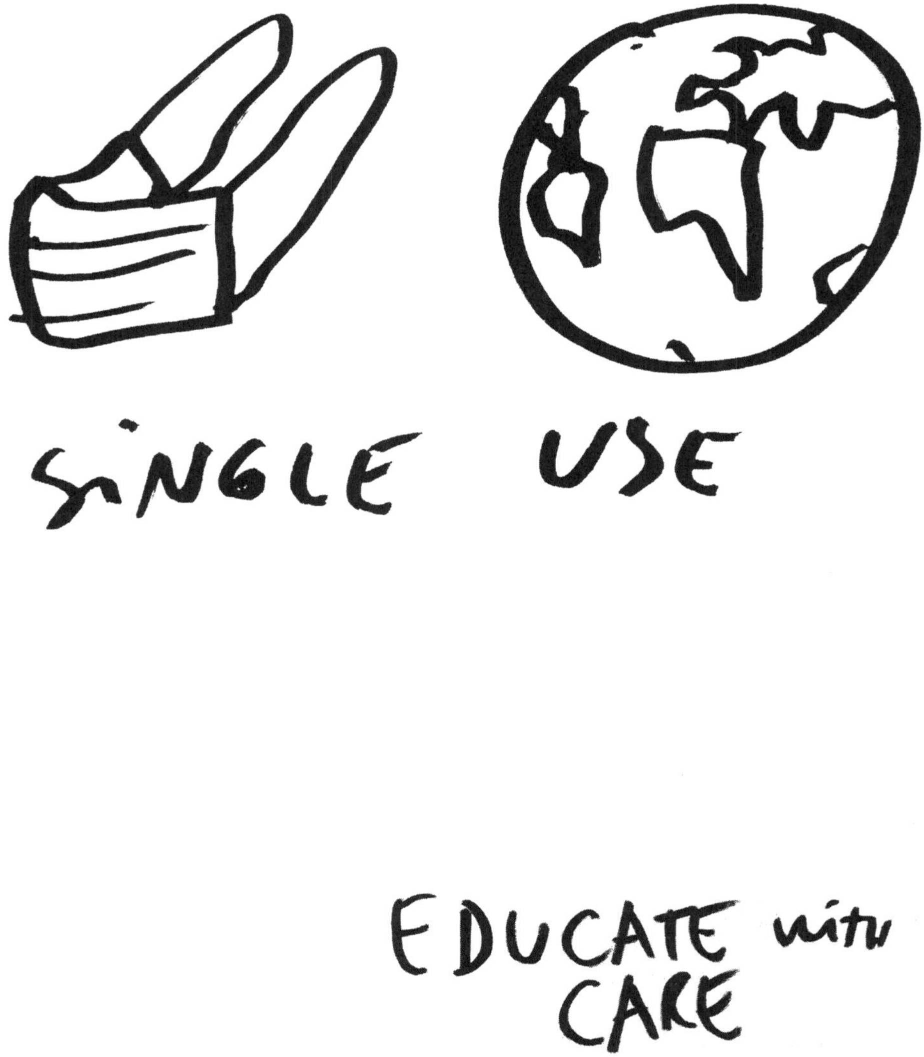
SINGLE USE
EDUCATE with CARE

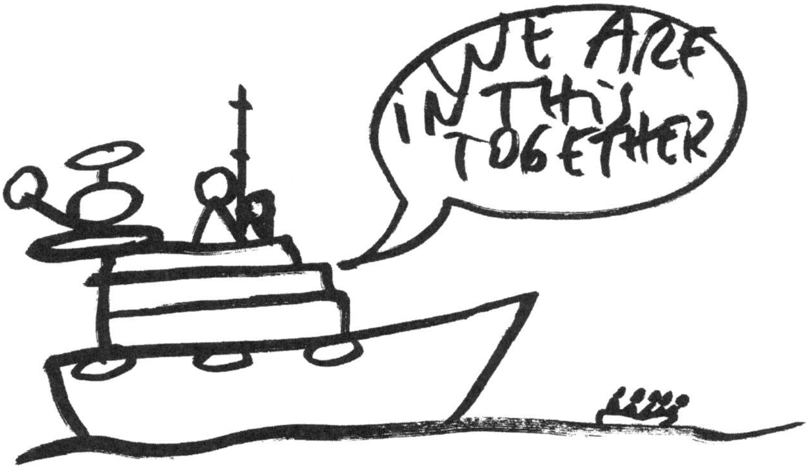
WE ARE
IN THIS
TOGETHER

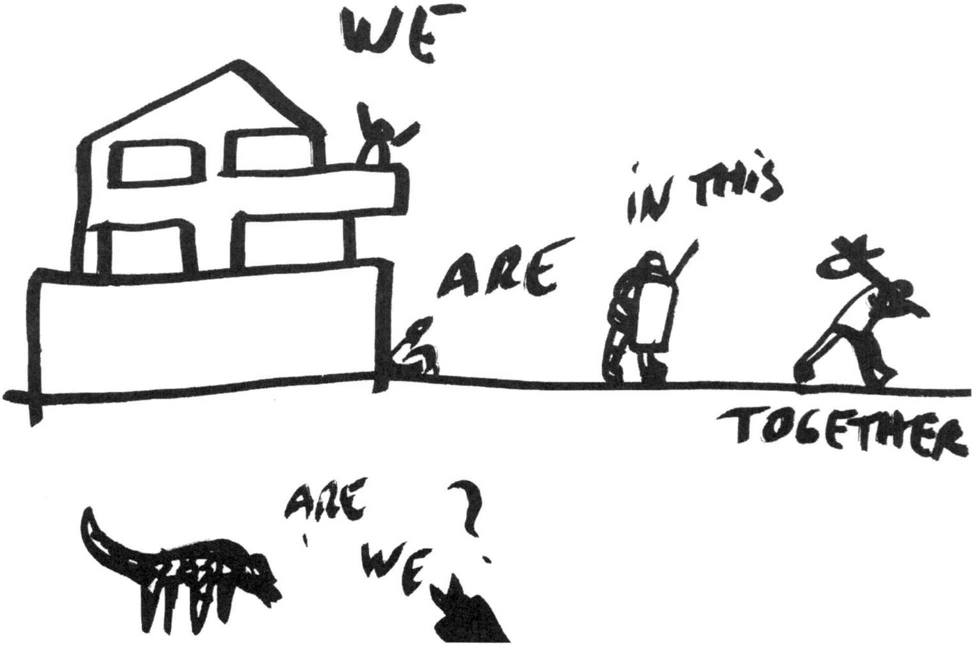
WE
ARE
IN THIS
TOGETHER
ARE
WE
?

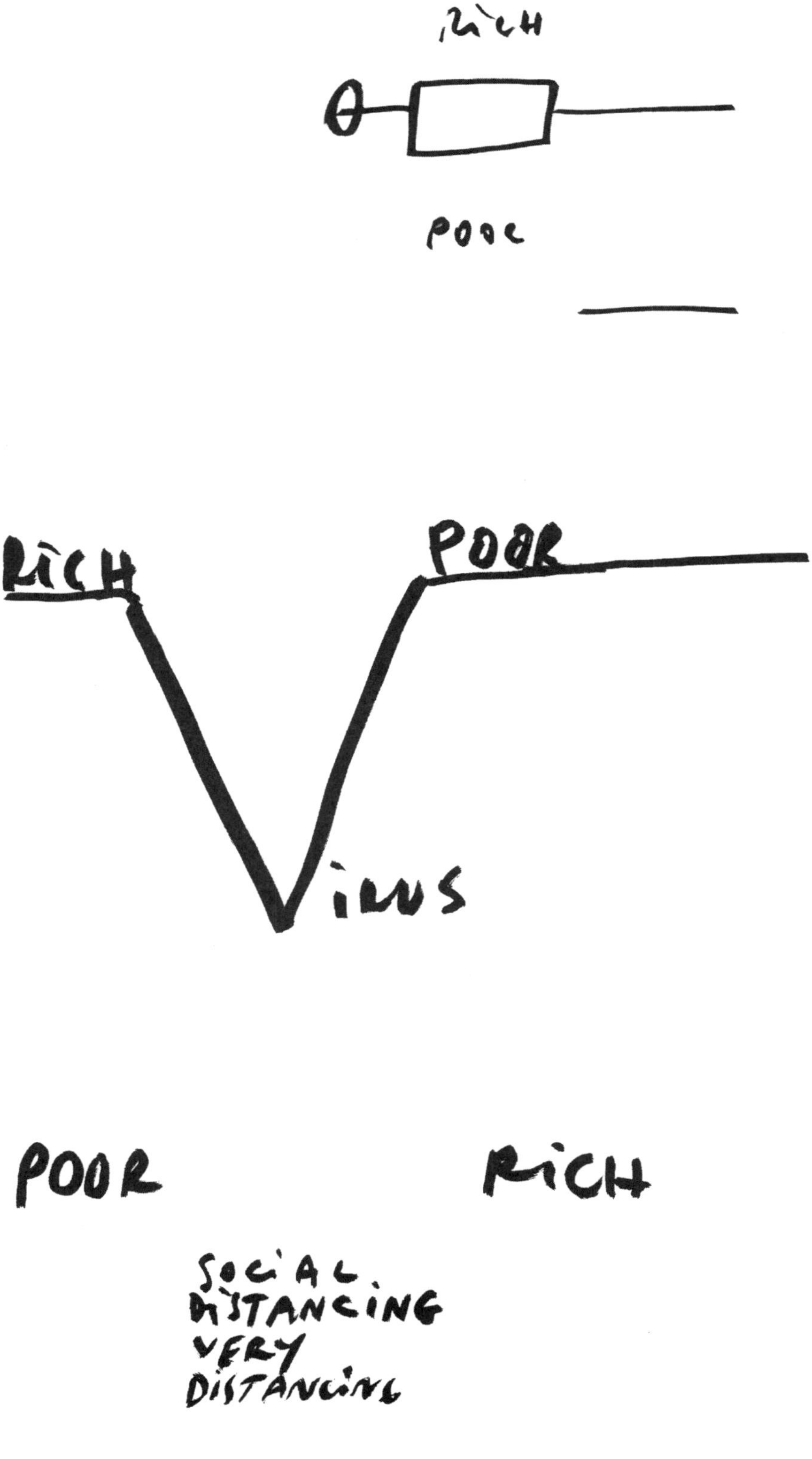
RICH
POOR
RICH
POOR
VIRUS
POOR
RICH
SOCIAL
DISTANCING
VERY
DISTANCING

Meet Me at 120 bpm

—Jammers

A: How do schools of fish swim in harmony? No single fish is in control, but every fish is in charge. In other words, each individual fish sticks together and swims together. I thought about how swimming in the ocean is similar to jamming. The school emerges when you have a certain number of fish following a unique set of local rules: keep swimming and stay close to your neighbor (but not too close). It's not because they like each other that much—it's a matter of survival.

Emergence: You can't understand it by taking it apart. If we reduce the school of fish to individuals, they will be eaten by predators. When many different species of fish swim casually, looking for food, the collective noun is a "shoal" of fish. Even if they're swimming independently, they behave as if they're connected. If they're shoaling, they're performing for a specific social reason (food, shelter, camouflage, etc.). As people, what are our reasons for jamming?

What is the Jamming Station?

How did we get here? What happened? What's inside? Who is the Jamming Station for? Between June 17 and 27, 2021, Rijksakademie Open Studios opened its doors to the public. This isn't unusual in and of itself, as this is an event that runs annually—being, most notably, one of the few times the Rijksakademie van beeldende kunsten, Amsterdam, and its studios (of the resident artists) are opened to the public. However, what made it unusual this time is that it took place in the midst of the ever-evolving-always-ongoing and precarious COVID-19 pandemic. It also happened at the beginning of summer as opposed to during the cold and looming winter month of November, as it usually does. In this way, the host site for what would come to be called the Jamming Station had been set up not only for that particular month and season, but continuously through the earlier jamming that occurred in many different forms throughout 2020 and 2021 in the same building.

The Jamming Station is an exercise in jamming by providing, activating, and managing a temporary communal space, albeit with restricted access and functionality, to jam. To jam is to come together. To come to the Jamming Station can also be to come to a space to rest or to take a break from one's journey around the routes of the Rijksakademie during the Open Studios event.

It is worth mentioning that during Open Studios 2021, the public had to pass through the Jamming Station before they could see the resident artists' studios, which consist of another forty-plus spaces. Open Studios happened when the COVID-19 regulations allowed three people per studio (with an exception of ten people permitted in the Jamming Station, due to its size) and always wearing a mask indoors. However, in the middle of the Open Studios event, the regulations were relaxed: five people could be in the same studio and were no longer required to wear a mask.

Despite the Jamming Station being the first stop on the tour route, many hosts and guests didn't necessarily experience it according to this design. While some visitors encountered it first, others didn't visit it until the middle or end of their journeys. Some didn't even notice there was a Jamming Station, because the door was closed.

As to when the door was opened or closed, there was no schedule. The Jamming Station had no particular timetable for when it was supposed to be activated; it happened when it happened. It takes at least two people to start jamming: one opens the door and turns on the equipment, and the next person enters the Jamming Station and starts playing with some instruments and then finds themselves submerged into the activity. In a way, the activation of the Jamming Station depends not just on the requirements for jamming, but also on one's availability of time and energy to be at the Jamming Station in the first place.

S: When we had all set up the Jamming Station, I think it was intended as a pre-rest room, because it comes before the more attention-demanding aspects of the building and event [of Open Studios].

T: It [the Jamming Station] was a space which related to the idea of opening our door/studio/mind/heart/ears. The Rijksakademie Open Studios in relation to the Jamming Station was about the idea of being ready to be a good host. Guests typically don't have the same intensity as us [hosts] because the input is so different.

If it's a wedding, for example, we are the house wedding band who have to entertain the guests. But the difference is that it's not ... It's discussed in the previous conversation[1] that we are the public, too. We are also the public of our own Jamming Station. We are already in the same position; we are no longer private in that sense. When someone new joins the room, it liberates us from being gatekeepers or merely audiences as well. Though, it's a bit different for us because we are familiar with the space. But during the jam, when it's happening, we are the players and spectators. We perform both roles at the same time. Inward-looking, deeper in, and still trying to understand and be self-reflective. This inward-looking approach is always in relation to what's happening outside.

S: And what's happening outside?

T: 2020. Clubs weren't open during that time. There wasn't any shared acoustic space for amplified sound amongst us that was accessible or even legal to do.

What is inside?

A drum set from Takeshi Ikeda, an organ from Simnikiwe Buhlungu, an organ from Özgür Atlagan, an electric guitar from Sungeun Lee, an electric bass from Diana Cantarey, an accordion from Daniel Aguilar Ruvalcaba, a shaker sculpture from Salim Bayri, a painting from Anh Trần, a poster from Penelope Koliopoulou, an electric keyboard from Togar, a reel-to-reel tape player from Simnikiwe Buhlungu, a painting from Salim Bayri,

1 The QR code leads to the Jamming Station's online material. The "previous conversation" mentioned is titled "Germination-State #04: Continue on jamming, on pajamas." This text was first published in (or is a re-edit and/or continuation of the conversation published in): Irene de Craen, Taylor Le Melle, and Natasha Soobramanien, eds., *We Had Plans* (Amsterdam: Rijksakademie van beeldende kunsten, 2021, 119–24). This book was published on the occasion of the 150th year of the Rijksakademie van beeldende kunsten, which happened to coincide with a global pandemic, during which resident artists continued to work collaboratively as well as individually on their respective practices, while also navigating what could be called expanded practice.

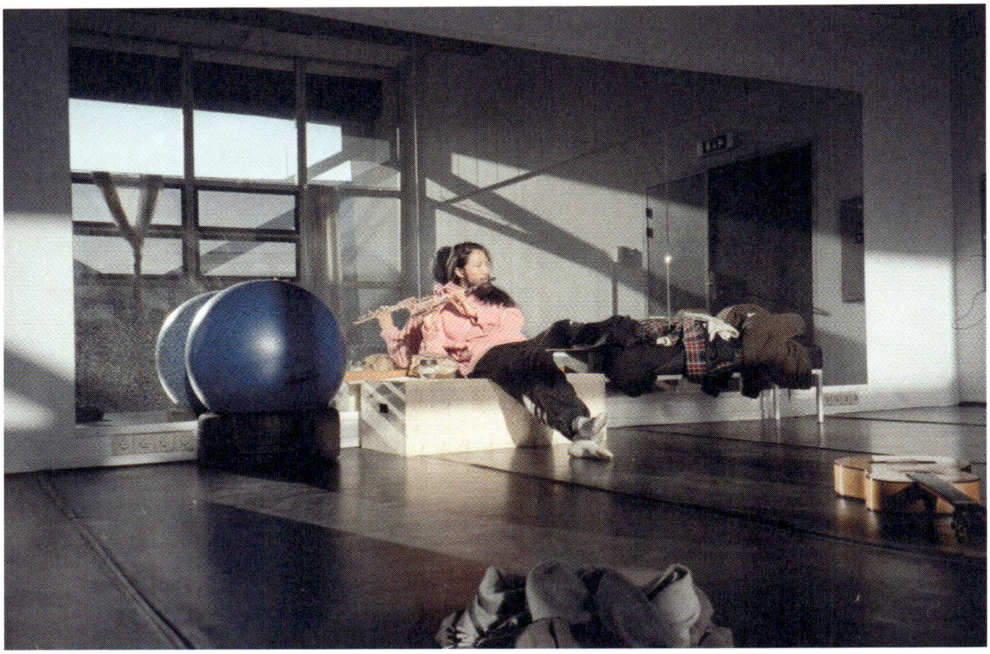

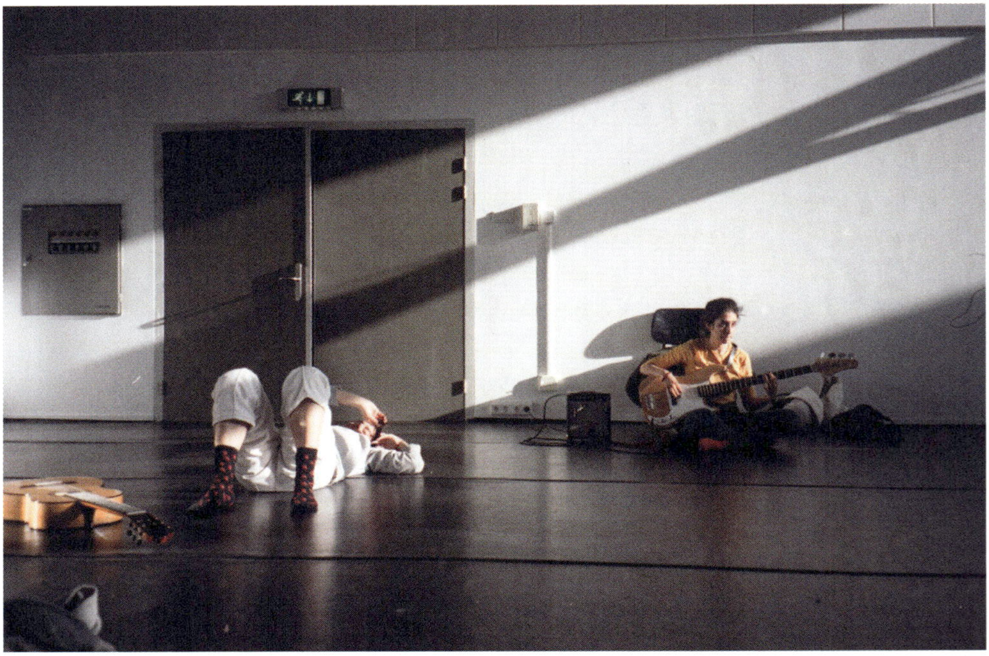

The Jamming Station at Rijksakademie Open Studios 2021
PHOTOS: Özgür Atlagan

a cardboard sign from Togar, a flute from Sungeun Lee, a surdo from Togar, fidget tubes and other musical instruments from Molly Palmer, a keyboard from Mette Sterre, chimes from Silvia Martes, clay sculptures and a collage from Tropical Tap Water, a sofa from Togar, wise words from Yazan Khalili, conviviality from Aldo Esparza Ramos and Tessa Mars, and microphones, mixers, cables, an amplifier, microphones, and microphone stands from the Rijksakademie Media Lab.

The musical instruments and equipment as well as paintings, posters, and sculptures voluntarily contributed by the various artists-in-residence somehow became the foundation of the Jamming Station.

For the usual jammers at the Rijksakademie, the Jamming Station, too, became an opportunity to continue the conversation around and on jamming. Why do we do it? Are we comfortable jamming in front of or with the public? Who is the public? What about the pandemic measures? Do we need to constantly clean the instruments with alcohol wipes so the next person entering the space can play them safely? What about our privacy? Who will be activating the Jamming Station from day one to day ten? Should we work in pairs? What about the number of jammers allowed in one room?

To prepare how we would operate the Jamming Station, we came together a month prior to Open Studios. We discussed things like how to feel comfortable in the space, how our sound could be made equal, and also how we, as the hosts of the Jamming Station, wanted to be perceived. We also decided where the drum set should be positioned, where the organ would sit best, and where the keyboard, the amplifier, the microphones, the sofa, the paintings, the posters, the sculptures, etc., should go.

D: I like to see how many different forms the jam has taken: jam in the Daylight Studio, radio, sparkling tap water, tropical tap water, agua mala, foamy jamming, hair cutting ... Like a broken gold vessel. How long could its pieces be left on the floor, with nobody sweeping them away? Or was it gonna be that someone would step on them and continue distributing their matter, like dust all around the cosmic carpet?

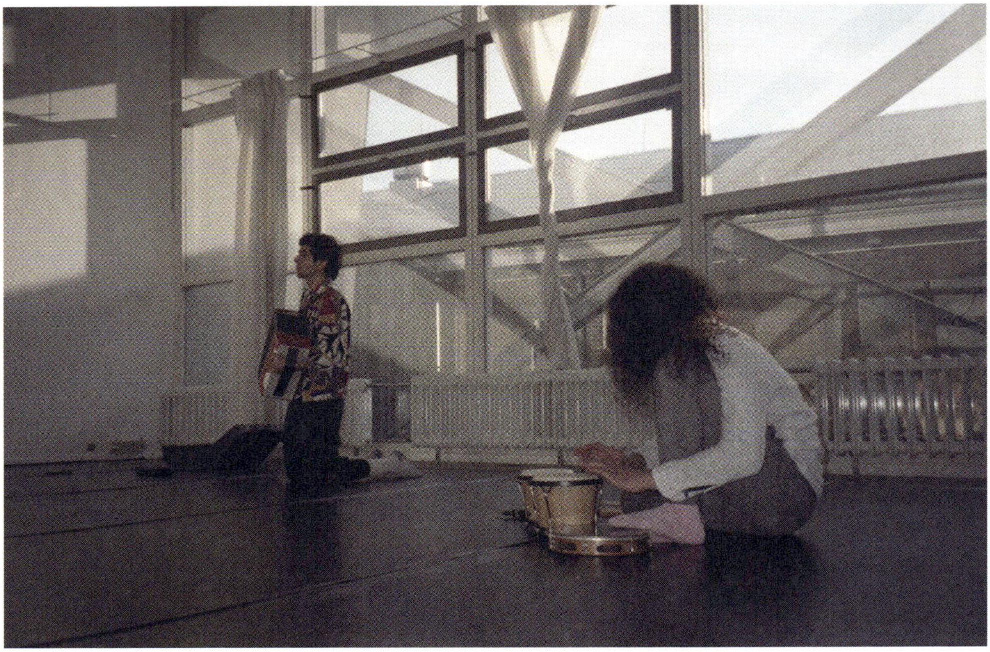

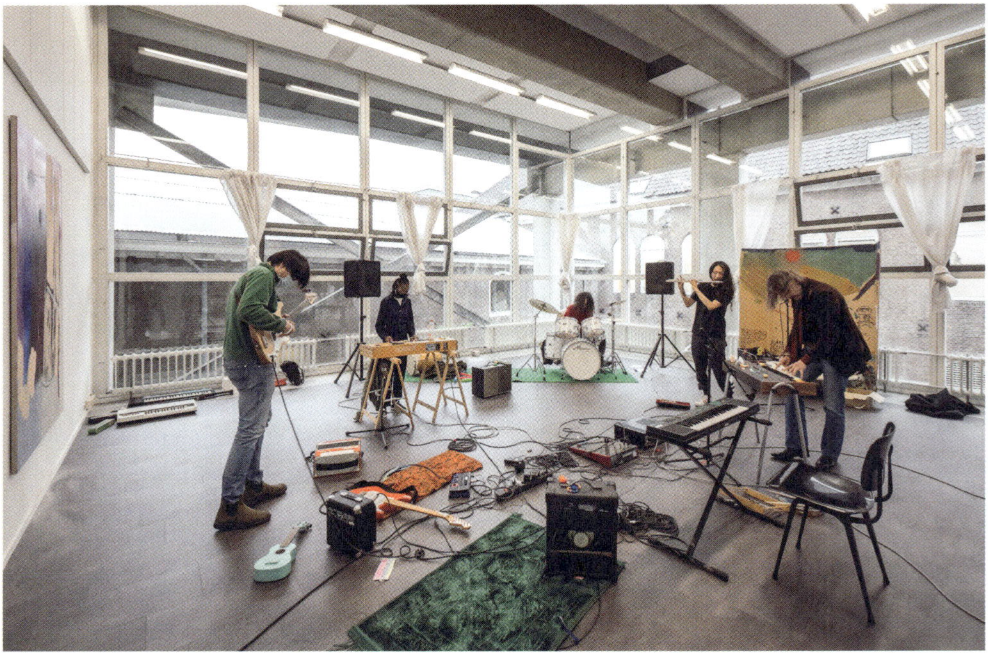

The Jamming Station at Rijksakademie Open Studios 2021
PHOTO (TOP): Özgür Atlagan
PHOTO (BOTTOM): Sander van Wettum

Who is it for?

There is a nonpermanence and a porosity to the various roles inside the Jamming Station: hosts and guests, listeners and players, convenors and contributors, askers and answerers. This is largely because the Jamming Station isn't a site of binaries—at least, it doesn't aim to be—and thus it is less about who is what and does what and more about what happens after we arrive in the same space. Ideally, the Jamming Station is for everyone.

Of course, one might argue and say that because we, the resident artists, set up the space, borrowed the equipment, prepared the installation, and cleaned and sanitized the instruments, we assumed the "role" of host in the name of technicianship, and so we are the ones who had autonomy and agency in steering the direction of the space. In recognition of this structure, which is maintained largely because the Jamming Station was based in our home at the Rijksakademie, it is easy to understand why the attempt at blurring the roles of "host" and "guest" might seem pedantic, if not futile. However, there is something admirable—and perhaps endearing—in offering up a space intended for private use (such as the Daylight and performance studio) to do something completely different: to be a hangout spot, a children's playroom, a space where tired visitors can nap, a meeting point for lost visitors, a "lost property" center, a space to take a break from art, a something room, a nothing room. Aside from yielding visual and sonic outputs, the Jamming Station existed as a site of publicly engaged possibilities within the context of the Rijksakademie Open Studios 2021.

T: ... because we are talking about how in a larger sense jamming is about the memory. The tendency to record.

S: Yes, this is a good one. The tendency to record. Because, I can't tell you when the first time we recorded the jam session was. When we did, I don't think it was with the intention to be heard; I think it's more an impulse to record something impulsive, and not to be heard.

T: But I think it also comes from the worry of it being lost, and being undocumented, because it is something where it cannot be predicted what's gonna happen; therefore to not record it [leaves] this impulsive behavior unanswered.

S: Do you think recording is a way to capture "what if" moments? To know that you have the recording going for that few seconds of bliss?

Considering that this activity of communal jamming was spawned in a moment of uncertainty and global pause, considering that we bought instruments either based on the need for specific sounds in our artistic practices or for personal desire, considering that, for us, jamming was a pastime and a way to get to know one another in a new country and new arts institution, it's quite difficult to articulate the sheer joy in seeing the Jamming Station grow its own legs and live its own life. And to live its own life not only in the constraints of the Rijksakademie, or the pandemic for that matter, but for it to become a truly public experience.

As mentioned earlier, lineage is a significant part of thinking about the Jamming Station. There were many exponents who defined its structure, and then there was this present moment, when, through the articulation of the pandemic, gathering and sharing an acoustic space changed. We jammed in studios, made food together, created clay sculptures together, had endless Zoom meetings, added and subtracted instruments, navigated laws and regulations, sustained resilience through jamming in response to pause—all so that the Jamming Station could come into being. So, that lineage and narrative is quite important.

T: Yes. We found the mechanism. That's what I will bring to the future: "Jamming happened in 2020." You know. That's how I think of it and will take it into the future. But for 2021, it's more "Jamming Station"—

S: It's the openness, no?

T: Ja. It's an evolution. It's what you said; it cannot happen without the lineage. Maybe there will be jamming in 2022, or outside of

Rijks, or when this is published, they'll invite us to jam [laughs]. Whatever! You know. Or we can install it. I don't know. The Jamming Station is a reflection of the willingness to do things together. You know.

The Jamming Station is a space that, by design, is meant to be shared. To play, to converse, to be loud, to allow oneself to not worry about making a mistake, a space to have a break from the mundane and the redundant. In that, it would be fitting to have the Jamming Station permanently installed at the Rijksakademie. At other art institutions and schools of varying levels. At corporate offices. At cultural monuments. At public transport stations. At health care facilities. It would be nice to live in a world where the Jamming Station continues on as part of our daily life. A space where one can enter and be together with others to jam.

[QUICK SIDEBAR: Yazan enters the room. It's an interesting conversation. Now we're talking about breaking power dynamics, about the jammer becoming a guest and the guests becoming the jammer. "Jamming is not a given," says Yazan. "There is a buildup and an entry, and once you enter it ... then you are there. Then the space is more fluid. Then it becomes this tradition of entering the room and not necessarily the actual jamming," he says. We bid him farewell.]

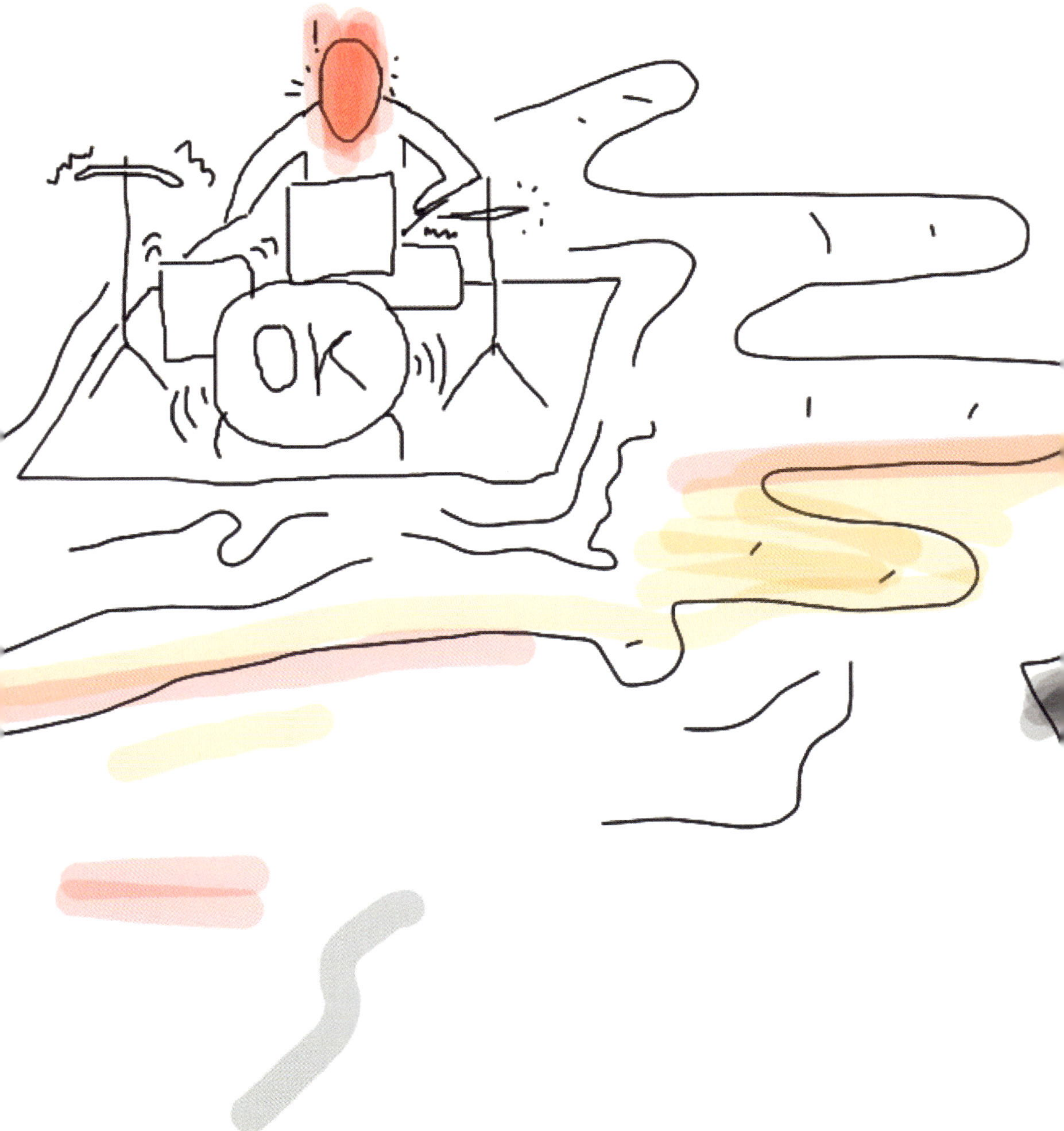

Pages 212–17: Jammers, *Collective Drawing Jam*, 2021

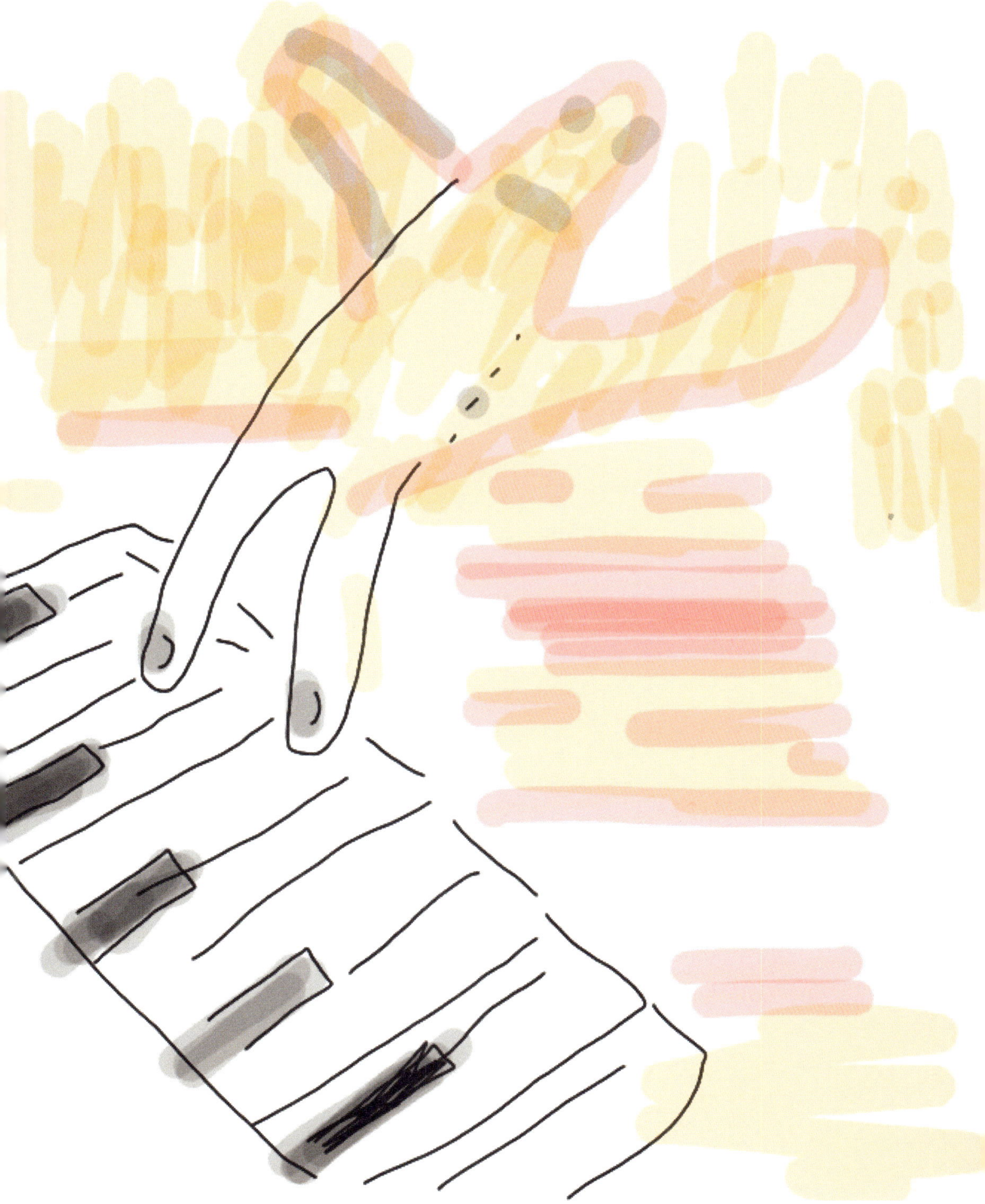

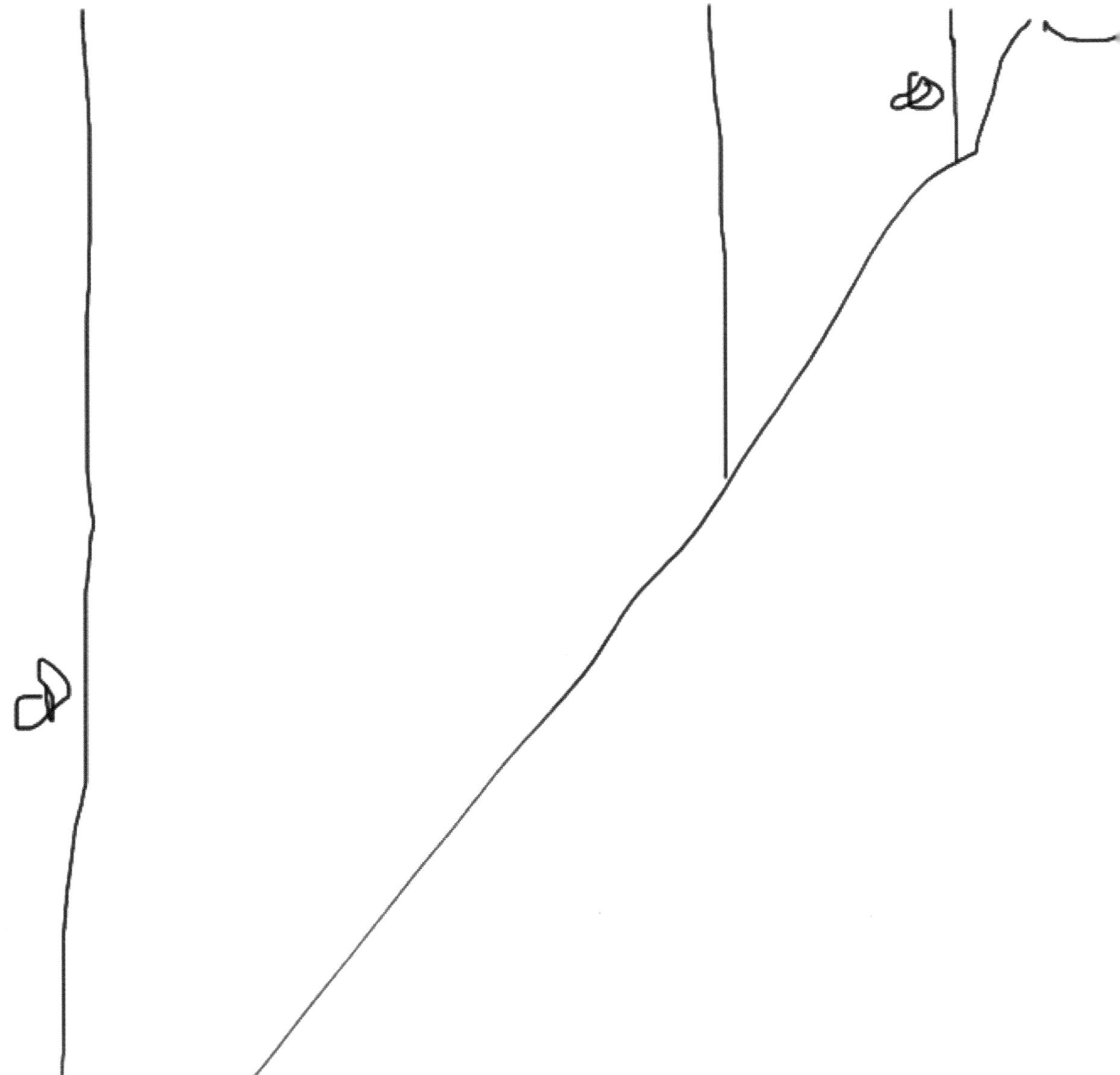

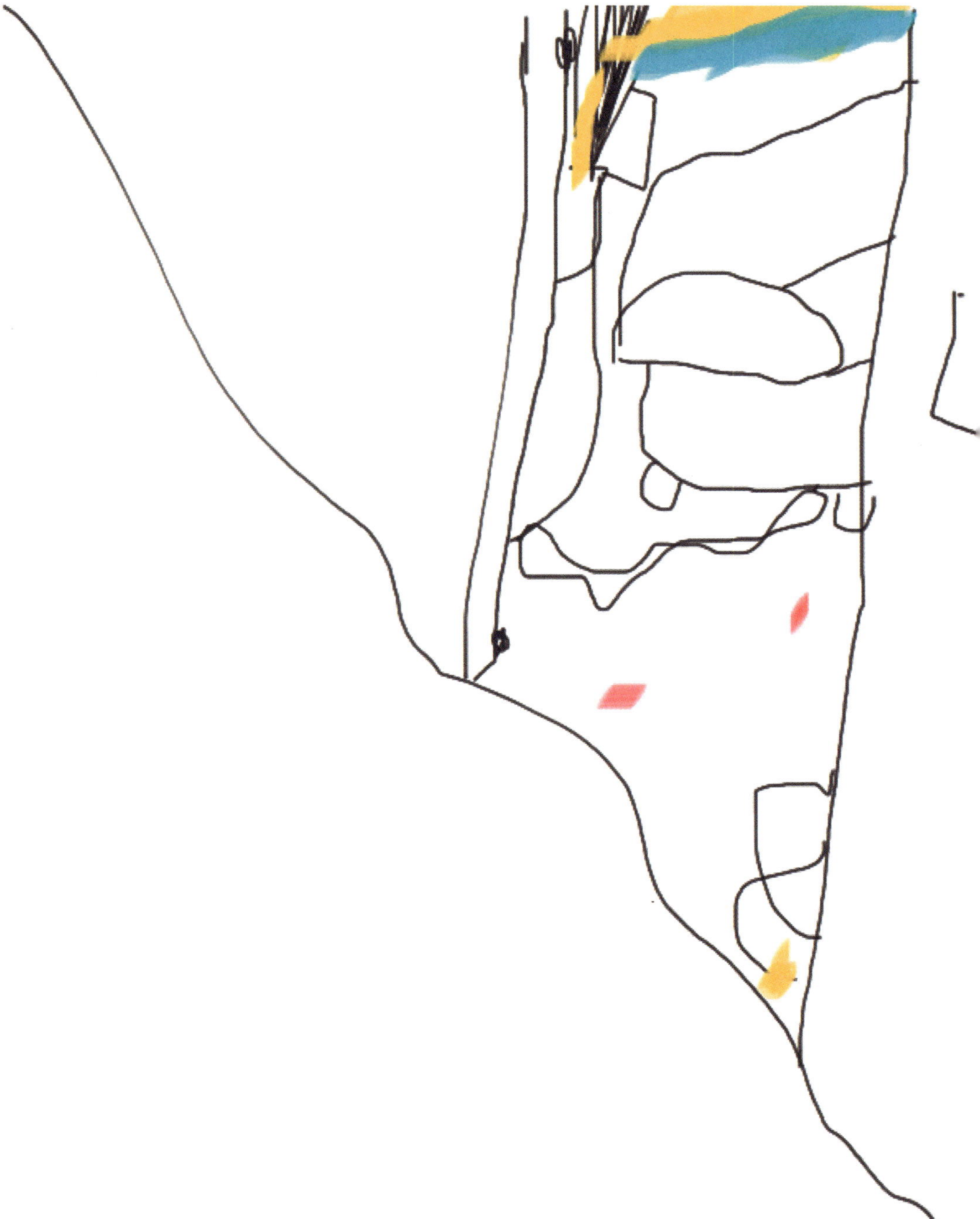

THAN

T O T

D

K YOU

tE

2UMS

Learning Strangeness

—Marina Garcés

Before they end up succumbing to burnout, today's students, workers, citizens, and consumers are first hounded by incessant demands for creativity, innovation, learning, and training. Since the onset of the COVID-19 pandemic, the language around self-reinvention has shifted to that of managing one's boundaries, with increasing cautiousness, since many have burned out part way through this process of reinvention. Even Simone Biles, the gymnast of the century, struggled to cope at the first Olympics of the post-pandemic era. And she's not the only one—millions of young people are suffering with poor mental health and thousands of workers are quitting their jobs, not only out of anxiety and fear but also because they do not want the "old normal" to ever come back.

Regardless of whether it results in success or failure, the imposed logic is the same: uncertainty itself is the only thing you can be certain of, at least when it comes to categorizing and evaluating life opportunities. In order to survive amid all this uncertainty, "learning" now means learning how to react quickly and effectively to whatever life throws at you, without breaking down. What kind of learning is this? It might seem open-ended and imaginative, but it actually underpins a new form of subordination: that of "adaptive servitude." When control takes the form of tireless calls for creativity, and even cooperation, how can the theoretical and practical languages of emancipation be articulated today?

The Instrument of Strangeness

The form of control obtained through means of uncertainty and instability demands novel responses that, at the same time, must guarantee security. That is, if you can successfully negotiate this overbearing uncertainty, you stay in the game: one more life is offered up to the market of opportunities. Producing something new, then, is the best way to prop up the existing state of affairs, and thus ensure its ongoing reproduction. This is the paradox of post-disciplinary capitalism, which uses the classic tools of obedience to segregate and repress, but not to bolster rights, support lives, or let projects flourish. Disruptive capitalism strengthens and reproduces its power via the logics of emergency and exception. This explains why, so often, any critique of hegemonic culture provokes responses that lean toward conservatism and the need to find continuities, rather than elements of change and transformation.

So, when we try to imagine other possible modes of doing, what might they be like? Emancipation is not a state of bliss, nor is it a promise of salvation. It is, rather, a relationship with the limits of control. To subvert these limits, the first step is learning how to perceive them. The writer and philosopher Albert Camus links the act of rebellion with the perceiving of a hitherto unapparent limit, after which collective dignity is duly called into question. In the same vein, another philosopher, Gilles Deleuze, notes the change in sensibility when something normal suddenly becomes intolerable, a situation that had previously gone unnoticed. Enlightenment-era thinking, which held sway up until Karl Marx, linked this potential of the limit with an exercise in awareness: to know in order to take action, to learn in order to transform. But, today, we could potentially claim that we know it all, and simply being aware of our world's current demands and limitations is no longer enough if we want to get by. We are apprentices in an imposed reality, one that is somehow both uncertain and irreversible. What, then, is capable of triggering such a change in our perception of limits?

The philosopher Gayatri Spivak writes that the imagination is the "instrument of othering."[1] The instrument of strangeness. I prefer to interpret "othering," here, as "strangeness" rather than "alterity." Alterity refers to the self/other binary, and it is thus linked with the semantic and political framework of identity. Strangeness, though, situates us within a different geography of limits: somewhere between the commonplace and the unusual, the familiar and the uncanny, between what we know and what we can't quite fathom. Strangeness is not clear-cut; it forces us to look closer, to dig deeper. It can come from a place of curiosity or discomfort, and it blends desire with fear. As such, whenever we perceive strangeness, it makes us feel strange, too. Just as acknowledging the other's alterity can be a way of affirming our own identity, the appearance of something strange makes us aware of the limits of our own frame of perception. This is why experiencing strangeness invariably sparks the imagination.

Spivak talks of the imagination as an instrument. If the magnifying glass is for enhancing vision, and if scales are for gauging weight, then the imagination is for revealing that the normal is in fact strange. The imagination shakes up the inertias of familiarity, challenging all our default or imposed assumptions and routines: it exposes us to all those things that otherwise pass us by. “This tastes strange” is what we say about a food we can’t quite place, when it’s still in our mouth and our brain’s neurons are darting around, searching for something to associate it with. Meanwhile, either we imagine that we have ingested something harmful, and we get scared, or perhaps we decide we have discovered a nice new flavor, and our curiosity is piqued. Similarly, when we come across a face that does not have the expected proportion or expression, or when we hear an idea that is not immediately acceptable, or when we are invited to move in a new way that breaks our body’s habits and reveals its coyness or clumsiness, we suddenly turn, for a moment, into that curious tongue, rolling around between desire and panic as it keeps on tasting that strange new thing, with no way back. That tongue is the instrument of the imagination.

Captured Imagination

The novelist George Orwell *imagined the imagination* as an animal in captivity, one that stops reproducing and soon dies. Centuries beforehand, Saint Teresa of Ávila referred to the imagination as a playful little lizard or a nocturnal butterfly, sneaking in between the window bars when we least expect it. Both images involve bars and captivity, but in opposite ways: for Orwell, the imagination is something that languishes behind bars, whereas for Saint Teresa the imagination arrives to shake up, with all its playfulness, the time we spend locked up in our domestic or domesticated prisons. They are not really opposing images, because both understand that the relationship between the imagination and the limits (the bars) is about being able to break through. The imagination dies only when the enclosure is absolute.

In his fiction, Orwell describes totalitarian configurations of power, their forms of governance, and their languages. Saint Teresa wrote about the houses, palaces, and monasteries where the religious and political power of her time was closely guarded, so that nothing unexpected could possibly get in and disturb the spirit. Saint Teresa also founded a network of convents where the doors did not entirely close. Pity the house where a lizard cannot sneak in. Or pity the lizard that can’t get out again.

Since today's power structures are now based on uncertainty, it might feel like there is no prison, no barred window, no locked house, and no captivity. All that's left is a harsh and stormy outdoors, where we must seek out fleeting shelter or powerful tools to aid us in this constant ordeal. In times of uncertainty, the imagination thrives. In times of danger, creativity increases. This is what feeds, orders, and produces the cognitive and economic programs of current capitalism, from basic education all the way up to global management. We could talk about how much imagination we need, today, to stay afloat in these waters, and we might get into a terminological (and political) debate about the differences between imagination, fantasy, creativity, and mere reaction. But if we look at the issue more carefully, we will find that imagination is being held captive in two ways.

Apocalyptic imagination

When any imaginable limit takes on the sense of an ending, it gives rise to what I have referred to, elsewhere, as the "apocalyptic dogma."[2] Under this dogma, the collapse of civilization is not just imaginable but irreversible. Historical events become prophecies, and prophecies (whatever they may refer to) only ever herald the end of the world. History becomes destiny, facts become oracles; the future is doomed and we become victims instead of subjects.

The famous quip that "it's easier to imagine the end of the world than the end of capitalism" has been repeated so often that we no longer know who to attribute it to. But is it really quite so straightforward? What world does this maxim refer to? And who is doing the imagining here? The relationship between us and the world, the one underlying the phrase, is described as a totality (all of us imagine the end of the whole world), but it does not interrogate its own point of view. Who is speaking in this phrase, and on whose behalf? Imagining possible worlds, such as those that have been destroyed by the present one, or those that we could create were it not for the current limits, is overshadowed by that one representation of totality: the world's complete annihilation.

In October 2021, as I write these words, we are in the midst of living through a global pandemic, but the modes of production, consumption, and work remain unchanged. Furthermore, we are in fact heading back into the same normality we left behind, albeit far more aware, this time around, of its sheer impossibility (this being a more accurate term than the ambiguous "unsustainability"). The government of Austria recently announced its plan to ready its population for a Europe-wide power blackout, an event forecasted to occur sometime before 2025. To modify the aforementioned maxim, we could say that it's easier to imagine such a blackout than the measures that might prevent it. In terms of educating the population, from children right up to broad social behavior patterns, this suggests that we are taught to accept the inevitability of damage rather than how not to cause it in the first place. Using the imagination as a social and collective practice for outlining other possible worlds is thus reduced to one single possibility: All or nothing. Doom or salvation. The world as we know it or apocalypse. We no longer limit ourselves to imagining specific, individual collapses. As we catastrophize, under this tyranny of totality, what collapses is imagination itself: it withers away, just like Orwell's listless and sterile animal, trapped in captivity.

Disruptive imagination

The other side of this imagination, amid its own total collapse, is imagination as the endless production of creative responses to uncertain situations. Today, creativity and innovation are part of a paradigm that not only needs to produce novelty but also must take place within an ever changing framework and system of references. That's why I call it "disruptive." The imagination, as the ability to perceive and transgress the limits of the possible, is thus trapped, as it is being forced to work in contradictory, perverse ways. Instead of an art of negotiating limits, imagining becomes the limitless producing of images for a disjointed reality.

There are many overt examples of this relationship between imagination and disruption. In teaching, it is not only clear, but in fact explicit: the brightest pupil, today, is the one who successfully studies for the future—and yet, according to some, we have literally no idea what that future will be like. Periodically, experts and media claim that around 80 percent of the jobs and professions that will soon dominate the labor market do not yet exist. We read such numbers, but we tend not to imagine them. If we try to imagine what that 80 percent means, we can immediately tell that either the corresponding study is false or that it labels certain future professions as "not yet existing" instead of, quite simply, evolving out of ones we already have today. Yet the message gets through, and we take it on board: we lifelong students (as we all are now) don't really know why we are studying, other than to acquire skills that might help us adapt better to a fickle social reality. Studying for a future that we know nothing about means, on a deeper level and with political consequences, accepting that we will play no role in the construction or creation of that future. Otherwise, we would perhaps know something about, at least, its fulfilled or unfulfilled potential. This arrangement might seem like a release of sorts, like a freeing from responsibility, but it is more like a condemning to servitude or, more specifically, to adaptive servitude. Similarly, migratory processes today are not just about one dangerous journey—which the migrant might or might not complete—for these processes also entail migrants' incorporation, often for life, into a system that constantly processes them in terms of in/out, in terms of being/not being. As a result, the migrant is then forced to undertake the never-ending, limitless task of managing their own existence with regard to regulations and legislation.

Adaptive servitude is the antithesis of being trained for strangeness, as proposed by Spivak. In today's world, defined as it is by permanent disruption, no room exists for experimenting with strangeness. Strangeness emerges, precisely, wherever there is a potential relationship between what we know and what we don't. What exists in that space between knowing and not knowing? It is, in fact, the work of the imagination. Imagination is the living link between what there is and what there isn't, between the known and the unknown, the certain and the uncertain. Training for strangeness means, then, once again considering the imagination's work as an art of limits, one that lets us shape contested worlds. We do not want a blackout. But neither do we simply want to defend the status quo. If we are to stop being servants to uncertainty, we must become apprentices of strangeness.

Learning to Read (Again)

There's nothing stranger than listening to a child as they learn how to read. The words and expressions they otherwise use with great verbal agility suddenly regress, and the child starts babbling, monotonously. It's like a not-very-human voice struggling to advance through the terrain of meaning, traversing a dense forest where everything is obscure and unfamiliar: the forest of the written word. But compared to a child learning to read, the way illiterate people react to written text is even more disconcerting. Their faces fill with discomfort and shame, and their inability reveals, at the same time, an expropriation and a humiliation. Illiterate people are denied access to something they know is theirs: language, and all it expresses, locked up behind those little arbitrary signs.

Given how the written word expropriates language, the battle for literacy has been a key practice of emancipation in a range of contexts. These include popular and revolutionary movements, women's groups, autodidacticism, and learning groups of people deemed unproductive, such as elderly people. The philosopher and educator Paulo Freire practiced and analyzed the power of literacy in all its facets: as he saw it, literacy is not just about learning how to read the dominant written text but also about the chance to probe it, to enter into dialogue with its meaning, and to debate its consequences.

The activity of reading, when reduced to literalness, is often presented as a matter of mere recognition: to recognize written words in order to obey them. To read while nodding along, as sacred texts are read. Or to read mechanically, just as we are encouraged to do at school: the education system's superficial textbooks are invariably designed for learning without asking any questions. These are all ways of trying to reduce reading to literalness. "You've not read that very well" is the teacher's disapproving summary, and we are forced to read it again.

"Reading well," in contrast to our teacher's admonition, is in fact about creating a strange language for the written word. With a babbling voice, a distant gaze, an inquisitive attitude, an unexpected response: reading awakens and trains the imagination. This is not because it invites us to conjure up or enter worlds unlike our own, but rather quite the opposite: it allows us to cross the limits of our world, without being held back by them. There is another famous phrase, this time by feminist civil rights activist Audre Lorde, which says, “The master’s tools will never dismantle the master’s house.” But I’m not so sure. Reading is a contested community, and it goes beyond the dichotomy of inclusion/exclusion or approval/rejection. Learning to read makes us strangers among strangers. That’s why I feel it is crucial, today, that the emancipatory practice of becoming literate should extend to all areas of life. If the future looks dark, that’s because our present has turned opaque: even if we know how to read the words, we don’t know how to read our world, our times, all our different forms of knowledge.

Encountering Strangeness

Strangeness cannot be planned. It is always the effect of an encounter with something that challenges or distorts what we know, what we expect, or what we recognize. I earlier noted how unsettling a strange flavor can be, whereby we turn into a tongue that laps at the edges of danger or discovery. That tongue is a muscle of the imagination, and the act of tasting provides a useful reference image when it comes to situating ourselves, in an embodied and practical way, within a relation of learning. Here, the critical imagination allows us to learn how to read the limits of our present without being held back by them.

Imagining the world

Imagination and fantasy are not the same thing. Fantasy works with the absence of limits, whereas the imagination explores what can happen when we have a looser relationship with them. If the world itself is a boundary, if we use the term “world” to mean “finite” (as opposed to the “infinite universe”), then imagining the world entails acknowledging its limits as an inherent part of our lives, rather than as an imposition. Humankind has imagined many different possible forms for the world—for this earthly world, but also for the world of each individual. The Latin for “world,” *mundus*, stems from the term for “cleanliness and neatness,” and it could even refer to the jewelry box where people’s most valuable belongings were kept. Imagining the world can be an invitation to play around like this: little children fill boxes and treasure chests with the things they stumble upon, from broken bits and bobs and stones to bottle caps and any other such trinkets from the worlds of others. Thinking about these containers, packed full of things, refutes the tempting idea that there might be exclusive worlds of our own, or entirely abstract worlds. We are always in the worlds of others, trying to sort out what they leave behind, strange things that can end up becoming familiar to us.

Imagining time

If we are always in the worlds of others, that's also because we are always living in times that are not exclusively ours. A fiction has been created, today, that suggests there is one time for people who live in the present, and it belongs to them, while other people either aren't there yet (children and young people) or their time is mostly behind them (the elderly). The expression "back in my time" perfectly shows this keenness to claim the meaning of a given moment, normally the most productive years of a person's life. Who is living in "their time"? The act of learning to read and the things left behind from times past both show us that temporality is an exercise of the imagination, and imagining time rather invites us to live the present as times shared among strangers. If we do this, the meaning of memory and its conflicts, as well as that of the future and its plans, opens up in multiple directions. The limits no longer separate a before and an after, or an after in relation to some absolute ending—instead, the limits become time-spanning bridges.

Imagining knowledge

If the world is not exclusively ours and the times do not belong to us, then all we know about them is but a partial, deficient sense of their meaning. Learning to read means placing what-we-know and what-we-don't-know into a live relationship. Otherwise, there would be no reading, nor any journey, and there wouldn't be any blank spaces, and so no questions would arise from them. Modern culture has been built upon the fear of ignorance, with social punishment as the price to pay for it. Illiteracy has long been one of the forms of this exclusion and fear. But ignorance itself does not exist. It is, instead, always some form of expulsion, an exclusion from whatever has been granted legitimacy as a form of knowledge. In reality, as is repeated constantly in the roots of all known cultures, including Western culture, knowing means learning not to know. At the point where what-we-know and what-we-don't-know come together and cannot possibly be separated by even the sharpest scalpel, right there is where we find strangeness. It is the raw material of the imagination, and a prerequisite for any kind of learning.

Translated from Spanish by George Hutton.

NOTES

1 Gayatri Spivak, *Death of a Discipline* (New York: Columbia University Press, 2005).

2 Marina Garcés, *Nueva ilustración radical* (Barcelona: Anagrama, 2018).

Dan Perjovschi

LIFE
QUARANTINE

Drawings (2020–21)

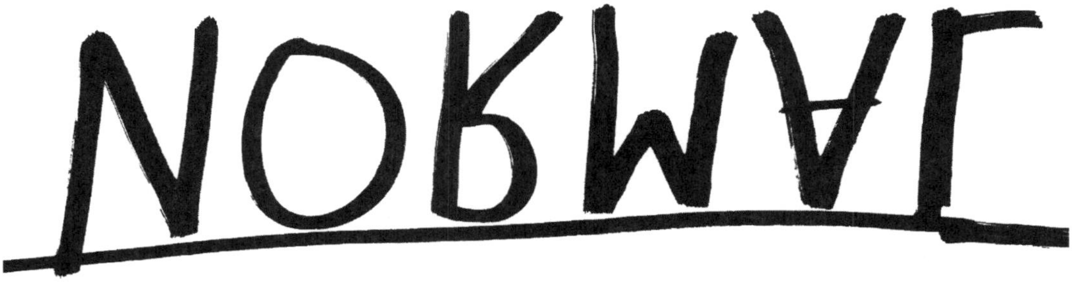
NORMAL

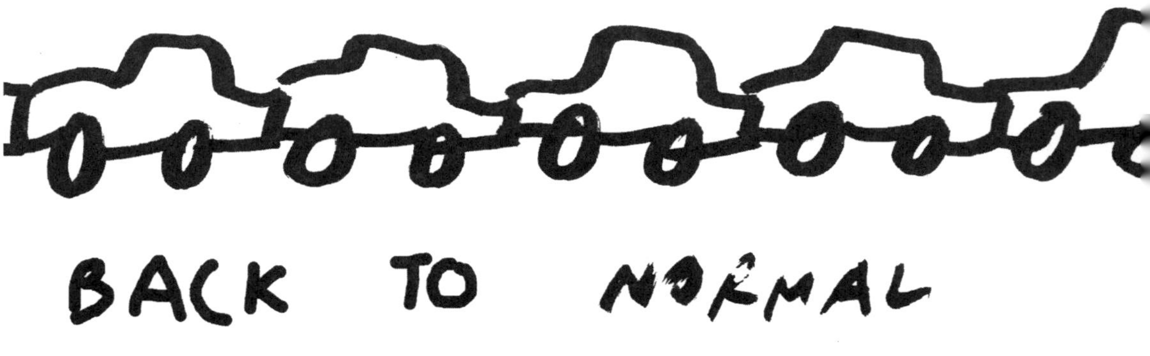
BACK TO NORMAL

THE SHOW
MUST GO ~~ON~~

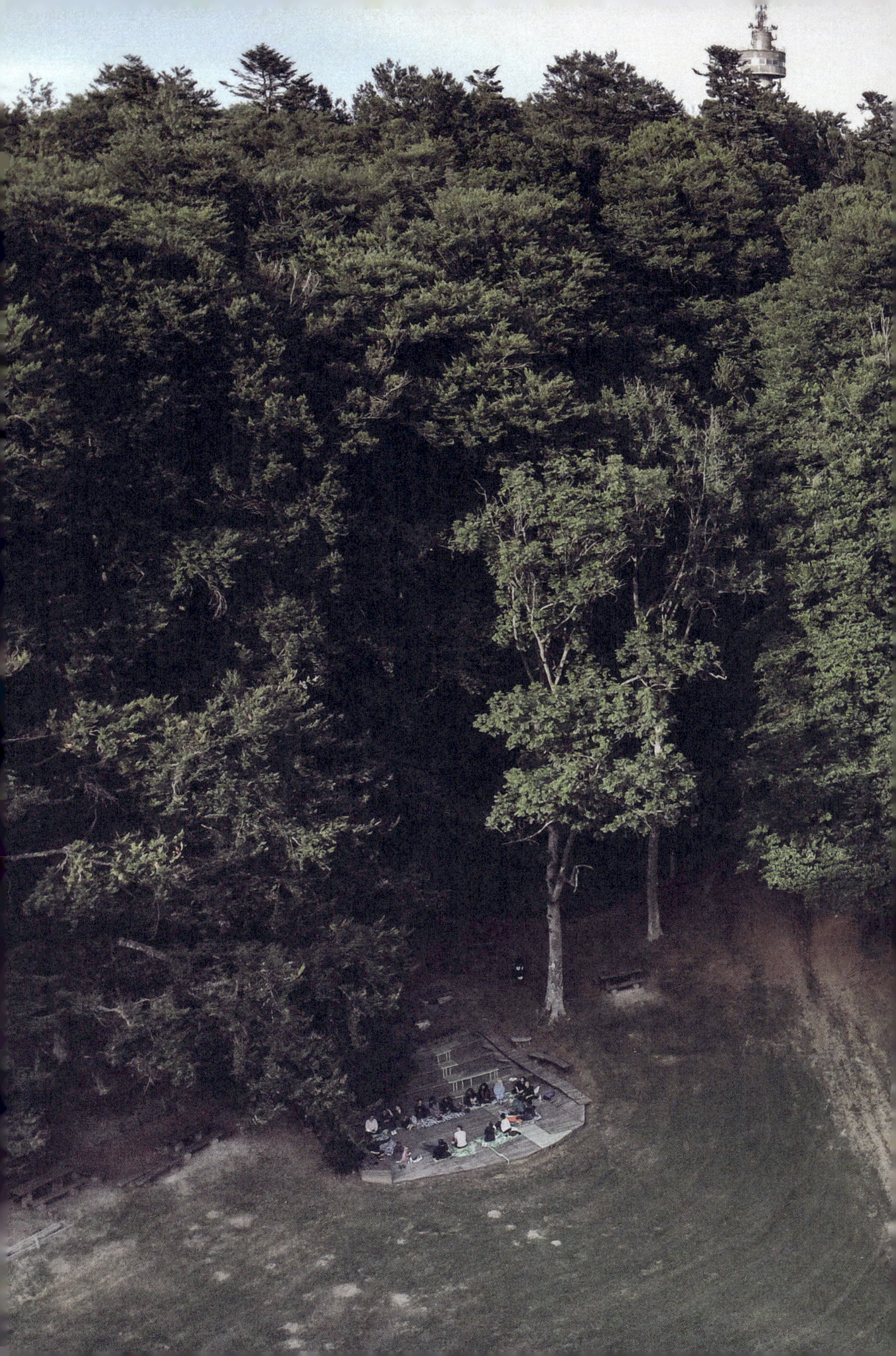

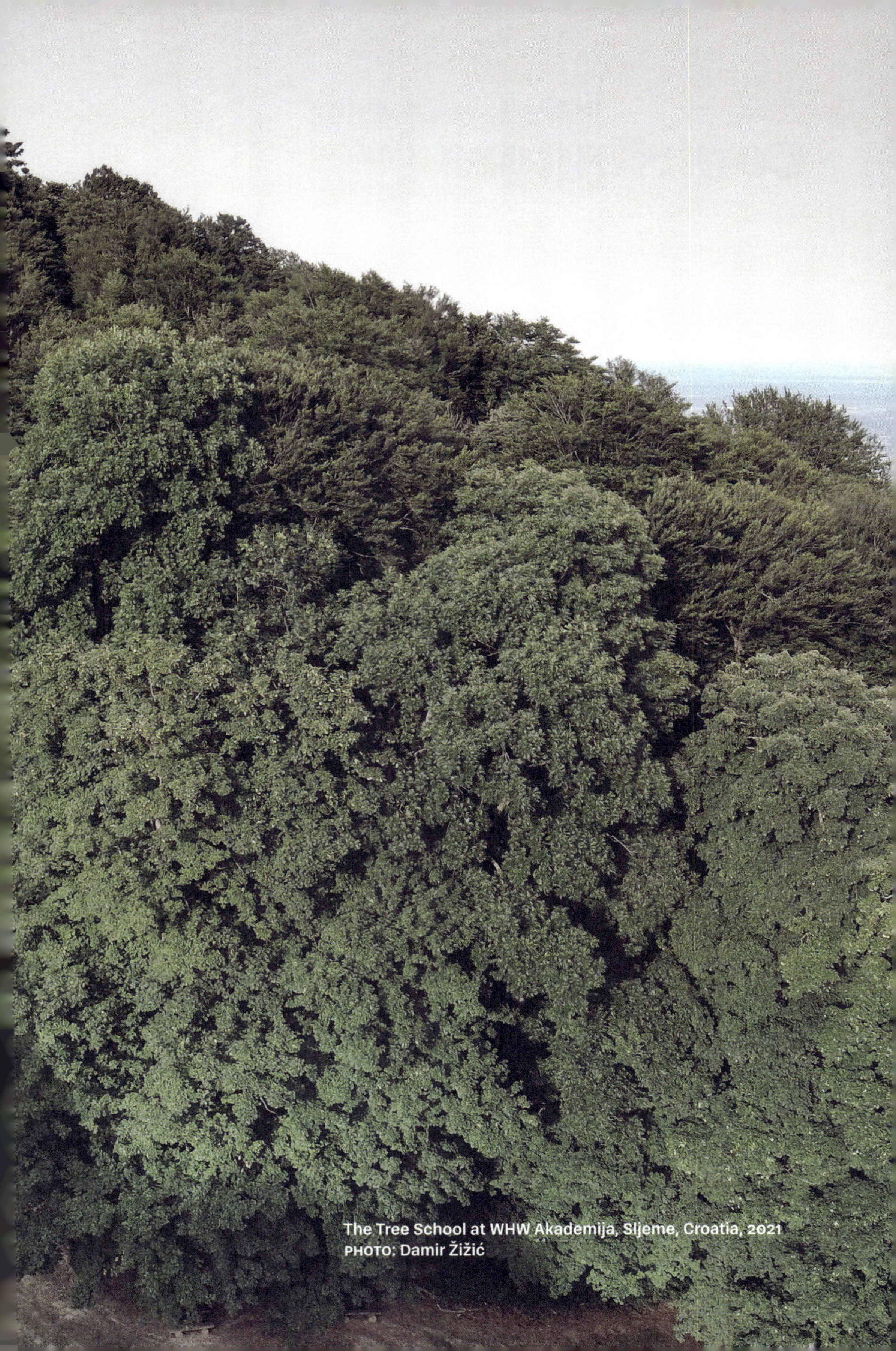

The Tree School at WHW Akademija, Sljeme, Croatia, 2021
PHOTO: Damir Žižić

Contributors

Luna Acosta is a visual artist, teacher, and researcher from Colombia, currently based in Barcelona. Her work explores narrating geographies and territories and elucidates the interrelationships between landscape transformations, human and nonhuman migratory fluxes, and the updated colonial order. She develops listening and meeting devices that orbit between textiles, electronics, installation, and performance. Acosta has participated in multiple group exhibitions and artistic residencies in South America and Europe.
https://lunaacosta.net
Instagram.com/palabraluna

CAConrad has been working with the ancient technologies of poetry and ritual since 1975. They are the author of *AMANDA PARADISE: Resurrect Extinct Vibration* (Wave Books, 2021). Other titles include *While Standing in Line for Death* (Wave Books, 2017) and *Ecodeviance* (Wave Books, 2014). *The Book of Frank* (Wave Books, 2010/Chax Press, 2009) is now available in nine languages. CAConrad has received a Creative Capital grant, a Pew Fellowship, a Lambda Literary Award, and a Believer Book Award. They teach at Columbia University in New York City and Sandberg Art Institute in Amsterdam.
https://linktr.ee/CAConrad88

DAAR – Decolonizing Architecture Art Research, founded by Sandi Hilal and Alessandro Petti, is an architectural collective that combines conceptual speculations and pragmatic spatial interventions, discourse, and collective learning. DAAR's artistic research is situated between politics, architecture, art, and pedagogy. In their practice, art exhibitions are both sites of display and sites of action that spill over into other contexts: built architectural structures, the shaping of critical learning environments, interventions that challenge dominant collective narratives, the production of new political imaginations, the formation of civic spaces, and the redefinition of concepts.

Yael Davids is an artist and a Feldenkrais instructor whose works examine the capacities in which the body operates as a documentary vessel—in connection to collective heritage, political narrative, and private biographies. Inspired by Dr. Moshé Feldenkrais, she experiments with somatic learning and alternative systems of knowledge transfer and production. Composed of performative, sculptural, and archival elements, Davids's works often take the form of choreographic assemblages.

Eva Ďurovec was born in former Czechoslovakia and is currently based in Košice and Berlin, where she studied spatial strategies at the Weissensee School of Art and Design Berlin. In her work, she deals with living space and life fulfillment in the context of social, economic, and environmental crises and issues of corporate power and kleptocracy. Ďurovec creates journals and objects combining autoethnographic research.

Marina Garcés is a Spanish philosopher and essayist. She teaches at the Universitat Oberta de Catalunya in Barcelona, where she coordinates the Master of Philosophy for Contemporary Challenges and the research project Ecologies of Imagination. She is part of a critical and experimental thinking collective called Espai en Blanc (Blank Space). Her main field of work is politics and critical thought, with a focus on the need to construct a philosophical voice that can speak out for commitment, action, and emancipation on the basis of awareness of our interdependence in a shared world.

Teuta Gatolin is an intermedia artist from Croatia, currently researching storytelling ecology, trickster mythologies, and the possibilities of imagining (and hopefully finding paths to) futures outside the capitalist narrative. She studied new media arts and animated film at the Academy of Fine Arts, University of Zagreb, as well as journalism and media studies in the university's Faculty of Political Science. Gatolin's works are process-based and incorporate various mediums such as text, textiles, installations, virtual reality, sound, and more. She likes to collaborate.

Yayo Herrero is a Spanish anthropologist, engineer, professor, and ecofeminist activist. She has coordinated the activities of Ecologists in Action, an umbrella organization of Spanish environmental NGOs, and has participated in numerous social initiatives that promote human rights and social ecology. Currently, she is Professor at the National University of Distance Education and General Director of FUHEM – Fundación Hogar del Empleado, both in Madrid. Herrero's research focuses on the current ecological crisis derived from the capitalist development and production model.

Max Jorge Hinderer Cruz is a Bolivian German writer, curator, and philosopher. He has been Artistic Director of the Akademie der Künste der Welt, Cologne, since January 2022. Prior to that, in 2019–21, he was Director of Bolivia's Museo Nacional de Arte (National Museum of Art) in La Paz. In 2008–11, Hinderer Cruz was the curator of the exhibition and publication project *Principio Potosí / The Potosí Principle* (together with Alice Creischer and Andreas Siekmann). He is the co-author, together with Sabeth Buchmann, of the book *Hélio Oiticica and Neville D'Almeida: Block-Experiments in Cosmococa—Program in Progress* (Afterall and MIT Press, 2013).

Margherita Isola is an artist from Italy leading a nomadic lifestyle, and is currently based in Barcelona. Trained in contemporary dance at Accademia Isola Danza, Venice, and holding a degree in cultural anthropology, she has been working as a visual artist since 2008. Isola's practice is a mix of media, performance, installation, textile art, collage, public art, and community works. She addresses issues related to feminism, migration, colonialism, the capitalization of life, and rethinking new forms of coexistence and interconnection. Recently, her work has focused on plants, care, and healing practices.

Jammers is a group of of individuals with a wide array of personal and creative pursuits—made up of current and past artists-in-residence at the Rijksakademie van beeldende kunsten, Amsterdam, and beyond—who find ways to come together to jam, in whatever shape or form, in a time when gathering is rendered a precarity. "Jamming" (verb: to gather through an activity) became a mechanism for the "jammers" (noun: a person who jams) to gravitate toward one another in the middle of a global pause. The moment created thereby, constantly in flux, moves and shifts through surrounding structures via the reverberations of the jamming itself.

Pablo Martínez is a researcher and educator. He worked as Head of Programming at the MACBA – Museu d'Art Contemporani de Barcelona from 2016 to 2021, where he also directed the Center of Studies and Documentation and its exhibition program, the Independent Studies Programme, and the *et al.* series of essays (Arcàdia). He worked as Head of Education and Public Activities at CA2M – Centro de Arte Dos de Mayo, Madrid (2009–16) and Associate Professor of Contemporary Art in the Faculty of Fine Arts of the Universidad Complutense de Madrid (2011–15). He's a member of the editorial board of L'Internationale Online as well as of the art and visual culture journal *#Re-visiones*. Martínez is a founding member of Las Lindes (est. 2009), a research and action group working on education and cultural and artistic practices. He obtained his doctorate in 2022 with a dissertation that analyzed images of crowds and focused on the funeral of the anarchist Buenaventura Durruti.

Dan Perjovschi is an artist and writer born and living in Romania. Unsparing toward popular clichés circulating in the news media, Perjovschi raises questions about politics, religion, the role of the individual in the collective, and the relationship of the global and the local. Sketched with a few strokes, his drawings are pictures and texts on walls in art institutions and function as a visual diary as much as a microcosm of what's going on in and around the exhibitions. His work comments, with piercing irony, on the absurdities and cynicisms of society. Perjovschi has received the George Maciunas Prize (2004), European Cultural Foundation Prize (2012, with Lia Perjovschi), and Rosa Schapire Art Prize from Kunsthalle Hamburg (2016).

Emily Pethick is Director of the Rijksakademie van beeldende kunsten, Amsterdam. Until 2018, she was Director of the Showroom, London, for ten years. Pethick was also Director of Casco – Office for Art, Design and Theory, in Utrecht, the Netherlands (2005–08) and Curator at Cubitt, London (2003–04).

Pirate Care is a transnational research project and a network of activists, scholars, and practitioners who stand against the criminalization of solidarity and for a common care infrastructure. It was initiated in 2018 by Valeria Graziano, Marcell Mars, and Tomislav Medak.
https://pirate.care

The Sensing Salon is a studio practice, conceived by Valentina Desideri and Denise Ferreira da Silva, that expands the image of art beyond objects, events, and discourse to include the healing arts. Through formats that facilitate collaborative studying and experimenting with different practices and tools for reading (e.g., tarot and astrology) and healing (e.g., reiki and political therapy), it fosters a form of sociality that attends to the deeply implicated existence of everything in this world, both human and nonhuman. The Sensing Salon takes different shapes according to the context in which it takes place and each iteration involves different guests and participants.

Cecilia Vicuña is a poet, artist, filmmaker, and activist whose works explore language, memory, dissolution, extinction, and exile. Central to her practice are pressing concerns of the modern world, including ecological destruction, human rights, cultural homogenization, and economic disparity, particularly the ways in which such phenomena disenfranchise the already powerless. Vicuña was appointed the 2015 Messenger Lecturer at Cornell University, Ithaca, New York.

What, How & for Whom / WHW is a curatorial collective. Its members are curators Ivet Ćurlin, Ana Dević, Nataša Ilić, and Sabina Sabolović and designer and publicist Dejan Kršić. Since 2003, WHW has run the program of Gallery Nova, a city-owned gallery in Zagreb. In 2018, the collective initiated an independent educational program, titled WHW Akademija, based in Zagreb. WHW members Ivet Ćurlin, Nataša Ilić, and Sabina Sabolović have been Artistic Directors of Kunsthalle Wien in Vienna since 2019.
WHW activities in Zagreb, including WHW Akademija and Gallery Nova, are led by Ana Dević in collaboration with curators Ana Kovačić and Martina Kontošić, and financial manager Gordana Borić as members of the WHW Zagreb team.

Thank You

Our heartfelt gratitude goes to all the participants of the programs that inspired this book and nourished our practices: all the artists, thinkers, activists, and educators who took part in the Independent Studies Program at the MACBA, the Rijsakademie residency program, and WHW Akademjia in 2020 and 2021.

We would like to thank all authors and contributors for their thoughtful and inspiring work, without which this book would not have been possible. The editorial team would also like to express its gratitude to the following people, whose efforts in different ways helped the production of this book and the project *Education from Below*:

Gordana Borić
Sanja Iveković
Hannah Dawn Henderson
Martina Kontošić
Ana Kovačić
Liza May Post
María Salgado
Branka Stipančić
Virág Szentkirályi